Denied Promotion

By A Tree

The Book of Amazing Football Facts

Les Scott

Aureus Publishing

First Published 2022
Digital Edition 2022
©2022   Les Scott
©2022   Digital Edition Les Scott
©2022   Aureus Publishing Limited

Front cover: St. Albans City AFC Hatfield Road Terrace at their Clarence Park ground.

Paperback ISBN : 978-1-899750-55-9
EPUB ISBN : 978-1-899750-56-6

Printed in Great Britain.
A catalogue record for this book is available from the British Library.
Aureus Publishing Limited
Tel: 00 44 (0) 1656 880033
E-mail: sales@aureus.co.uk
Web site: www.aureus.co.uk

Acknowledgements

I am greatly indebted to the following for their expertise and help in the production of this book.

Meuryn Hughes at Aureus Publishing; Julian Alexander at Soho Agency; Celtic FC; Jimmy Greaves; Leicester City FC; Nick Johnson; Christien Phillips; Don Mackay; Neil Baker at Leek Town FC; Phil Sproson; John McGowan, Leigh Page, Andrew Hippisley, David Tavener, and St. Albans City AFC;   Sunday Sun (Reach plc); Sunderland Echo, The Sentinel (Stoke-on-Trent).

For Susan Millard, for your unflagging encouragement and support; also, Lauren, Ruby, Danni, Natasha and all the children.

This book is dedicated to all the club secretaries of English, Scottish and Welsh clubs who, in the 1960s, indulged a young boy by complying with his polite written request for a programme and, 'if possible a printed autograph sheet', of their respective club. They could never have known the excitement and absolute joy their replies brought me. Forever grateful.

All the facts detailed in 'Denied Promotion Because Of A Tree' are correct as at April 2022.

Contents

GATESHEAD A.F.C. Ltd.

Division IV   Monday, Septembe

GATESHEAD v COVEN

Official Programme
3d.

TO

HOGG

SILVER

Ho

WEST HAM
UNITED

BOLEYN GROUND : LONDON E.13

EVERTON   No. 55
FOOTBALL LEAGUE : Division I
SATURDAY 11th MAY 1963 at 3 p.m.

THE FOOTBALL
LEAGUE TROPHY

SEASON 1967-68

FOOTBALL LEAGUE
DIVISION 1

F.A. CUP WIN
1950, 1896, 1960
LEAGUE CHAMP
1931, 1933, 1934,
1938, 1948, 1953

ARSENAL
v
MANCHESTER UNI

SATURDAY 24th FEBRUARY

ARSENAL STADIUM   KICK-O

Colour Special
Official Programme
1/-

R. & L. NEWMAN   ROVER   LAND ROVER   AUSTIN
LOW ROAD GARAGE   W. N. WILSON & Son Ltd.
Ironworks Road, Barrow-in-Furness   3209 ULVERSTON 3208
Phone 3470   USED CARS A SPECIALITY

You always Win at   Quality . Service . Economy
BOWMAN'S   E. HOLME LTD.
167 RAWLINSON STREET   COKE COAL SOLID FUEL
CARPETS and FLOORCOVERINGS   Tel. Barrow 1102

Barrow
AFC

HOLKER ST. GROUND
Barrow-in-Furness

OFFICIAL
PROGRAMME 6d   SPATIARI UT   PROGREDIARIS

R. RODGER   SUNLIGHT
Coal, Coke and Fuel Merchant   CHINESE RESTAURANT
9, LAWSON STREET   84 DUKE STREET
Barrow 1531   Barrow-in-Furness, Lancs.
Deliveries in your area .   TEL. 1031
WEEKLY   OPEN 11-30 a.m. to 11-30 p.m.
FORTNIGHTLY   (Monday to Saturday)
MONTHLY   Open Sunday from 12 noon to 11-30 p.m.
All Orders Promptly Delivered   SPECIAL LUNCH
                      Monday to Saturday 11-30 a.m. to
                      2-30 p.m.

Introduction

ootball is a game of opinions, as the man standing next to me in the pub would no doubt disagree. What even the most inexorable football fan can not argue against, however, are facts. In the opinion of someone, a team may have been unlucky to lose, the fact is, that team lost. Like the game itself, football facts are organic, continuously developing, perpetually in a state of addendum. There are football facts which record success, such as the first team to win the English league and cup 'double' in the twentieth century, or, the first British club to win the European Cup. This book is no place for facts of such laudable achievement, for they are more than adequately recorded in other tomes. Furthermore, facts such as the first substitute in an English league match, or, who is England's all time leading goalscorer are far too familiar to fans of football ever to give the reader a reward for reading.

What this book attempts is to document the curious, oddball and extraordinary football facts, the vast majority of which will, hopefully, be unfamiliar to even the most committed lover of the game. Facts whose diffuseness exemplifies the richness and abiding attraction of football. A game which, by turn, rewards its ardent followers with mostly angst, trials and tribulations tempered by the occasional triumph and success. Peculiar, bizarre, funny and fantastic football facts are this book's remit. The sort of football facts which, hopefully, will give the reader a reward for reading by telling him or her, something they did not know and reinforce the notion that football is indeed the manifestation of human nature and, as such, has a place in the best of all possible worlds. Above all, football facts which will entertain and engender laughter in the reader.

So where did all these facts come from? From research of league tables - anyone can do research, it is how you interpret research which is key; poring over season-by-season club records looking for strange sequences of results and goalscorers; the reading of a few thousand match programmes dating from the 1940s which, in addition to now serving as poignant social documents, invariably reveal long forgotten gems of facts; checking thousands of team line-ups, on the look-out for strange combinations of names or rare first-team appearances vis-à-vis the length of time a player had been with the club. Press cuttings going back to the 1930s; interviews with players and managers.

In addition to writing football books, I am fortunate to work as a football journalist and match-data analyst which, over the years, has afforded me the privilege of attending some seventy games a season. Every season produces a myriad of eye-catching curious facts, occasionally some of the jaw-dropping variety, each season serving as a passing parade of the peculiar, phenomenal and curious. All such facts were duly noted.

I often hear someone bemoan, 'Football isn't what it used to be'. Thank heavens for that. I dread to think what sort of game we would now have should football have stood still and stagnated. For sure, contemporary football is very different to the game I followed as a boy, then, for over twenty-years as a player in the ranks of league youth/reserve teams and non-league clubs. Football in the past was, to my mind, more authentic but it was neither better nor worse than the contemporary game, just different. Whenever I hear someone lament, 'football has changed', I am often given to thinking they themselves have changed as much as football has; as have footballers over the years. In researching this book, I was constantly reminded of that fact when looking at photographs of players from the thirties or forties and being taken aback as to how old they looked compared to contemporary footballers. Furthermore, one could, more often that not, correctly guess the position of the player simply by his physical appearance. In contemporary football, in terms of physical appearance, it is difficult to differentiate between a full-back and a central-midfield player.

Given football has changed over the years there are still, of course, innumerable constants. The infinite pleasures and dark despair all football fans experience following the fortunes of their team. No matter your age, Saturday evenings spoiled should your team have lost. Reading football websites or newspapers with gusto should your team have won. Conditions familiar to any person who has given their heart to a football club. 'Hope is the thing with feathers' wrote Emily Dickinson. It isn't often the 19th century American poet is referenced in terms of football but, whatever the era, football fans of every hue perpetually live in hope that one day it will be their team which takes off and produces the success they have always dreamed of.

Another constant of football, of course, are facts. Here I return to the meat and indeed the purpose of this book, to record, hopefully for your entertainment, some of the little known amazing, unusual and incredible incidents to have occurred in football. The nuts and bolts of the game, which go no small way to affording football its colour, fascination and compulsion. I feel this in-keeping, for I have always been of the opinion football is, in essence, entertainment. As the man standing next to me in the pub would no doubt disagree.

Les Scott
2022

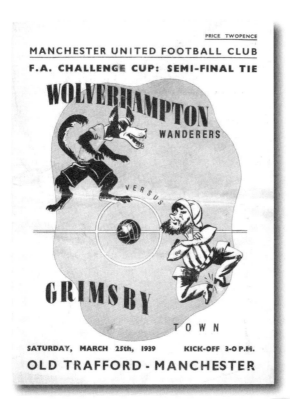

PRICE TWOPENCE

MANCHESTER UNITED FOOTBALL CLUB

F.A. CHALLENGE CUP: SEMI-FINAL TIE

WOLVERHAMPTON
WANDERERS

VERSUS

GRIMSBY

T O W N

SATURDAY, MARCH 25th, 1939   KICK-OFF 3·0 P.M.

OLD TRAFFORD · MANCHESTER

OLD TRAFFORD GATE RECORD IN DANGER

SCORES OF CROWD CASUALTIES

AMAZING scenes occurred at the Wolverhampton Wanderers v. Grimsby Cup tie at Old Trafford, Manchester, this afternoon.

An hour before the start the ground record of 73,000—set up at the Bolton Wanderers v. Sheffield United semi-final some years ago— seemed likely to be beaten.

Casualties occurred by the dozen and a small army of ambulance men and stretcher bearers could hardly keep pace with the demands made on them.

Ugly-looking sways in the crowd were almost continuous, and crushing cases were numerous.

Women Victims

Dozens of women were among the casualties.

Outside the gates ambulances were waiting to rush the more urgent cases away.

10

Attendances

The highest attendance at Old Trafford was not for a Manchester United game. It was for a Grimsby Town match. On 25 March 1939, Old Trafford's record attendance of 76,962 was achieved for the FA Cup semi-final between Grimsby Town and Wolverhampton Wanderers.

County's unlucky thirteen. On 7 May 1921, Stockport County's Division Two game against Leicester City attracted just 13 paying spectators. County had been ordered to play the game at Old Trafford as their own ground, Edgeley Park, had been closed by the FA due to a crowd disturbance. It is thought the game was actually watched by in excess of 4,000 spectators, the vast majority of whom stayed behind after watching the Manchester United game which had taken place previously. Not much in the way of entertainment, County's game against Leicester City ended goalless.

Maine Road multi-tasks. In 1946-47, Manchester City's Maine Road ground was used by both City and Manchester United - Old Trafford being closed due to bomb damage. Maine Road was also the venue for an England v Wales International, an FA Cup semi-final and the Rugby League Championship Play-Off Final. The aggregate attendance at Maine Road for all fixtures was 2,250,511.

I was there, kind of. Colchester United had an attendance of 19,072 for their 1st Round FA Cup tie against Reading on 27 November 1948, but supporters never saw the game. The match was abandoned after 35 minutes due to thick fog. Colchester had never previously enjoyed such a large attendance and never have since.

Seventy years later, history repeated itself at the Wham Stadium, home of Accrington Stanley who were entertaining Sunderland on 8 December 2018. The attendance of 5,257 was a record for re-formed Accrington but the fans never saw the game out, it was abandoned after 72 minutes due to a waterlogged pitch. Of the 5,257, record crowd, 2,804 were from Sunderland.

Second Division Newcastle United's average attendance at St. James' Park in 1947-48 was 56,299.

In 1949-50, Notts County's average home attendance in the Third Division South was 35,013.

The highest aggregate attendance for a single day's fixtures in English football is 1,272,185 which occurred on 27 December 1949. There were 44 matches in the Football League, which produced an average attendance of 28,913.

The highest attendance for a game in the second tier of English football (Championship equivalent) is 70,302 for the Second Division meeting between Tottenham Hotspur and Southampton at White Hart Lane on 25 February 1950.

In their League Championship winning season of 1959-60, Burnley had an average home attendance of 26,869. Burnley's population in 1960 was 84,000. Burnley's average home attendance constituted 28.58% of the town's population, the highest percentage of average home support vis-à-vis population of any title winners of the modern era.

In 1960-61, Crystal Palace of Division Four had an average home attendance of 19,092. On 31 March 1961, Palace's game against Millwall at Selhurst Park attracted an attendance of 37, 774, the highest ever attendance for a fourth tier league match in English football.

On 17 October 1961, Rangers' friendly match against Eintracht Frankfurt at Hampden Park attracted 104,493 spectators - the highest attendance for a club friendly match in British football.

The highest attendance in English football where all the digits coincide is 33,333, Spurs v Ipswich Town on 30 August 1969. The highest worldwide attendance where all the digits coincide is 111,111 Santos v Flamengo (Brazil).

In 1966-67, Celtic achieved a unique quintuple, winning the Scottish

League, Scottish Cup, League Cup, Glasgow Cup and European Cup. In this 'annus mirabilis' Celtic scored 196 goals in major competitions, yet Celtic's average home league attendance was a modest 31,082, with four league matches attracting less than 20,000. Celtic clinched the Scottish League title in their penultimate game of the season, a 2-2 draw at Rangers. Celtic's following game, at home to Kilmarnock on 15 May 1967, prior to which they paraded the League Championship trophy, attracted just 19,097 spectators.

Celtic's average home league attendance in 1966-67 was bettered by ten English First Division clubs: Manchester United (average 53,854), Liverpool (46,388), Everton (42,606), Tottenham Hotspur (41,988), Chelsea (35,543), Leeds United (35,221), Newcastle United (32,081), Sunderland (31,737), Nottingham Forest (31,282) and Manchester City (31,208).

In 1969, Watford broke their record attendance for both League and FA Cup matches. On 3 February 1969, Watford's FA Cup Third Round replay against Manchester United attracted 34,099 spectators. On 20 August 1969, Watford set a new club record for a home league attendance, 27,968 for the Division Two match against Queens Park Rangers. As at 2022, neither record had been broken.

The Final of the European Cup Winners Cup of 1973-74, between AC Milan and FC Magdeburg (East Germany) in Rotterdam, attracted only 4,903 spectators. The lowest ever attendance for the final of a major European club competition.

After three matches had been played of the 1974-75 season, Carlisle United topped Division One for the first and, to date, only time in their history. Carlisle won their opening three matches without conceding a goal; 2-0 at Chelsea, 2-0 at Middlesbrough and 1-0 at home to Tottenham Hotspur. Carlisle were relegated at the end of the season with an average home attendance of 14,751 which constituted 16.39% of the city's population. The granting of city status to Carlisle in 1974 coincided with Carlisle United's promotion to Division One. Carlisle United play in the largest city in England. The city, which encompasses a large rural area, covers 402 square miles (1,039.97 square kilometres).

Crowded out. In 1976-77, Workington (Division Four) enjoyed only three attendances that exceeded 2,000. Against Halifax Town (2,081), Watford (2,009) and Huddersfield Town (2,133). It is thought away support was the reason these attendances exceeded the 2,000 mark. Workington failed to win re-election to the Football League and were replaced by Wimbledon. Workington, however, were not the worst supported team in Division Four that season. Southport also attracted only three attendances which exceeded 2,000 - Bradford City (2,302), Barnsley (2,308) and Workington (2,069). Again, it is thought away support helped these attendances exceed 2,000. Southport also had six attendances below 1,000 - Brentford (969), Swansea City (972), Scunthorpe United (941), Bournemouth (976), Colchester United (897) and Hartlepool United (880). Workington, however, never had an attendance below 1,000, their lowest being 1,034 for the visit of Stockport County.

Groundhog day. On 19 October 1985, the attendance for Torquay United's Division Four game against Northampton Town at Plainmoor was 1,282. Torquay then played two successive away games but returned to Plainmoor on 2 November to face Leyton Orient - the attendance for this game was also 1,282 (surely not the same people?). Both matches were drawn.

Not on a par with St. Andrews. On 9 September 1995, the attendance for England v Colombia at Wembley (0-0) was 20,038. Meanwhile, in the Midlands, the attendance for Birmingham City's Anglo-Italian Cup tie against Genoa at St.Andrews was 20,430 - 392 more than attended Wembley.

The attendance for the Scottish League Cup tie between Clydebank and East Stirling on 9 September 1995 was just 29, the lowest recorded for a post-war game in British senior football. At the time Clydebank were homeless and the tie was switched to the neutral venue of Cappielow Park, home of Morton.

Plenty in reserve. In 1998-99, the Pontins League (Central League) match between Sunderland Reserves and Liverpool Reserves at the Stadium of Light attracted an attendance of 33,513.

In 2005-06, the attendance for the Coppa Italia match between Juventus and Sampdoria was just 237. Juventus' record low attendance for a Coppa Italia tie was blamed on exceptionally cold weather and live TV coverage.

Despite being hugely popular in Brazil, football does not usually attract large attendances. For all there have been some 100,000 plus attendances in the Campeonato Brasileiro Serie A, the last in 1989, aggregate and average attendances do not feature in the top ten throughout the world. In 2019,

Flamengo's average attendance was 50,872, followed by Sao Paulo, 34,346. Five clubs in Brazil's top-flight had an average attendance of below 10,000, lowest being America FC, 6,407. The average attendance in Serie B in 2019-20 (pre Covid) was 5,086.

On 9 October 1976, the attendance at the Racecourse Ground for Wrexham's Third Division match against Lincoln City was 7,753. The attendance for the return fixture at Lincoln's Sincil Bank on 18 March 1977, was also 7,753.

On 5 January 1991, Chester City recorded the smallest ever attendance for a Third Round FA Cup match, 1,833 watching their tie against Bournemouth.

On 4 May 2013, Rangers created a world record attendance for a fourth-tier league game when 50,048 attended their match against Berwick Rangers at Ibrox.

In 2018-19, attendances in the EFL (Football League) exceeded 18.3 million, the highest figure since 1959. It was the third consecutive year cumulative attendances in the EFL exceeded 18 million. With Championship attendances in excess of 11 million, this made the Championship the fourth best attended league in the world, behind Bundesliga, Premier League and La Liga.

Albion Rovers' record attendance is 27,831 against Rangers on 8 February 1936. In 2021-22, the capacity of Albion's Cliftonhill Stadium was designated as being 1,238, the greatest percentage attendance reversal vis-à-vis capacity differential in British senior football.

On 13 November 2021, the attendance for Notts County's home game at Meadow Lane against Solihull Moors was 12,843, a record for the National League.

In 2021-22, three clubs in the North West Counties League (Level 9 - Step 5 in the National League System) had an average home attendance in excess of four figures. Macclesfield (3,200), AFC Bury (1,411) and Isle of Man (1,112). On 27 December 2021, Macclesfield's NWC league game against Winsford United attracted 4,353 spectators to their Moss Rose ground.

In the days before Health and Safety, they knew how to pack them in at Leicester City's Filbert Street.

Away the Lads

Can we play you every week? In 1898-99, Second Division, Darwen, conceded 109 goals in their 17 away games, an average of 6.4 per game.

Peeble Rovers first entered the Scottish Cup in 1907-08 when they were drawn away to Celtic; from which point Peeble never received a home draw in the Scottish Cup until 23 January 1926 when they defeated Keith 7-3, having previously been drawn away from home for 19 consecutive Scottish cup ties.

In 1930-31, Arsenal scored 60 goals away from home (21 league matches) in a title winning season in which the Gunners never failed to score when on their travels.

No victory for Nelson. Nelson did not secure a single point from their 21 away matches in Division Three North in 1930-31, the season in which the club lost their Football League status to Chester.

Just the ticket. The most goals scored by an individual player in an away match is seven. Ted Drake achieved this feat when scoring all of Arsenal's goals against Aston Villa at Villa Park on 14 December 1935. Arsenal won 7-1. Drake's rail ticket for the return trip with the Arsenal party was numbered 193517. As Drake wistfully bemoaned in his autobiography, 'I wish I'd kept that ticket.'

Middlesbrough are not the only team to score six away from home in the league and fail to win the game (22 October 1960, 6-6 at Charlton Athletic). On 21 April 1930, Arsenal scored six in their First Division match at Leicester City, 6-6.

Rovers like a roving. In 1946-47, Doncaster Rovers won 18, drew one and lost only two of their 21 away matches in Third Division North. Doncaster also won both their away matches in the FA Cup.

In 1947-48, Preston North End played successive away ties in the FA Cup in different rounds but on the same ground. In Round Five, Preston beat Manchester City 1-0 at Maine Road. In Round Six, Preston lost 4-1 to Manchester United, the tie also being played at Maine Road as Old Trafford was unavailable due to bomb damage during WW2.

Doncaster Rovers twice won Division Three North in the late 1940s, on each occasion securing more points away from home than they did home matches. In 1946-47, 37 points away from home from a total of 72; In 1949-50, 28 points from away matches from a total of 55.

Seven of Doncaster Rovers' first nine matches of the 1950-51 season were away from home, which included five consecutive away matches. Laudably, Rovers only lost one, their opening day fixture at Leeds United (3-1). Having been unbeaten in five consecutive away matches, Doncaster returned home on 30th September only to lose to Blackburn Rovers.

Pointless trips. Crewe Alexandra did not win an away game from 25 December 1954 to 24 April 1957, a total of 56 matches.

On 27 September 1958, British Railways launched a new type of football excursion, 'The Away Day Special'. On the same day, eight of the twelve matches in Division Three resulted in victories for the away team, the most away wins in any division of the Football League on a single day. Furthermore, Colchester United drew at Tranmere Rovers as did Southend United at Rochdale. The only two teams to win at home were QPR (2-1 v Bury) and Plymouth Argyle (3-1 v Bournemouth).

OUR VISITORS

Here are pen pictures of some of the Grimsby Town players:
CLARRIE WILLIAMS (goalkeeper) Joined Grimsby from Doncaster Rovers in 1953. Teetotaler and non-smoker and plays tennis for relaxation.

A 1958 pen picture of Grimsby goalkeeper Clarrie Williams.

Pen pictures of the away team were a regular feature in match programmes for decades. The pen picture of Grimsby goalkeeper Clarrie Williams appeared in Charlton Athletic's programme for their Second Division match against Grimsby Town on 6 September 1958. Inadvertently, the entry says more about the culture of smoking and drinking amongst footballers at the time than it does about Williams.

He had to Leggat. Fulham were defeated 3-2 at Bolton Wanderers on 19 September 1959. After the game, Fulham's Graham Leggat boarded the team coach that was to take the Fulham party to Manchester Piccadilly station to catch their train to London. Leggat, however, disembarked to talk to one of the Bolton players. Not noticing Leggat was on the club carpark, the coach pulled away from Burnden Park with Leggat running after it. The coach accelerated away leaving Leggat in a quandary. Eventually one of the Bolton officials managed to garner the help of the local police who placed Leggat in one of their squad cars and set off in pursuit of the Fulham team coach. The police caught up with the coach some three miles from Manchester.

Nottingham Forest's visit to Fulham on 13 September 1960 would no doubt have provoked comment from Forest fans when they bought the match programme.

On 9 October 1961, Gillingham travelled the 345 miles to Barrow for a midweek league match. As Barrow had no floodlights at the time, kick-off was set for 5.15pm. Gillingham were due to catch the 9.05 train from Euston, but heavy traffic resulted in their team coach arriving late and the Gillingham party missing their train. Undaunted, Gillingham directors then chartered a plane, whose take-off was delayed. Eventually Gillingham arrived at Blackpool airport, eighty miles from Barrow. The kick-off was put back to 5.30 with Gillingham travelling in taxis, in part with a police escort. Gillingham arrived with minutes to spare. After 76 minutes of the game, Gillingham were trailing 7-0. Light was fading, so Barrow switched on their training lights which only illuminated part of the pitch. With darkness descending on Holker Street the referee abandoned the game with the score at 7-0. The Football League ordered the result to stand, a decision which prompted Gillingham director, Clifford Grosmark, to remark, 'Thank heavens for that'. In the Gillingham team for this match was Billy Jervis, it was the only game he ever played for the club.

They scored away goals for their own team on their home ground. Peter Farrell (Everton) scored for Eire (The Republic of Ireland) against England at Goodison Park on 21 September 1949; Jim McLaughlin (Swansea Town) scored for Northern Ireland against Wales on 15 April 1964 at the Vetch Field home of Swansea Town.

On 6 September 2006, Germany won 13-0 away from home against San Marino in a European Championship qualification match. Seven different German players featured on the score sheet with Lucas Podolski scoring four. Some consolation for San Marino was the attendance of 5,217. San Marino having a population of little over 27,000.

From 5 April 2003 to 25 September 2004, Arsenal did not lose a single away game in the league - 27 matches.

In 2010-11, Hull City lost 4-0 at Burnley on 28 September. Hull then went 14 consecutive Championship matches undefeated away from home, the run coming to an end on the final day of the season in a 3-0 defeat at Bristol City.

Chelsea and Manchester City jointly hold the record for the most consecutive away wins in the top flight - 11. Chelsea achieved this by winning their final three away matches of 2007-08 and the first eight away games of 2008-09. Manchester City by winning their final away game of 2016-17 and first ten away matches of 2017-18.

Between 3 March and 26 October 2013, Arsenal won twelve consecutive away matches in the league.

Carlisle United's 1-0 win at Bradford City in League Two on 5 December 2020, was the Cumbrians' first league victory at Valley Parade since a 2-1 win in Third Division North on 27 October 1951 - 69-years.

'Players and managers may come and go, but we never do well there.' When Fulham won 2-0 at Everton on 14 February 2021, it was the Cottagers' first League victory at Goodison Park in 74-years, a period which dates back to 1949. Fulham had never won in their previous 22 League visits to Everton, the previous occasion on which the West London club left Goodison undefeated in a League match, was on 5 September 1959 following a goalless draw.

More than my job's worth. On 20 January 2021, Queens Park Rangers players were initially refused entry to the Cardiff City stadium, for their Championship match against Cardiff City, by a steward. The Rangers' players were wearing the wristbands which had been issued to them but, according to the steward, these were, 'not the correct wristbands.'

On 9 February 2021, Exeter City made the 333- mile journey north to play Barrow in League Two. The game was scheduled to kick-off at 6.30pm, with Referee Ross Joyce having passed the Holker Street (Progression Solicitors Stadium) pitch fit for play at 4pm. A sudden drop in temperature, however, necessitated the referee making a second pitch inspection at 5.30pm, which he deemed to be 'frozen and unfit for play'. The Exeter party immediately boarded their team coach and headed for home - a pointless round trip of 666 miles, which Exeter repeated on 13 April when they lost the rescheduled game 2-1.

Of the ten ties in the Coup de France of 10 February 2021, nine resulted in victories for the away team. The only exception being Brest 2 Rodez 1.

Cambridge United won promotion from League Two in 2020-21 having won 43 points away from home as opposed to just 30 from their 23 home games. Cambridge recorded the biggest away win of the season in League Two, 5-0 at promotion rivals Morecambe (on 19 September 2020), a feat Cambridge equalled when winning 5-0 at Scunthorpe United (17th October 2020). Cambridge were also involved in the highest aggregate score in the division, when losing 5-4 at Harrogate Town (30 April 2021).

Throw-back to Doncaster Rovers of the late 1940s. When Norwich City won the Championship in 2020-21, the Canaries won more away matches (15) than home games (14).

In 2020-21, Manchester United became only the fourth team to remain undefeated away from home across an entire top-flight season, equalling the achievements of Preston North End (1888-89), Arsenal (2001-02) and also (2003-04).

AS Venus from Mahina, on the Tahiti island of French Polynesia, are thought to have made the longest ever trip for a 'domestic' game. Clubs based in French overseas territories and protectorates are allowed to enter the Coup de France, the French equivalent of the FA Cup. AS Venus entered the Coup de France for the first time in 2021-22 and were drawn away to French fourth tier club, Trelissac, 10,000 miles away. Venus were defeated 2-0 on 13 November 2021, their 20,000 mile round trip, surely the longest ever undertaken by a club for a domestic competition.

We always do well there. On 20 November 2021, Sheffield Wednesday enjoyed a 3-2 victory at Accrington Stanley. It was Wednesday's first visit to Accrington Stanley since they achieved a 4-2 victory on 24 September 1892 - 129 years.

On 27 November 2021, Accrington Stanley won 1-0 at Lincoln City. It was Accrington's first victory at Sincil Bank since a 3-2 win on Christmas Day 1947, thereafter there had been no Accrington successes in 17 visits (14 league, one League Cup and two EFL Trophy).

Bookings and Dismissals

Child's play. Hull City's Arthur Childs is the only player to be sent off for wearing 'inappropriate boots'. Childs was dismissed minutes into Hull's Second Division match against Port Vale in 1929-30. Shortly after the incident, the laws of the game were changed to allow a player with incorrect attire back onto the pitch once the problem had been rectified. Arthur Childs also became the first player to be sent off in an FA Cup semi-final when playing for Hull against Arsenal at Villa Park on 26 March 1930 in a semi-final replay. On this occasion, Childs was dismissed for a foul on Arsenal's Jack Lambert.

Browned-off. With two players falling ill, Wrexham made an urgent telephone call home for Ambrose Brown to join their team for their Christmas Day game at Hull City in 1936. At some cost, Brown travelled on the day by a series of trains and taxis before finally arriving at Boothferry Park with only half an hour to kick-off. Brown was sent off in the first minute of the game for dangerous play.

Not a single player was sent off in Division Three North in the 1946-47 season.

Short on Christmas good will. On Boxing Day 1959, referee Jack Sturgeon dismissed all twenty-two players and thus abandoned a very ill-tempered Southern League game between Dartford and Gravesend.

Hales-fellow-not-well-met. On 6 January 1979, Charlton Athletic's Derek Hales and Mick Flanagan were sent off for fighting one another during Charlton's 1-1 draw at home to Maidstone United in the 3rd round of the FA Cup. Without both players for the replay, Charlton won 2-1.

Nothing to crow about. Jason Crowe came on as a substitute for Arsenal in their League Cup tie against Birmingham City at Highbury on 14 October 1997. Crowe, making his Arsenal debut, replaced Lee Dixon at the beginning of the first period of extra time but was only on the pitch for 33 seconds when he was dismissed for a foul on Birmingham's Martin Connor.

Pepper not a man for all seasons. Nigel Pepper joined Aberdeen from Bradford City in November 1998 for a fee of £300,000. Pepper was sent off on his Aberdeen debut six minutes after coming on as a substitute. Following his suspension, again having come on as a substitute, Pepper was sent off after just 17 seconds.

Chic red card man. Chic Charnley's playing career spanned 1982 to 2003 during which time he played for a variety of clubs including Partick Thistle, St. Mirren, Dundee, Hibernian and Bolton Wanderers. During his twenty-year career Charnley was sent off 17 times. When at Partick Thistle, he and two team-mates were approached by two teenagers during a Thistle training session in Ruchill Park. The teenagers attacked Charnley with a samurai sword, despite sustaining a stab wound to his hand, Charnley laid out his assailant with a single punch.

Player issued five red cards in a single game. In 2000-01, former Dundee United and Scotland midfielder, Dave Bowman, was red carded four times for persistently arguing with match officials, refusing to leave the pitch and making a crude gesture when playing for Forfar Athletic in a 5-3 defeat against Berwick Rangers. The following season, Bowman was red-carded five times in Forfar Athletic's Scottish Second Division match against Stranraer for similar behaviour. Given his previous disciplinary record, Bowman was banned for 17 matches which ruled him out for six months.

Not thinking outside the box. On 13 August 2000, Sheffield Wednesday goalkeeper, Kevin Pressman, was sent off after only thirteen seconds for handling outside his penalty area during Wednesday's League One game against Wolves at Molineux.

Change as good as a rest. On 27 January 2002, Liverpool's Jamie Carragher was dismissed during his club's FA Cup tie against Arsenal at Highbury for throwing a coin at Arsenal supporters. Referee Mike Reilly had already dismissed Arsenal's Martin Keown and Denis Bergkamp; as the referee ordered Bergkamp from the field, a coin thrown from the crowd struck Carragher, who threw it back and was himself dismissed for 'ungentlemanly conduct'.

Technically, Keith Gillespie was sent off after zero seconds whilst 'playing' for Sheffield United against Reading in the Premier League on 20 January 2007. Gillespie appeared as a second-half substitute, before play resumed, however, Gillespie was sent off for 'violent conduct' having appeared to 'throw an elbow in the direction of Reading's Stephen Hunt.'

The most yellow cards received by a Manchester United player is 136, Paul Scholes, in 702 appearances between 1993 and 2013.

Brief Church service. Simon Church was a substitute for Reading's Championship match at Bristol City on 19 December 2009. Church was booked after thirteen minutes for rising from the bench and too vigorously protesting a penalty award for Bristol City. Late in the game, Church came off the bench and scored Reading's equaliser in the 90th minute, only to then receive his second yellow card for exuberant celebration and was consequently dismissed.

After the brawl is over. The League Two game between Bradford City and Crawley Town on 27 March 2012 resulted in five players being red-carded after the final whistle. A tetchy game 'kicked-off' after the final whistle, which resulted in red cards for Bradford City's Andrew Davies, Luke Oliver and Jon McLaughlin and for Crawley's Pablo Mills and Claude Davis.

Given short shrift. Former Manchester City striker Edin Dzeko was sent off for pulling down the shorts of an opponent whilst playing for Bosnia-Herzegovina against Greece in a World Cup qualifying match on 13 November 2016. To add to Dzeko's chagrin, from the free-kick, Greece scored to tie the game at 1-1.

Paying by card? In 2020-21, 47 red cards were issued in the Premier League, in the Championship the number of red cards issued was 48. In 1965-66, nine players were sent off in Division One.

Champions

In 1912-13, Sunderland gained only two points from their first seven league matches and were second bottom of Division One. Sunderland then won 25 of their remaining 31 matches to finish as League Champions. Sunderland's first league win of the season did not arrive until 12 October, a 4-0 home win over Middlesbrough. That same season Sunderland were also beaten FA Cup Finalists.

When Huddersfield Town were crowned League Champions in 1924-25, Huddersfield won more points from away matches than they did at home - 28 from home games, 30 away. The only instance of this happening regarding the English League Champions.

In 1937-38, only 16 points separated champions Arsenal from relegated Manchester City and West Bromwich Albion - the closest points margin in the history of English top-flight football (42 match season). Relegated Manchester City were reigning League Champions. Arsenal won only two more away games than relegated West Brom.

On 22 February 1939, Everton travelled to Molineux as leaders of the First Division and were beaten 7-0 by Wolverhampton Wanderers. The joint highest defeat by a leading team in the English top-flight, Everton, however, finished the season as English League Champions.

1952-53 produced the smallest winning margin by English League Champions. Arsenal and Preston North End both finished on 54 points and had identical results, 21 wins, 12 draws and 9 defeats. Arsenal scored 97 goals and conceded 64, whereas Preston scored 85 and conceded 60. Teams level on points were separated by goal average, Arsenal's goal average of 1.51 was 0.1 better than that of Preston (1.41). Had goal difference been in use at the time, Arsenal would still have won the title, by a margin of +8.

When Liverpool won the First Division title in 1965-66, they used only 14 players throughout the season. A feat equalled by Aston Villa in 1980-81. Nowadays a Premier League club will use more players for a single game.

Should three points for a win have been awarded in 1974-75, Ipswich Town would have been League Champions. Champions Derby County finished on 53 points; runners-up Liverpool on 51 points with Ipswich Town, also 51 points, third on goal difference. Ipswich won 23 matches whereas Derby County won 21 and Liverpool 20. Should three points have been awarded for a win, Ipswich would have won the League title ahead of Derby on goal difference of plus 4, both teams finishing with 74 points.

The First Division title race of 1974-75 was one of the most competitive in the history of English football. During the course of the season, the leadership changed hands 21 times among ten clubs.

Burnley, Portsmouth, Preston North End, Sheffield United and Wolverhampton Wanderers are the only clubs to have won all four divisions in English football.

In 1980-81, Villa won the League Championship and the FA Cup for Tottenham Hotspur. Aston Villa won the First Division and Ricardo Villa scored Spurs' winner at Wembley in the FA Cup Final replay against Manchester City.

On the final day of the 1990-91 season, West Ham United and Oldham Athletic had both sealed promotion from Division Two to Division One (top-flight) but were contesting the title. Should West Ham beat Notts County at Upton Park the title would be theirs. With ninety minutes played West Ham were losing 2-1 to Notts County but the title still seemed destined for Upton Park as Oldham were losing 2-1 at home to Sheffield Wednesday. Football League officials were present at Upton Park along with the Division Two trophy and as the game entered added time, had the trophy engraved with West Ham United as Division Two Champions. Oldham Athletic then scored twice in three minutes of added time, their winning goal, a Neil Redfearn penalty, being the last kick of the match. Two days later, on 13th May, Oldham Athletic were presented with the Division Two Champions Trophy by Football League officials. The trophy was still engraved with West Ham United as Champions.

In 2004-05, Yeovil Town were champions of League Two, having lost only two fewer matches away from home than Cambridge United who were relegated to the Conference League.

Manchester City's title win of 2011-12 was the smallest winning margin of any Champions in Premier League history, but not the Football League. City finished level on points with Manchester United, both on 89, City claimed the title due to their better goal difference, +8 goals.

When Cardiff City won the Championship in 2012-13, the most goals an individual player scored was eight. The club's joint leading goalscorers were Aron Gunnarsson, Heider Helguson and Peter Whittingham, the latter's tally included four penalties. Champions Cardiff scored only six more goals than relegated Peterborough United.

Manchester City claimed a treble in 2020-21; City won the Premier League, their Under 23 team won the PL2 League and their youth team won the Premier League Under 18 League.

In 2020-21, Chelsea won the Champions League, finished 4th in the Premier League and were FA Cup runners-up, yet no Chelsea player reached double figures in terms of Premier League goals; the first time a club finishing in the top four in English top-flight football failed to have a player scoring ten goals or more since Everton in 1910-11. Chelsea's top goalscorer in the League was Jorginho with just seven goals.

Cheltenham Town were League Two Champions in 2020-21, the club's joint leading goalscorers were Alfie May and Andy Williams with just eight goals apiece.

Premier League regulations state the League Champions shall receive 40 League winners' medals 'for distribution among players, coaches and club officials.' A player who appeared in five matches or more is guaranteed a medal, otherwise it is at the discretion of the club. Club Officials?

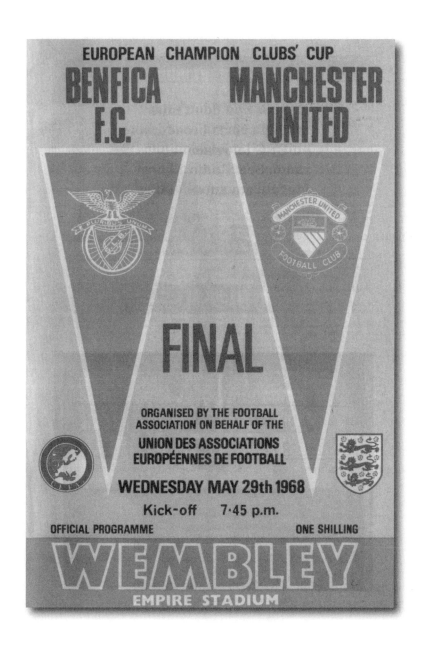

30

Curiosities

Five-a-side football was initiated by Queens Park. At a club meeting in 1876, the idea of playing four-a-side football in training was mooted by a member of the Queens Park committee. The motion was approved on the recommendation five-a-side be implemented as the club regularly had twenty players attend training, thus four teams of five could be better accommodated.

AC Milan was founded in 1899 as a cricket club by two English expatriates, Alfred Edwards and Herbert Kilpin, who later added football to the club's sporting repertoire. In honour of its English origins the club retains the English spelling of the city's name, as opposed to the Italian spelling 'Milano'.

In 1915, Manchester United's Enoch 'Nocker' West, along with three other United players and four Liverpool players, was found guilty of match-fixing. West received a thirty-year ban from the Football Association. He was 59 when his ban was lifted in 1945.

Popped into the refreshment kiosks. Between 1928 and 1935, Tom 'Pongo' Waring scored 159 goals in 216 League matches for Aston Villa. A Villa legend, Waring was known for his idiosyncratic ways. Before training on a Monday, Waring would make a tour of all the refreshment kiosks at Villa Park and decanter the remnants of lemonade bottles into larger bottles which he then took home. Waring continued this practice throughout his career at Villa Park.

To hide his premature baldness, Irish International Tommy Priestley, whose clubs included Chelsea (1933-34), always wore a rugby skull-cap, even when travelling to and from matches.

The last club to win either the Premier League or First Division whose first-choice strip is stripes was Sunderland in 1935-36.

At the start of the 1937-38 season, Wolverhampton Wanderers had forty professionals on their books, none were married.

Horace Gager captained Luton Town during the 1947-48 season, included in the Luton team were manager/player Dally Duncan, first team coach, Frank Soo and assistant coach/trainer, Sid Ottewell. As at January 2022, Luton Town boasted the oldest living former England International, goalkeeper, Roy Baynham, 92 years of age.

In 1950-51, all four Rotherham United teams were captained by players whose surname was Williams but none were related. First team - Horace Williams; Reserves - Danny; 'A' team - Ken; youth team- Bobby.

Following a friendly game against Boston United in April 1951, Southampton goalkeeper, Hugh Kelly, returned to the team hotel accompanied by a young woman. When Southampton trainer, Jimmy Easson, attempted to eject the lady, he and Kelly had an argument which resulted in Kelly striking Easson and giving him a black eye. Kelly was immediately placed on the transfer list and never played at any level for Southampton again.

Worth reviving. In 1952, the Football Association held a competition, 'Football in Art', in which professional and amateur artists were invited to submit work relating to football. The FA received over 1,700 entries which included paintings in oils and watercolour, drawings and sculptures. The judges were Professor William Coldstream (University College of London), Sir Phillip Hendry (Director of National Gallery), Phillip Jones (Director of the Arts Council) and Sir John Rothenstein (Director of Tate Gallery). 150 of what were considered the best entries were shown at a month-long exhibition staged at Park Lane House in London which attracted over 40,000 visitors.

Baden Powell was a winger who played for Darlington from 1950 to 1954; when Baden Powell retired as a player, he became a scout for the club.

Jimmy Seed (manager) and Sam Bartram (goalkeeper) spent twenty two years together at Charlton Athletic, from September 1934 to March 1956. From making his debut, to his retirement in 1956, Bartram was never dropped from the Charlton team.

Charlton Athletic goalkeeper, Sam Bartram, enjoyed 22-years with the club and was never dropped from the team, making 623 senior appearances. Bartram, seen here in action against Cardiff City on 11 October 1952, having parried an effort from Cardiff's Ken Chisholm, is unable to prevent George Edwards scoring for Cardiff from the rebound. Charlton won 3-1. On 29 March 1947, Bartram suffered food poisoning but played in the FA Cup semi-final against Newcastle United at Elland Road with a hot poultice strapped to his stomach.

Tommy Lawton, at the time with Brentford, appeared alongside Diana Dors, Thora Hird, James Hayter and John Laurie in the 1953 film 'The Great Game'. Lawton played himself, many of the scenes in this football comedy-drama were shot at Brentford's Griffin Park.

The Lincoln City team of 1958-59 included David Short, who was 5'2" tall and George Long, who was 6'3" tall.

Former Dundee United skipper, Neil Paterson, became a football journalist and screenwriter when his playing days were over. Paterson is the only former player to have won an Academy award, for his screenplay for the 1959 film 'Room at the Top'.

Former Crewe Alexandra manager, Dario Gradi, attended Loughborough University between 1960 and 1963, among his fellow students were Bob Wilson (Arsenal) and Barry Hines, author of 'Kes'.

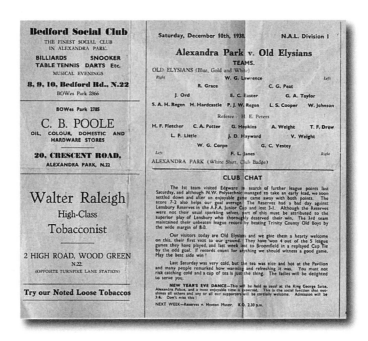

Match programme from 1938-39, Alexandra Park FC (still going) of the Southern Amateur League, the curiosity being the advert for the tobacconist.

Nurses no grudge. Mel Nurse was playing for Middlesbrough in 1963 when, after a night out in the town, he was pulled over by the police who had mistaken him for Great Train Robber, Ronnie Biggs. Nurse was released when his identity had been verified.

The entire Alloa Athletic team and Hibernian centre-forward, Brian Marjoribanks, appeared in a 1963 episode of the popular BBC drama series, 'Dr. Finlay's Casebook', filmed at Alloa's Recreation Park ground. Marjoribanks appeared in numerous plays and TV dramas before becoming the anchor of BBC Scotland Sports for 18 years.

Pedrag Lukic is the only former member of the Communist Party in an Iron Curtain country to become a director of a Football League club. A native of Yugoslavia, Lukic came to Britain and eventually became a director of Stockport County in November 1964.

Little pomp for the occasion. Following their goalless draw at Leicester City

Match programme from the first leg of the 1965 League Cup Final between Chelsea and Leicester City, the final in which Football League officials misplaced the winners' tankards. The bonus paid to the winners was £25 per player. In addition, £750 'talent' money was distributed to the winning team, £500 to the runners-up (Leicester City), After expenses had been deducted, each club received 40% of the match receipts (two legs) with 20% going to the League Cup pool.

which gave Chelsea a 3-2 aggregate win in the 1965 League Cup Final, Football League officials could not find the winners tankards with which to present Tommy Docherty's side. It was whilst the Chelsea players were showering that club secretary John Battersby entered their dressing room with a large cardboard box containing the tankards, saying, 'Help yourselves, one each.'

Bob Wilson and Charlie George were teammates when Arsenal won the 'double' in 1971. They first met when George was a pupil and Wilson his teacher at a secondary school in Islington.

Following a press report intimating Leicester City's Alan Birchenall had 'been asleep' when presented with a chance during a match in the 1970s, Birchenall took to the pitch for his next match at Filbert Street wearing a dressing gown over his strip.

Stamp issued by Equatorial Guinea to commemorate the finals of the 1974 World Cup. England get a mention, albeit England did not qualify; England have also acquired George Best who, in turn, has the looks of John Noakes.

Not such a stupid boy. Actor Ian Lavender is an Aston Villa fan and grew up supporting the club. When filming began for the TV series 'Dad's Army', Lavender was allowed to choose his character's (Private Pike) scarf and chose to wear an old Aston Villa scarf.

Bournemouth had the longest continuous membership of the Third Division (in both its guises) from 1923 to 1970 - 47 years.

When Eamon O'Keefe (Everton, Wigan Athletic and Port Vale) made his debut for The Republic of Ireland Under 21s versus China in 1983 he was four months short of his 30th birthday.

The Division Two game between Sheffield United and Oldham Athletic on 9 February 1985 was postponed when workmen found an unexploded bomb from WW2 whilst digging up the road outside Bramall Lane.

Frank Worthington had numerous clubs but one not officially listed is Manchester United, for whom he played four times. At the end of the 1984-85 season, having left Southampton, Worthington joined Manchester United as a 'guest player' on their post-season tour of Australia and appeared for United against the Australia national team, Nottingham Forest and Juventus. Worthington made one more appearance for United, against Oxford United at the Manor Ground in Peter Foley's Testimonial match on 14 May 1985.

You go Ashkam. On 21 March 1987, Southampton's Jackpot Lottery Draw of £5,000 was won by Guy Ashkam, the club's financial director.

What inflation? In 1988, Doncaster Rovers' supporters launched their fanzine 'Popular Stand', cover price £1. 'Popular Stand' is one of the few fanzines to have survived into 2021-22, furthermore, 34 years on, it still costs just £1.

One for each goal conceded. Albion Rovers travelled to Partick Thistle for a Scottish League Cup tie on 11 August 1993. Albion's official away support was 11; they lost 11-1.

Swindon Town is the only English league club whose name does not contain any of the letters that appear in the word 'mackerel'.

Reds v Blues. Russian Premier Alexey Kosygin has a ball with Rangers players prior to their 2-1 win over Kilmarnock in 1967.

Many will be familiar with Oasis' first studio album 'Definitely Maybe' and the fact the album artwork features two footballers on the cover: George Best, featured in a photograph on the windowsill, and Rodney Marsh, of whom a framed picture is posed before the fireplace. There is, however, a third footballer who appears on the inside gatefold of the vinyl album. Liam Gallagher is pictured reading a newspaper and on the back page of the newspaper is a photograph of Leicester City's Matt Elliott in the 1994 First Division play-off Final against Derby County.

On 11 February 1967, Russian Premier Alexey Kosygin attended the Scottish First Division match between Kilmarnock and Rangers at Rugby Park.

On 1 April 1995, Torquay United wore the colours of arch-rivals, Exeter City, for their Division Three match against Hereford United at Plainmoor. The April Fool's Day prank on their fans somewhat backfired, Hereford won 1-0.

In 1994-95, the Chester City fanzine was edited by the Reverend Colin Mansley; in the Chester City team at that time were Eddie Bishop, Chris Priest, Graham Pugh and Wayne Parsonage.

Tommy Lawton, whose clubs included Burnley, Everton, Chelsea, Notts County and Arsenal, who scored 22 goals in 23 official Internationals for England, died in November 1996. Lawton's ashes are kept in the National Football Museum in Manchester.

The Dutch club Ajax is named after Ajax, in Greek legend son of Telamon, king of Salamis, noted in the Iliad for his strength and bravery.

The person with the most clubs named after him is the 15th/16th century Portuguese explorer Vasco De Gama, who has five clubs named in his honour, the most famous being CR Vasco De Gama (Brazil). Curiously, none of the five clubs are Portuguese.

Ibrox, home of Rangers, derives its name from an old Scottish term, 'Y brocks' meaning badger ford.

Some Guys Have All The Luck. On 9 March 2003, reggae star, Maxi Priest ('Some Guys Have All The Luck', 'Wild World' etc) played for Southall in their 3-0 home defeat to Feltham in the Spartan South Midlands League. Priest was in attendance to watch his son (Marvin) play for Southall, however, due to illness and injuries, Southall were short on players and Maxi Priest was named as substitute. An injury to a Southall player early in the second-half saw Priest senior, at 41 years of age, called into action.

Oldham Athletic, Fleetwood Town and Forest Green Rovers are the only English League clubs situated in a town which does not have a railway station. Oldham Mumps, Oldham Wenther and Oldham Derker were converted to tramstops in 2010, thus ceased to be linked to the national network. In 2009, the Association of Train Operating Companies proposed a new station in Fleetwood as part of a plan to expand the national network, locals were told to, 'watch this space'. As at 2022, they were still space watching. Forest Green Rovers are based in Nailsworth, however, FGR's New Lawn stadium is three miles from Stroud railway station, albeit less than the distance between some clubs and the mainline railway station in their town/city, such as Oxford United, Salford City and Coventry City. Four clubs in Scotland play in towns that do not have a railway station, Kelty Hearts (a village), Peterhead, East Fife and Forfar Athletic, the latter who, ironically, play at Station Park. East Fife play in Methil, for all there is no railway station, there are plans to reopen the line from Thornton Junction which received Government support in 2019.

The number one shirt is usually afforded to goalkeepers but there have been exceptions. Edgar Davids wore a number one shirt when playing for Barnet (2012-14) and Derek Riordan when playing as a striker for Hibernian in 2009-10.

Supporters acquire former cannabis farm. In August 2018, Newport County Supporters Trust took control of the nearby Ivy Bush Inn after the pub had its licence revoked following a police raid in which a cannabis farm was found in the upstairs rooms. The premises, which now houses a fine collection of County artefacts and memorabilia, functions as the headquarters of the Newport County Supporters Trust and, on match days, welcomes away supporters.

Watford's nickname is the Hornets, yet the club badge features a hart (male deer). In 1959-60, Watford changed the colours of their strip from blue and white to gold and black; following a vote by supporters, the team adopted the nickname of the Hornets. A hart appears on the club badge to symbolise Watford were, and still are, since Barnet dropped into the National League, the only league club in Hertfordshire.

In 2020, 80% of footballs used across the world were manufactured in Pakistan.

In 2020-21, the Northern Premier League South East and the North West Counties League First Division South were the only two leagues to have three of the four cardinal geographic direction points in their title.

Five players with same name as the club they played for. In 2020-21, Ross County had five players whose first name was Ross - Ross Laidlaw, Ross Draper, Ross Stewart, Ross Doohan and Ross Munro.

No one noticed until the 1997 Charity Shield match between Chelsea and Manchester United was underway (United 4-2 on penalties after 1-1), that United's David Beckham had a slight problem with the name on his shirt, Beckham being spelt as 'Beckam'.

It is a common misconception that Queen of the South is the only football club mentioned in the Bible - 'The queen of the south will rise up at the judgement' (Genesis 10:7). There are five other football clubs that appear in the Bible. Bury - 'Bury your dead in the choicest of our tombs' (Genesis 23:1); Arsenal - 'The Lord has opened his arsenal and brought out the weapons of his wrath' (Jeremiah 50:25); Hearts - 'Cleanse your hands, you sinners and purify your hearts' (James 4:8); Wolves - 'Beware of false prophets, which come to you in sheep's clothing but inwardly they are ravening wolves' (Matthew 7:15). There is, of course, two books of Corinthians, as in the Brazilian football club.

Germany and Bayern Munich goalkeeper Manuel Neuer provided the voice-over for the character Frank McCoy in the German version of the Disney-Pixar animated film 'Monsters University'. Neuer also won the German celebrity edition of 'Who Wants To Be A Millionaire', the 500,000 Euros prize money was donated to charity.

Theory Henri. Frank Leboeuf, who won the World Cup and European Championship with France and played 144 league matches for Chelsea, played Henri, the Swiss doctor, in the Oscar nominated and BAFTA winning film 'The Theory of Everything'.

The only manager to have managed a Premier League club and to have acted in a major film is Carlo Ancelloti who played the 'Devil's Player', a 'hit man', in the 1983 film, 'The World of Don Camillo'.

Crystal Palace's new strip for 2004-05 was replaced after just one match when the club were alerted to a problem regarding the club badge.

Out of the left field. Former Arsenal and Chelsea midfield player, Emanuel Petit, a World Cup winner with France appeared in an episode of the drama series, 'The Bill'.

The only footballer to have been mentioned in a Monty Python sketch is former Sunderland and Aston Villa striker, Kevin Phillips, as in 'Kevin Phillips Bong, slightly Silly Party' in the Python sketch 'Election Night Special'. Obviously not a specific reference to the former England striker.

In 2007, Australian club Sydney FC spent 10,000 (Aus) dollars promoting a poll to find a nickname for the club, a mark of the quality of suggestions can be gauged by the winner - 'Sky Blues'. Following a party to launch the nickname, neither club nor anyone else has ever used it since.

Ground hop without leaving your seat. Should you journey on the Plymouth to Aberdeen train you would pass, and get a glimpse of, 20 English and Scottish league grounds.

Dale tries luck with chip shot. On 23 November 2019, during Crewe Alexandra's League Two home match against Morecambe, Crewe winger, Owen Dale, cut inside from the right and shot at goal. The ball cleared the roof of the Gresty Road stand, bounced on the road outside then proceeded to travel through the open door of the chip shop that faces the stadium and over the counter, scattering assistants. The incident provoked much mirth in the press box, who had a good view of the event courtesy of the gap between Crewe's main stand and Gresty Road stand.

In 2021-22, Arsenal did not qualify to play in European competition for the first time in 25 years.

As at 2021-22, only two clubs in the Premier League had strips made by British kit manufacturers, Burnley and West Ham United, both with Umbro.

When Ruben Colwill scored after ten minutes for Cardiff City at Luton Town on 27 November 2021, it was the first time Cardiff had scored in the first half of a league match since Keifer Moore netted against Wycombe Wanderers on 24 April 2021 - a sequence of 22 matches.

Carbon football print? Manchester United travelled by air for their Premier League game at Leicester City on 16 October 2021. United flew from Manchester airport to East Midlands airport, then travelled by coach for the 22-mile journey to Leicester. The journey from Manchester to East Midlands airport is 83.2 miles, it was estimated the flight took around ten minutes.

The pyjama game. Following their 3-0 victory over Ayr United in the Scottish Championship on 18 December 2021, Queen of the South players Josh Todd and Wullie Gibson gave an interview for TV in which Todd wore a tracksuit, and, Gibson, Christmas pyjamas.

On 21 December 2021, League Two club, Oldham Athletic, banned three supporters from all first team and youth games for three years for 'promoting their dislike of the club'. Something of a misnomer as the three supporters in question were ardent Oldham Athletic fans and rather than the club, it was the club's hierarchy, in particular the club owner, who had been the subject of their protests. Non executive club director, Richard Bowden, resigned his post, citing the letter informing the supporters of their ban, 'erroneously states the board approved the action taken'.

Wrexham were included in the simulation video game FIFA 22, the first non-league club to feature in the series.

Debuts

Such was the excitement and interest surrounding Tom 'Pongo' Waring's £4,700 transfer to Aston Villa from Tranmere Rovers in 1928, a crowd of 23,667 turned up at Villa Park to see his debut for Villa reserves against Birmingham City reserves. Waring scored a hat-trick in a 6-3 victory.

Andy Cunningham made his debut for Newcastle United at the age of 38 years and two days against Leicester City in a First Division match on 2 February 1929, having been transferred from Rangers for a fee of £2,500.

Most goals scored by a player making his debut in senior football is eight. On 2 January 1930, Jim Dyet, netted eight in, now defunct, King's Park's 12-2 victory over Forfar Athletic in Scottish League Division Two.

Swindon Town's debut as a Football League club took place on 28 August 1930, they beat Luton Town 9-1, the highest margin of victory by a club playing their first game in the Football League.

Stan Milton made his debut in goal for Halifax Town against Stockport County on 6 January 1934. It was far from a dream debut, Milton conceding 13 goals. Stockport's 13-0 victory is the joint highest total scored by a club in English senior football and the record margin of victory.

Shop-window job? Fullback Norman Young signed for Aston Villa in April 1926 but had to wait ten years before making his first team debut in 1936. Having made his debut, he was sold two days later to Barnsley.

Neil McBain, a centre-half, made his debut for New Brighton at the age of 51 years and 4 months in their 3-0 defeat against Hartlepools United on 15 March 1947. McBain was manager of New Brighton but due to a plethora of injuries had to name himself in the team as the goalkeeper.

McBain holds the record for being the oldest player ever to have made a debut in the Football League. Having made his senior debut for Ayr United in 1911, McBain's playing career spanned 32 years.

Conceded nine goals on his International debut and retained his place for the next game. This dubious distinction is held by Hugh Kelly of Fulham, who played in goal for The Republic of Ireland when they lost 9-2 to England on 16 November 1949. Kelly kept a clean sheet in his next International appearance, a 0-0 draw against Wales in a World Cup qualifying match.

Bill Nicholson's first ever game as manager of Spurs on 11 October 1958 resulted in a 10-4 defeat of Everton at White Hart Lane. During his post-match interview Nicholson is quoted as saying, 'Ten goals will never be surpassed during my time as manager of Spurs.' Sixteen months later, Nicholson's Spurs beat Crewe Alexandra 13-2 in an FA Cup tie.

Trevor Chamberlain, for Fulham v Lincoln City on 20 November 1954; Micky Lill, Wolves v Preston North End, 7 December 1957; Peter Burridge, Leyton Orient v Stoke City December 27 1958; Alan Jones, Fulham v Bolton Wanderers 6 February 1960; Maketa Molongo for Brighton v Reading 7 August 2004 and Jamie Mackie for Plymouth Argyle v Brighton on 12 February 2008 - all scored within twenty seconds of making their debut for their respective clubs.

Ralph Brown made his debut for Aston Villa on 22 August 1961 in the League Cup Final first-leg against Rotherham United. Villa lost 2-0 but won the second leg 3-0 at Villa Park to become the first holders of the League Cup. Brown's debut was the only game he ever played for Aston Villa. In addition to receiving a winners tankard, which were awarded to League Cup winners rather than medals, Brown has the distinction of being the only player to have made his debut in a major Cup final and it being his only appearance for the club.

Jimmy Greaves scored on his debut for every senior team he played for - Chelsea v Spurs (23 August 1957); England Under 23s v Bulgaria (25 September 1957); England v Peru (17 May 1959); AC Milan v Botafogo (7 June 1961); Spurs v Blackpool - a hat-trick (16 December 1961); West Ham United v Manchester City (21 March 1970).

Following his transfer from Kilmarnock, goalkeeper Sandy McLaughlan made his Sunderland debut at home to West Bromwich Albion on 2 September 1964, his first touch of the ball was to pick it out of his net, West Brom having scored after 45 seconds. McLaughlan enjoyed a reputation for the power of his dead-ball kicks. McLaughlan's second touch of the ball, some minutes later, was to take a goal kick which sailed down the pitch, bounced once in the opposition penalty area and over West Bromwich Albion's goalkeeper Ray Potter's crossbar.

Goalkeeper Gordon Nisbet signed for West Bromwich Albion in 1968 and made his League debut against Coventry City on 12 August 1969. Albion coach Don Howe, however, noticed Nisbet had another string to his bow. Howe switched Nisbet to full-back, a position he fulfilled for 621 League matches, 136 of them for West Brom'.

Feet on Trevor firma. On 10 October 1979, Nottingham Forest issued a souvenir programme and invited national media to attend the match between their Midland Intermediate Youth team and Notts County Youths. The occasion was the debut of Trevor Francis, purchased from Birmingham City for £1million. Forest boss, Brian Clough, wanted Britain's most expensive footballer to make his debut in inauspicious surroundings which he felt would help Francis 'keep his feet on the ground.'

Marc's his debut with goal. Marc de Clerck made his debut in goal for Aberdeen at Berwick Rangers on 30 August 1980. Not only did the goalkeeper keep a clean sheet in a 4-0 victory, he also scored, a long clearance bouncing over the head of the Berwick 'keeper and into the net.

Brazil International, Socrates, signed a one month contract with Garforth Town of the North West Counties League, making his debut as a substitute on 20 November 2004 against Tadcaster Albion. It was Socrates' only appearance in English football. During the second half, Socrates twice excused himself from the bench to visit the changing rooms. The Garforth manager later discovered the Brazilian World Cup winner had drunk two bottles of Budweiser and smoked three cigarettes whilst in the dressing room.

Jonathan Woodgate was transferred from Newcastle United to Real Madrid in August 2004. but did not make his Real debut until 22 September 2005 against Atletico Bilbao, a game in which he scored an own goal and was sent off after 65 minutes.

On 8 August 2009, Michael Theoklitos made his debut in goal for Norwich City in a 7-1 home defeat to Colchester United. Theoklitos never played for Norwich again. Theoklitos was chosen as the substitute goalkeeper for an EFL Trophy match against Gillingham but did not turn up. His contract with Norwich was later terminated by mutual consent.

Reading signed goalkeeper Mikkel Andersen from AB Gladsaxe (Denmark) on 26 January 2007. Andersen did not make his first team debut for Reading until 20 September 2014 in a 1-0 defeat away to Sheffield Wednesday. Andersen spent eight years at Reading making three League appearances before joining FC Midtjylland in 2015.

The youngest player to score on his league debut for Manchester United is Marcus Rashford who scored in United's 3-2 victory over Arsenal in 2016. It was, however, not Rashford's first senior goal for the club, on 25 February 2016, he scored twice in a Europa League game against FC Midtjylland having come on as a substitute.

Directors and Club Owners

The only director to be selected, on merit, to play for his club is Vivian Woodward. In 1907-8, Woodward was a director of Tottenham Hotspur when selected to play for Spurs. Woodward had joined Spurs as a player in 1901, making 131 League appearances, scoring 61 goals.

In 1946, Ken Friar, aged twelve, was employed part-time in Arsenal's box office, which became his full-time employment when he left school in 1950. Friar went on to serve Arsenal for over seventy years, as club secretary, managing director, club director and, in 2020 upon his retirement, was appointed life president of the club.

In October 1953, all seven Newport County directors resigned en bloc with the team bottom of Division Three South. Billy Lucas joined the club from Swansea Town as manager and, along with the club secretary, ran the club until new directors were appointed.

Bob Lord became a director of Burnley in 1951 and Chairman in 1955. The early years of Lord's chairmanship were the most successful in the club's history. He invested heavily in the club and was once asked what he would have been should he not have been chairman of Burnley. Lord replied, 'A millionaire'. Lord's response to football journalists he thought had slighted him was to ban them from Turf Moor. In 1966, Lord banned three newspapers and six individual journalists from the Turf Moor press box and fined Burnley players if they spoke to the press without prior permission, however, due to adverse publicity and pressure from within the club, Lord had to relent. Lord, of whom Tommy Docherty once said, 'Was a chairman seemingly intent on keeping his Christmas card list very short', was, however, one of the few chairmen to give wholehearted support to the PFA's campaign to end the maximum wage in the early 1960s.

During October 1966, Third Division, Workington, increased membership of their Board of Directors to 15. The increase meant Workington had more directors than it had full-time professional players (12).

WORKINGTON A.F.C. — MEMBERS FOOTBALL LEAGUE.
NORTH REGIONAL LEAGUE.
REGISTERED OFFICE: BOROUGH PARK, WORKINGTON.
Phone: Workington 3736.
Directors: T. Kirkpatrick (Chairman), R. J. S. Atkinson, J. Z. Bridgewater, D Coveney,
E Firby, H. Horsley, R. A. Keenan, T. Kirkpatrick, J. W. Mason, H. Moffat, M. Nilsson,
E. D. Smith, R. Tognarelli, H. Walker, J. Wannop.
Secretary: Norman Conquest.   Manager: G. Ainsley.   Financial Sec.: W. Knowles.

A page from Workington v Oxford United match programme of 11 February 1966. Workington had increased the number of club directors to 15, three more than the club had full-time professional players. Note the club secretary, who had previously served Hastings United in the Southern League.

Only manager to have been sacked and refused to leave the club. On 15 November 1966, Hartlepool United Chairman, Ernest Ord, sacked manager Brian Clough's assistant, Peter Taylor, as a cost-cutting measure. Brian Clough refused to accept the decision, so, Ord subsequently sacked Clough as well. Clough refused to go and organised a boardroom coup which resulted in Ord being ousted as chairman.

On 29 March 1969, Manchester City defeated Everton 1-0 in the FA Cup semi-final at Villa Park. Following what had been a very tight and highly contested game, Manchester City Chairman, Albert Alexander, visited the City players in their dressing room. 'Mr Alexander congratulated the team on reaching Wembley', adding. 'Getting to the FA Cup Final will be very good for this club. It will bring in much needed extra-revenue to allow us to bring in some better players.' As told to the author by Mike Summerbee.

Tommy Docherty's term as Chelsea manager ended in 1967. In 1972, Docherty was appointed manager of Manchester United. On his first trip back to Stamford Bridge as United manager, Docherty met the Chelsea President, Viscount Chelsea, in a corridor within Stamford Bridge. After exchanging pleasantries, Viscount Chelsea told Docherty, 'Tommy, when you left Chelsea, many people at this club passed some very undeserving comments about you. But I wish you to know, I have never, at any time, told anyone, you now live in the North of England.' As told to the author by Tommy Docherty.

For 117 years Nottingham Forest were not run by a board of directors but by a committee. The club eventually became a limited company with directors in 1982, two years after the club's second (and back-to-back) success in the European Cup.

Brian Clough twice applied for the vacant manager's job at his former club, Sunderland, but was rejected on both occasions by the club's directors. Decisions which still evokes ire among Sunderland supporters to this day.

EXCLUSIVE

I'll talk to Sunderland

IT IS still on the cards that Brian Clough may leave Nottingham Forest and join Sunderland, he revealed today in an exclusive interview with the Evening Chronicle.

As he left his detached home in his white Mercedes car to see this afternoon's big match between Forest and Everton, Clough said: "I want to talk to the Sunderland directors, and I certainly would consider any offer which they would make.

"I hold no grudges against Sunderland Football Club for turning me down twice. In fact I feel flattered that they want me now. I still feel sentimental as far as Sunderland town is concerned.

And Brian Clough dropped a broad hint that he wants to return to Wearside when he said: "If my chairman changes his mind I will talk to Sunderland."

Mr. Clough had earlier slammed the door and refused to say anything. He shouted "No" before closing the door.

Two hours later, Clough, his attitude as inconsistent as ever, got out of his Mercedes, shook hands, smiled and said: "Ask me questions, but for God's sake don't quote anything which has been said in the newspapers this week."

BRIAN CLOUGH talks to Chief Reporter MIKE CURRIE

He has been widely quoted as saying: "The slate will be clean by this weekend."

He said he meant by this that as no change of thought had been given by his directors, he would have to remain at Nottingham.

In the meantime Cloughie said he was giving all his attention to this afternoon's top-of-the-table clash

To the everlasting angst of their fans, the Sunderland Board didn't want to talk to Brian Clough.

George Herd made 318 senior appearances for Sunderland between 1961 to 1970, yet rarely travelled with the team to away matches. Herd could not get a good night's sleep in hotels, only in his own bed at home. With the exception of long-haul journeys, Sunderland club directors took it in turns to collect Herd from his home on a Saturday morning and drive him to away matches.

Comedian Jasper Carrott was once a director of Birmingham City. Other celebrities, apart from those whose affiliations to clubs is well known, who have been directors of clubs include: Sir Richard Attenborough (Chelsea); Frank Carson (Newport County); Willie Carson (Swindon Town); Tommy Cannon (Rochdale); Billy Cotton senior (Queens Park Rangers); Jim Davidson (Bournemouth); Fred Dinenage (Portsmouth); Arthur English (Aldershot); Brian Moore (Gillingham); David Milliband (Sunderland).

In 1990, Heart of Midlothian Chairman, Wallace Mercer, proposed a merger between Hearts and local rivals Hibernian. The move caused an uproar and was seen as a hostile take-over by Hibernian fans who persuaded Kwik-Fit owner, Sir Tom Farmer, to acquire a controlling interest in Hibernian, thus preserving the independence of the club and securing its future.

Steve Gibson, who owns Middlesbrough, is a life-long supporter of the club and, as a boy, attended Boro' home games with his pal, Chris Kamara. Steve Gibson is the longest serving owner/chairman of a club in English senior football, having assumed control at Middlesbrough in 1986.

The second longest serving chairman/club owner is Paul Scally who took control of Gillingham in 1995 for the sum of £1. One of Paul Scally's sons, Adam, has been editor of the club's match day programme for a number of years.

In 1995, Doncaster Rovers chairman, Ken Richardson, hired two criminals to burn down Rover's Belle Vue stadium in an attempt to make an insurance claim after having his plans for a new stadium rejected by the local council. Richardson was prosecuted and sentenced to four years imprisonment.

David Sullivan owns 51% of West Ham United, David Gold 35% with 10% owned by the Straumur Investment Bank, Iceland's only investment bank.

Los Angeles FC of the MLS are part owned by actor/comedian Will Ferrell and NBA legend Magic Johnson.

Zlatan Ibrahimovic owns 25% of Swedish club Hammarby. Brazil's Ronaldo, owns 82% of Spanish La Liga club Real Valladolid.

Three-time Grammy award winning DJ Diplo, Didier Drogba and Fall Out bassist Pete Wentz, have part-ownership of USL club Phoenix Rising FC.

Though he no longer has a stake in the club, Elton John still regularly attends Watford home matches. In 2018, Elton's son, Zachary, joined the Watford Academy.

Little Mix's Jade Thirwall is part-owner of Northern Premier League Premier Division club, South Shields, her home-town club, and is the club's honorary president.

American actor, Matthew McConaughey, who won an Oscar for his role in 'Dallas Buyers Club', is part owner of Austin FC.

Hollywood actors Ryan Reynolds and Rob McElhenney, who own Wrexham, are not the only celebrities with a stake in British clubs. Los Angeles Lakers legend, LeBron James has a 2% stake in Liverpool. James bought his stake for $6.5million in 2011 and, according to 'Business Insider' in 2019, his stake was estimated to be worth $32million.

Mark Palios is one of the few examples whereby a former player has become the club's owner. Palios played over 250 games for Tranmere Rovers, he also played for Crewe Alexandra. The former Football Association Chief Executive and his wife, Nicola, took control of Tranmere Rovers on 11 August 2014.

Though he does not have a stake in the club, Led Zeppelin's Robert Plant is Vice President of Wolverhampton Wanderers.

Lee Power, whose clubs as a player included Norwich City, Bradford City and Peterborough United, was chairman of Swindon Town, having taken control of the club in December 2013. Power was also chairman/owner of Irish club Waterford.

Eminent football writer, Ian Ridley, was once chairman of Weymouth and St. Albans City.

American actress and comedian, Mindy Kaling, writer and star of the US TV series 'Office', owns a 1% stake in Swansea City.

In March 2008, it was reported that John Batchelor had made a bid to purchase Mansfield Town. Initially, Batchelor's bid had a lukewarm reception from Mansfield fans until he announced his plan to change the name of the club to that of Harchester United, the name of the football club in the fictional TV series, 'Dream Team'. The mayor of Mansfield, Tony Egginton described Batchelor's idea as 'absolutely bizarre'. Batchelor's attempted take-over of Mansfield Town met with strong opposition and failed.

The second largest shareholder of Forest Green FC is former Arsenal full-back, Hector Bellerin, who, when an Arsenal player, became a club director in September 2020.

A rare instance of a club chairman visiting an opponents' ground which bears his name - Rangers' chairman Douglas Park visited coincidentally named, New Douglas Park, home of Hamilton Academical.

Re-cycling bin, Stafford, 2021

English and Welsh Clubs

On 11 April 1955, Accrington Stanley did not field a single English player in their team for their Third Division North fixture against York City. The Stanley team comprised eleven Scots, as chosen by their Scottish manager, Walter Galbraith. The game ended 2-2 before a healthy crowd of 15,598.

AFC Wimbledon played 78 consecutive Combined Counties League games without defeat between February 2003 and December 2004. AFC Wimbledon are the first club formed in the 21st century to become a Football League club.

Dave Smith's tenure of management at Aldershot spanned three decades. Smith was appointed manager in 1959 and held the position solely until 1967, when he became the club's General Manager, a post he held until 1971.

Arsenal's Division One match against Sheffield United on 22 January 1927 was the first ever English League game to be broadcast on radio.

Aston Villa won two major trophies on the same day. On 18 April 1897, Aston Villa won the FA Cup, beating Everton 3-2 at Crystal Palace. On the same afternoon, Derby County lost 1-0 at Bury. Derby were the only club who could overtake Aston Villa at the top of Division One. Derby's defeat left them seven points behind Villa with only three games remaining, thus Villa won the 'double' of FA Cup and First Division title on the same day.

Barnsley had successive managers in the 1980s all of whom had previously played for Leeds United. Allan Clarke 1978-80; Norman Hunter 1980-84; Bobby Collins 1984-85 and Allan Clarke again, 1985-89.

Barrow were voted out of the Football League in 1971-72 and spent 48 seasons in non-league football before returning in 2020-21. In 1968-69, Barrow topped Division Three for one day, the highest position the club has ever held.

In 2009-10, Birmingham City played twelve successive Premier League matches with the same starting eleven. The twelve-match sequence began on 21 November with a 1-0 victory over Fulham and ended on 7 February with a 2-1 win against Wolves.

Boston United were members of the Football League from 2002-03 until 2006-07. Boston's inaugural season in the Football League began with a deduction of four points by the FA for 'irregularities regarding the registration of players' and also, without their manager, Steve Evans, who received a lengthy ban.

It is a common misconception that Bournemouth changed their name to AFC Bournemouth in 1972. For all the club has operated under this name since '72, the club's official registered name remains Bournemouth and Boscombe Athletic FC, the name it has been registered under since 1923.

Blackburn Rovers are the only English club to have won major honours in the 19th, 20th and 21st centuries (Football League Cup winners 2001-02).

Blackpool were the first club to be promoted from all three divisions of the Football League via the Play-Offs, rising from Division Three (now League Two) to the Premier League in eight seasons.

Bolton Wanderers had the most players of any League club on active service during World War Two. 32 of the 35 pre-war professionals saw action in the British forces. The sole fatality was team captain Harry Goslin, who had risen to the rank of Lieutenant, and was fatally wounded by shrapnel on the Italian front in December 1943.

Bradford City are the only professional club in England to wear claret and amber shirts, colours they have worn since the club's formation in 1903. The colours were inherited from Manningham rugby league club with whom the club merged. Claret and amber were the colours of The Prince of Wales' Own West Yorkshire Regiment, which was based at Belle Vue Barracks on nearby Manningham Lane. From 1903 to 1908, Bradford City used the barracks as changing and club rooms. When performances were poor, City fans would gather at the Barracks to voice their disapproval to the players, hence the term 'barracking', the word 'barrack' coming from the French 'baraque' meaning a hut made of planks of wood.

Bradford Park Avenue is one of the few teams in the world to have been re-founded as the same club after going into liquidation (1974). Reformed in 1984, BPA began their climb up the football pyramid by re-starting as a club in a Bradford Sunday league.

Brentford are the only club to have completed the transfer of a player in the House of Commons. In November 1964, Brentford manager Malcolm MacDonald met with Club Chairman, Jack Dunnett MP, along with Northern Ireland international Ian Lawther, whose transfer from Scunthorpe United was completed in the Commons.

Striker Johnny Dixon, who played for Brighton in 2008-09, left the club and became a television and film producer. His credits include 'Come Dine With Me', 'Don't Tell The Bride' and 'The Valleys'.

Bristol City staged a Lacrosse International between England and a combined Scotland/Wales team at Ashton Gate prior to their game against Nottingham Forest on 14 October 1978.

In 1958-59, Bristol Rovers' average home attendance in Division Two was 35,922, the ninth highest in English football. Neighbours Bristol City boasted an average home attendance of 43,335, the highest in Division Two and only bettered that season by Manchester United and Arsenal, the latter by only a few hundred.

Burnley, who finished below half-way in the Second Division in 1978-79, beat Celtic twice in the Anglo-Scottish Cup, this in the season Celtic won the Scottish Premier League. Burnley won only four away games that season, one being at Celtic.

Brian Barry-Murphy scored in the 12th minute for Bury against Wrexham at Gigg Lane on 27 August 2005. Barry-Murphy's goal made Bury the first club to have scored a thousand goals in each of the four tiers of English League football.

Carlisle United's Ivor Broadis was the first manager ever to transfer himself. In January 1949, Broadis was player-manager at Carlisle United when he received a bid from Sunderland for himself. Broadis arranged his own transfer, Carlisle receiving a fee of £18,000 from Sunderland for his services. During his six years as a Sunderland player, Broadis continued to live and train in Carlisle. Broadis was the oldest surviving England International (14 caps) until his death in 2019 at the age of 96.

Charlton programme seller, turned turnstile operator, went on to play for the club, and England. Rob Lee sold programmes at Charlton Athletic then became a turnstile operator at The Valley before signing as a professional for the club in 1983. Lee went on to play in excess of 300 matches for Charlton before moving to Newcastle United where, again, he clocked-up in excess of 300 games. Lee won 21 caps for England.

Chelsea appointed three player-managers in succession, Glen Hoddle (1993-96), Ruud Gullit (1996-98) and Gianluca Vialli (1998-2000) the latter being the last full-time player-manager in the Premier League. There was a precedent, Chelsea's first ever manger, John Tait Robertson (1905-06) was also player-manager.

Cheltenham Town's former players include cricket great, Gilbert Jessop, Wisden cricketer of the Year in 1898 and often referred to as 'the fastest run-scorer English cricket has ever known'.

Chesterfield won the last ever Anglo-Scottish Cup competition, staged in 1980-81. In the two-legged final, Chesterfield beat Notts County 2-1 on aggregate, perhaps their most notable performance, however, was their quarter-final victory over Rangers. Having drawn 1-1 at Ibrox, Chesterfield won the second-leg 3-0 against a Rangers team who went on to win the Scottish Cup.

In May 1953, Colchester United appointed Ron Meades as player-manager. Meades' CV stated he had been with Cardiff City and more recently manager of Wadebridge Town in the Western League. Meades' CV did not ring true with Arthur Wood, the Colchester United reporter for the local newspaper. Wood did some investigating and discovered Meades was a fraud. After four days as manager, he was asked to leave the club by the Colchester directors.

Coventry City were the last ever winners of the Southern Floodlit Cup. In 1959-60, Coventry defeated Southend United, Fulham, Southampton, and, West Ham United 2-1 in the Final. The competition ceased because, as the Football League stated, 'Floodlit matches are no longer a novelty for supporters as evidenced by the poorly attended Final at Coventry's Highfield Road which drew an attendance of only 12,345.'

Crawley Town appointed Dermot Drummy as Manager in May 2016. Regarding playing personnel, Drummy promised to 'bring in a few new faces', and that summer he signed 22 new players.

Crewe Alexandra have arguably the most successful of all youth policies. In 2021-22, eight of the regular starting eleven had graduated through the club's Academy system as had been the case in 2020-21. In previous seasons Crewe fielded teams in which the entire starting eleven were Academy graduates. Players Crewe developed and sold include: David Platt, Robbie Savage, Dean Ashton, Danny Murphy, Geoff Thomas, John Pemberton, Neil Lennon, Ashley Westwood, Seth Johnson, David Vaughan, Luke Varney, Nicky Maynard, Nick Powell, Perry Ng, Harry Pickering, Ryan Wintle and Charlie Kirk.

Crystal Palace are the only English club which does not have a vowel in the first five letters of its name.

On 16 May 2010, Dagenham and Redbridge created a record score in the Play-Offs by beating Morecambe 6-0 in the first leg of their League Two tie. Josh Scott scored four, the highest individual goals tally by a player in a Play-Off game.

In 1948-49, Darlington broke their record attendance at Feethams three times in the same season, including twice in successive matches. The ground record stood at 12,868 but was broken with the visit of Rotherham United on 9 October with an attendance of 14,590. Darlington's next home match, on 23 October against Doncaster Rovers, drew a new record attendance of 15,326. On 12 March, the record was broken for a third time when 17,978 saw a 1-0 defeat against Hull City.

Derby County won the FA Cup in 1946 beating Charlton Athletic 4-1 (after extra time). The Derby Manager, Stuart McMillan was only a part-time manager. McMillan divided his time between managing County and as the publican of the Nag's Head pub in Derby.

Doncaster Rovers were involved in the longest ever competitive football match in English football. On 30 March 1946, Doncaster's Third Division North Cup tie at Stockport County was 2-2 after 90 minutes. Competition rules stipulated in such a situation the teams would play-on until one team scored. After two hours and twenty three minutes of play with neither team having added to their score and darkness descending, the referee brought the game to an end. Doncaster won the replay 4-0.

Everton have lost more FA Cup semi-finals than any other club. As at 2020-21, Everton had lost in 13 FA Cup semi-finals. Everton also hold the record for having lost the most FA Cup Finals, having been beaten eight times.

Exeter City toured Argentina and Brazil in 1914; on 21 July 1914, Exeter played the first Brazil national team, Brazil won 2-0.

Fleetwood Town won the North West Counties Premier League title in 2004-05 and in 2011-12 won the Conference League to secure a place in the Football League. In May 2014, Fleetwood beat Burton Albion at Wembley in the League Two Play-Off Final to gain promotion to League One, it was the club's sixth promotion in ten years. Defender Nathan Pond played in seven divisions for Fleetwood throughout the course of all six promotions.

Forest Green Rovers under the chairmanship of Dale Vince became the world's first vegan football club in 2015. The club's home, the New Lawn, boasts numerous eco-friendly innovations and in 2018 became the first football club in the world to be certified carbon neutral.

Fulham can boast two players who are the only footballers from their country to have played in the Premier League: Zesh Rehman (Pakistan) and Kevin Betsy (Seychelles).

The current Gateshead were formed in 1977. Gateshead FC which competed in the Football League from 1930 lost League status in 1960. It was only the second time Gateshead FC had ever applied for re-election to the Football League (previously 1937); the club had no creditors and had an average home attendance in 1959-60 of 3,412 (lowest in the Football League). In the days when away teams shared a portion of home gate money, many visiting Fourth Division clubs didn't cover their expenses for what was a long trip. Following their expulsion from the Football League, Gateshead applied to join the Scottish League but their application was rejected.

Prior to 1983, clubs shared gate money from League matches. The home club retained 70%, the visiting club received 25%, with 5% going to the Football League. The system was scrapped following pressure from clubs such as Liverpool, Manchester United and Arsenal. Featured, cheque received by Sunderland from Birmingham City for their 25% share of the gate money for the Division Two match played at St.Andrews' on 9 October 1979. Note, the match was played on the Saturday, the cheque sent on the following Monday.

Gillingham hold the record for having conceded the fewest goals in a 46-match season. In 1995-96, Gillingham finished as runners-up in League Three (now League Two) conceding only 20 goals. Gillingham conceded only six goals in 23 home matches and had 29 clean sheets.

Halifax Town, now known as FC Halifax Town after the original club went into administration in 2008, appointed eight managers who had at least two spells managing the club. Willie Watson 1954-56 and 1964-66; Alan Ball senior 1967-70 and 1976-77; George Kirby 1970-71 and 1978-81; George Mulhall 1972-74, 1986, 1996 and 1997-98; Billy Ayre 1984 and 1986-1990; Kieran O'Regan 1996, 1997 and 1998; Tony Parks 2000 and 2001; Neil Redfearn 2001 and 2002.

On 29 October 1965, Hartlepool United appointed Brian Clough as manager. The club were so strapped for cash that on 15 January 1966, the club could not afford to hire a team coach to take the team to Barnsley. Clough, his assistant Peter Taylor and the players travelled in their cars and came away with a 2-2 draw. Taylor then managed to borrow a coach from a friend for away games, and he and Clough passed their test as coach drivers and took it in turns to drive the team to away matches for the remainder of the season.

Hereford United hold the record for the biggest win by a non-league club against League opposition in the FA Cup. Hereford beat Queens Park Rangers 6-1 in Round Two in 1957-58.

It is well known that in 1957-58, Huddersfield Town led Charlton Athletic 5-1 at The Valley with only thirty minutes remaining only to lose 7-6. Not so well known is that the Huddersfield manager that day was Bill Shankly... you can imagine... the train Huddersfield caught home from Euston arrived into Manchester 76 minutes late.

Hull City is the only English League club whose name contains letters you cannot shade in, as in letters forming a circle or half-circle.

Between 1985 and 2000, Mick Stockwell played 610 games for Ipswich Town fulfilling every outfield position.

Leeds United were the first club to sell replica shirts, as the result of a kit deal with Admiral in 1973-74.

Leicester City are one of only two clubs (other being Brighton) to win the

Charity Shield despite not having won the League Championship or FA Cup in the previous season. On 7 August 1971, Leicester City beat Liverpool 1-0 at Filbert Street. Leicester (Second Division champions) and Liverpool (FA Cup runners-up) contested the Charity Shield as 'double' winners, Arsenal, chose not to participate due to European commitments.

Barry Hearn became chairman of Leyton Orient in 1995 after the club was put on sale for £5 by then chairman Tony Wood. The sale was the subject of the Channel Four TV documentary 'Orient. Club for a Fiver'. Under Hearn's stewardship, Leyton Orient enjoyed one of the most successful periods in their history. When Hearn sold the club to Italian businessman Francesco Becchetti, Orient suffered two relegations in three years under 11 different managers.

Lincoln City were the first club to suffer automatic relegation from the Football League, in 1986-87. Lincoln City were also the first club to add the suffix 'City' to their name, acquired in 1884.

The flagpole situated between the Kop and Kenny Dalglish stands at Liverpool's Anfield came from 'The Great Eastern', an iron sailing steamship designed by Isambard Kingdom Brunel. The flagpole was erected in 1892 by Everton, who played at Anfield prior to the ground becoming the home of Liverpool.

Maidstone United are the only Football League club never to have played a league match on their home ground. Maidstone won promotion to the Football League in 1989-90 and remained a league club until the club went into liquidation in August 1992. Having won promotion to the Football League, Maidstone's Athletic Ground was not deemed suitable for league football. During their entire period as a Football League club, Maidstone ground-shared with Dartford at the latter's Watling Street ground, with a view to constructing a new stadium in Maidstone itself, however, the plan never came to fruition.

On 10 November 2019, Macclesfield Town were forced to play loan and youth players in their (pre-Covid) FA Cup 1st round tie against Isthmian Premier Division side Kingstonian. Macclesfield's first team squad went on strike over unpaid wages and the League Two club fielded a team comprising five loanees and six youth team players. The club's administrative staff were also out on strike and it was only as a result of help from volunteers that the tie went ahead. Only 200 match programmes were produced for the tie which Kingstonian won 4-0. Many Macclesfield supporters boycotted the game, the attendance of 996 included over 300 from Kingstonian.

Manchester City are the only club to be relegated in English football with a positive goal difference. In 1937-38, City were relegated from Division One having scored 80 goals and conceded 77.

Two men have managed Manchester United twice, Walter Crickmer (1931-32 and 1937-45) and Sir Matt Busby (1945-69 and 1970-71).

Mansfield's net gain. In 1999, Mansfield Town signed Michael Boulding from non-league Hallam. Boulding swapped tennis for football, having previously played at Wimbledon and been a member of the Great Britain Davis Cup team.

Middlesbrough were the first football club in the world to launch its own TV channel. Boro TV began broadcasting in 1997, a year ahead of MUTV.

Millwall played in the UEFA Cup in 2004-05. Millwall lost 3-0 to Manchester United in the 2004 FA Cup Final, as United had already qualified for the Champions League, Millwall were granted a place in the UEFA Cup. Millwall played in the first round proper, losing 4-2 on aggregate to Ferencvaros (Hungary).

Milton Keynes Dons player-coach, Dean Lewington was, at 2021-22 the current longest-serving player for a single club in English football, having joined the club in 2004. Lewington is also the only former Wimbledon player remaining from Wimbledon FC's relocation to Milton Keynes.

As at January 2022, Morecambe had never been relegated at any level of football throughout the entire history of the club, which dates back to 1920.

Newcastle United were the first club to have an official photographer, Gladstone Adams, in 1908. Adams' other claim to fame is that he invented windscreen wipers for cars.

Northampton Town's swinging sixties. Northampton Town began the 1960s in Division Four, during the decade they won three promotions in five years reaching the First Division in 1965-66, the club's only season in the top flight. Northampton then suffered three relegations and, at the end of the decade, in 1969, found themselves back in Division Four.

Norwich City have the world's oldest football song, 'On the Ball, City'. The song is older than the club which was founded in 1902. The composition of the song is often attributed to Albert Smith, who became a club director when Norwich City were formed, with the original lyric tweaked to accommodate 'City'. The song is still played and sung at Norwich home matches to this day.

Nottingham Forest won promotion to the First Division when the team was 40,000 feet in the air. In 1976-77, Nottingham Forest had completed their fixtures and were mid-air on their way to an end of season break in Mallorca when they received news that Bolton Wanderers, the only team that could overtake them should they win their remaining two matches, had lost their penultimate game at home to Wolves.

Three Notts County players missed the same penalty during County's Division Two game against Portsmouth on 22 September 1973. Kevin Randall missed the initial penalty which was ordered to be retaken because the goalkeeper had moved off his line. Randall declined responsibility for the retake, so, Don Masson stepped up. Masson also put his penalty wide, but the referee ordered the kick to be retaken yet again, adjudging a Portsmouth player to have encroached into the penalty area. The third attempt at the penalty, by Brian Stubbs, was also placed wide of the goal. No matter, Notts County won 2-1.

Oldham Athletic were founder members of the Premier League in 1992. Oldham Chairman Ian Stott chaired the first meeting of Premier League club owners.

The only time in their history when Oxford United qualified to play in Europe, they were denied. Oxford United won the League Cup in 1985-86 and thus qualified for the UEFA Cup, however, a subsequent UEFA ban on English clubs in European competitions following the Heysel Stadium disaster, denied Oxford what would have been their first ever sojourn into Europe. The club have never since qualified for Europe.

In 2010-11, Peterborough United were promoted from League One despite having conceded more goals (75) than any other team in the division. Peterborough scored 106 goals, more than any other club in the top four leagues.

Plymouth Argyle is situated in the largest city in England never to have hosted top-flight football. There is no definitive explanation for the origin of the suffix 'Argyle'. One explanation is that the club was named after the Argyll and Sutherland Highlanders regiment who were stationed in Plymouth in the 1880s. The other theory suggests the name may have come from 'The Argyle Tavern' where club founders may have met in 1886, as the original name of the club was simply Argyle FC.

Portsmouth are the only English League club whose home ground is not located on the English mainland. Fratton Park is situated on Portsea Island off Portsmouth.

Port Vale began the 1919-20 season playing in the Central League but ended the season playing in Division Two. Following the expulsion of Leeds City from the Football League on 4 October 1919 for having made illegal payments to players, Port Vale were re-admitted to the Football League, having resigned in 1907. Port Vale took over Leeds City's remaining fixtures, and their first game in Division Two was a 2-0 defeat at South Shields on 18 October, followed by a 1-0 home defeat to Tottenham Hotspur. Despite their inauspicious and handicapped start, Port Vale finished a creditable 13th in Division Two.

Preston North End were the original 'Invincibles'. In 1888-89, Preston won the inaugural Football League Championship, and, the FA Cup, the latter without conceding a goal. Preston are the only club to date, to go through an entire season unbeaten in both League and FA Cup.

Queens Park Rangers have moved ground location more times than any other League club - 18 times. From the club's formation in 1886 to their move back to their current stadium in 1963, Queens Park Rangers had more grounds than they had managers (13), a situation which remained the case until the early 1970s.

When Reading were admitted to the Football League in 1920, the club was granted special dispensation by the League from having to change their shirts should there be a colour clash because the club is situated in the Royal County of Berkshire (club's nickname 'The Royals'). Whilst this privilege was adhered to for a number of years, following WW2, it seemingly became forgotten. The special dispensation allowing Reading not to have to change their shirts, however, has never officially been revoked.

Rochdale were admitted to the Football League in 1921-22, joining the newly formed Division Three North. Rochdale spent 47 years in that division until the creation of Division Four in 1959. Rochdale won promotion from Division Four in 1969 only to return in 1974. Rochdale then spent 36 years in Division Four until securing promotion in 2009-10. Rochdale's 36 consecutive seasons in the fourth tier of English football is a record. Rochdale also hold the distinction of having played the most seasons in English football without ever having graced the top two tiers or having been relegated to the Conference League. As at 2021-22 that stood at 94 seasons and totalled 100 years.

Rotherham United finished in ninth place in Division Two in 1951-52. Of their regular starting eleven, all but one hailed from Yorkshire, the one exception being Colin Rawson, who was born in Nottinghamshire.

Rushden and Diamonds were promoted from the Conference League to the Football League in 2000-01 and lost league status in 2006. The club was owned by Max Griggs, President of the R Griggs Group which owned the shoe manufacturer Doc Marten's. Griggs, feeling he could take Rushden and Diamonds no further forward, sold the club in 2005 to a supporters group for £1. The club entered administration in 2011, their home, Nene Park, a Championship standard football ground, was demolished in 2017.

Salford City's nickname 'The Ammies' originates from the club's name from the early 1960s to early 1970s - Salford Amateurs. The club song is 'Dirty Old Town', penned by Ewan McColl in 1949 which describes his home town of Salford.

Scunthorpe United were the first English club in the modern era to move to a new, purpose-built stadium, Glanford Park, in 1988. Scunthorpe's previous ground, The Old Show Ground, is now a Sainsbury's. For a number of years there was a plaque next to the delicatessen counter marking the location of the centre-spot at the Old Show Ground. For reasons best known to themselves, Sainsbury's removed the plaque. There is now, however, a carved stone commemorating the site's previous use as Scunthorpe United's ground which is set in the exterior wall of the 2011 store extension - it's next to the cashpoints.

Sheffield United's badge was designed by legendary Notts County manager Jimmy Sirrel. Between spells as Notts County manager, Sirrel was manager of Sheffield United, 1975 to 1977. For decades the Sheffield United badge had been the city's coat of arms but during Sirrel's tenure as manager, Sheffield City Council copyrighted the coat of arms which negated it being used by United. Sirrel sat at his desk and designed a new badge for the club, the one which is still used by the club to this day.

As at 2021-22, Sheffield Wednesday were the last club outside of the top tier of English football to have won a major trophy. Wednesday, then in Division Two, beat Manchester United 1-0 in the League Cup Final of 1991.

In 1906-07, Shrewsbury Town's Billy Scarratt played in all eleven positions for the club. This included three successive FA Cup ties when he played in goal in which he only conceded once. Despite playing in all eleven positions, Scarratt ended the season as Shrewsbury's leading goalscorer with 14 goals.

Southampton are the only club in the history of the Premier League to have lost two matches when one of their players had scored a hat-trick. In both instances the hat-trick man was Matt Le Tissier; the first being on 8 May 1993, lost 4-3 at Oldham Athletic; second, on 19 August 1995, lost 4-3 at home to Nottingham Forest.

Southend United were formed in 1906 and were admitted to the Football League in 1920. In 1971-72, Southend finished as runners-up in Division Four and were promoted to Division Three despite having won only one of their opening six games and only one of the last seven matches of the season. It was the first promotion in the history of the club. Southend were demoted from the Football League at the end of 2020-21 for the first time in 101 years. On the day Southend lost their League status, the 'Southend Echo' conveyed their 'congratulations' to the club stating, 'Everything that could have been mismanaged at the club, has been.'

Southport were voted out of the Football League in the summer of 1978 and replaced by Wigan Athletic. Southport were the last club to leave the Football League through the re-election process. In 1975-76, Southport were drawn at home to Newcastle United in Round Two of the League Cup. Southport, however, conceded home advantage in the hope of receiving a financial windfall from a tie at St.James' Park. Southport lost 6-0 but the attendance of 23,352 was little short of the aggregate total of Southport's first 18 League matches of the season.

Stevenage were the first club to win a trophy at the new Wembley. On 12 May 2007, Stevenage defeated Kidderminster Harriers 3-2 in the final of the FA Trophy. The attendance of 53,262 was a record for the competition.

Stoke City were looking forward to their overseas tour in the summer of 1939. Where were City headed? Poland. Needless to say, the tour never went ahead.

Stockport County designate the number 12 shirt to 'Blue and White Army', a tribute to the club's supporters being considered the team's 12th man and in recognition of the support the club has received since dropping out of the Football League. Attendances at Edgeley Park are often in excess of 4,000 and in 2019-20, County had an average away attendance of 902.

On 1 February 2003, Sunderland trailed Charlton Athletic 3-0 after 31 minutes in the Premier League with the London side not having had a shot on target. All three goals Sunderland conceded were own goals, Steven Wright (24 minutes), Michael Proctor (28 minutes and 31 minutes). Sunderland lost 3-1.

On 18 March 2000, Swansea City's Walter Boyd came on as a substitute in the Division Three game against Darlington and, before play had resumed, was sent off by referee Clive Wilkes for having elbowed Darlington's Martin Gray. The referee's report stated Boyd was 'dismissed after zero seconds on the field of play.'

Swindon Town are the only club to have won a Play-Off Final at Wembley and not be promoted. On 28 May 1990, Swindon beat Sunderland 1-0 in the Division Two Play-Off Final but were denied promotion to the First

Division after admitting breaching Football League regulations which included illegal payments and falsifying an attendance. Sunderland were promoted in their place.

Torquay United's League (Worthington) Cup tie against Portsmouth in 1999-2000 was postponed due to a solar eclipse. Torquay police requested the tie be postponed as they did not have the manpower to cope with both the League Cup tie and the crowds wanting to view the solar eclipse from the town's seafront.

Tottenham Hotspur were the first British club to win two different major European trophies. The European Cup Winners Cup in 1963 (first British club to win a major European competition) and the inaugural UEFA Cup in 1972.

Tranmere Rovers were the first English League club to have foreign owners. In July 1984 the club was sold to Californian attorney, Bruce Osterman.

Walsall's Jack Flavell, who played for the club in the 1950s, also played cricket for Worcestershire. Flavell played in four tests for England and was Wisden Cricketer of the Year in 1965.

On 26 August 1980, Watford were defeated 4-0 by Southampton at the Dell in the 2nd Round of the League Cup first leg. The second leg took place at Vicarage Road on 2 September, Watford winning 7-1 to clinch the tie 7-5 on aggregate. The biggest deficit a team has overturned in the League Cup.

West Bromwich Albion are the only club to avoid relegation from the Premier League when heading into the final game of the season bottom of the league. In 2004-05, West Brom' won their final match of the season, on 15 May beating Portsmouth 2-0, results elsewhere conspired to relegate Southampton, Norwich City and Crystal Palace.

West Ham United are the only club to have had a manager who, unbeknown to the club's board, resigned and appointed his own successor. In 1974-75, Ron Greenwood resigned as manager of West Ham, appointed himself as the club's General Manager and appointed his assistant, John Lyall, as team manager without first informing the club's directors.

Wigan Athletic failed in 34 applications to be elected to the Football

League. In the summer of 1972, the club applied to join the Scottish League Second Division but were rejected. Wigan Athletic were finally elected to the Football League in 1978.

Wolverhampton Wanderers scored from the first ever penalty kick to be awarded in world football. On 14 September 1891, Wolves' John Heath scored from the spot in the Division One fixture against Accrington Stanley at Molineux. Wolves went on to win the game 5-0.

Promising career understatement. Workington lost their Football League status in the summer of 1977, being replaced by Wimbledon. In 1968-69, Workington gave a Football League debut to locally born goalkeeper John Burridge against Newport County on 8 May 1969. Burridge's second touch of the ball resulted in him punching a corner into his own net. The local newspaper, 'Evening News and Star' reported, 'Despite his error, Burridge gave a competent display and looks to have a promising career ahead of him'. John Burridge went on to play for 29 clubs, clocking-up 768 league games in English and Scottish football, playing his final game in 1997 at the age of 46.

Formed in 1864, Wrexham are the oldest football club in Wales and the fourth oldest professional club in the world. In November 2020, the club was taken over by Hollywood actors Ryan Reynolds and Rob McElhenney. Wrexham's home, the Racecourse Ground, is the world's oldest international stadium that continues to host international matches.

Wycombe Wanderers were founded in 1887 but did not have a manager until 1968. Though Wycombe had a coach, team selection and the acquisition and release of players was handled by a club committee. In December 1968, eighty one years after their foundation, Wycombe appointed Brian Lee as the club's first ever manager.

The pitch at Yeovil Town's original home, The Huish, had an 8 foot (2.4m) drop from side-line to side-line.

Jimmy McCormick resigned as manager of York City in September 1954. York then went eighteen months without a manger during which time they enjoyed one of the most successful periods in their history, reaching the FA Cup semi-final in 1955, narrowly losing to Newcastle United in a replay. York eventually appointed Sam Bartram as manager in March 1956.

FCZ-Revue

Herausgeber und Inseratenannahme: Sekretariat des FC Zürich, Lutherstrasse 2, 8004 Zürich, Telefon 39 70 86.
Druck: Albert Spillmann, Buchdruck-Offset, Heinrichstr. 217, 8005 Zürich, Tel. 42 00 50 / Fotos: Horvath Pressefoto

| Matchprogramm Nr. 16 | Saison 1976/77 | Preis Fr. 1.50 |

Heute im Programm

EUROPACUP

Halbfinal

Mittwoch, 6. April 1977, 20.00 Uhr

Stadion Letzigrund

FC Zürich — FC Liverpool

Ein wichtiges Tor für den FCZ im Europacup auf dem Weg in den Halbfinal: In der letzten Spielminute gegen Dresden in Zürich erzielt Risi das 2:1

Europe

The longest European competition was the inaugural Inter-Cities Fairs Cup which spanned three seasons. The competition began on 4 June 1955 and was completed on 1 May 1958 when Barcelona beat a London X1, 6-0 in the Final second leg to win 8-2 on aggregate. Competition rules stated only one side from each city was allowed to compete, hence cities such as London picked a representative team.

Despite finishing fifth in the Scottish League in 1954-55, Hibernian were invited to participate in the European Cup, which was not strictly based on league position at the time. The teams who finished above Hibernian - Aberdeen (Champions), Celtic, Rangers and Hearts did not participate through choice or for the fact their grounds did not meet European Cup requirements, such as for floodlights. Hibernian were the first British club to participate in the European Cup and reached the semi-finals only to lose to Stade Reims.

Hibernian are the only club to play home and away European ties against foreign opposition without leaving their own country. In the second round of the 1955-56 European Cup, Hibernian beat Djurgardens IF 3-1 at Easter Road. Severe winter weather prevented Djurgardens from playing the second leg on their home ground in Sweden. UEFA switched the tie to Partick Thistle's Firhill stadium where, on 28 November 1955, Hibernian won 1-0 to clinch the tie 4-1 on aggregate.

Birmingham City were the first English club to reach a European Final. The Inter Cities Fairs Cup took place between 1958 and 1960, Birmingham lost 4-1 on aggregate to Barcelona. Birmingham City were also the first British club to appear in two European Finals. After their defeat in 1960, Birmingham reached the Final of the Fairs Cup the following season (competition played over a single season), losing the 1960-61 Final 4-2 on aggregate to

Roma. Much has been written about Manchester United being pioneers of European competition for English football, Birmingham's pioneering European exploits are often unsung.

Brentford's Ken Coote played in the first European Final involving a British team. Above, the London line-up from the Chelsea programme for the Fairs Cup Final first leg between London and Barcelona on 5 March 1958. The first British player to score in a European Final was Jimmy Greaves, in this, a 2-2 draw.

Burnley were eliminated from the European Cup by Hamburg in 1960-61, Hamburg winning 5-4 on aggregate. At the time Burnley enjoyed a reputation for having an excellent youth system which produced several players for the first team. The Hamburg team which defeated Burnley, however, comprised entirely of players who had graduated through the club's youth system, including West Germany internationals Gert Dorfel and Uwe Seeler.

In 1966-67, Clyde finished third in the Scottish First Division, behind Rangers and champions Celtic. As a result of their league position, Clyde qualified for Europe and entered the Inter Cities Fairs Cup. UEFA, however, withdrew Clyde, citing a rule which stipulated only one team per city could enter the competition, in this case, league runners-up, Rangers. Clyde appealed against their withdrawal, arguing they were not, in fact, from Glasgow but Rutherglen. UEFA rejected Clyde's appeal, stating their non-membership of the Lanarkshire FA and their participation in the Glasgow Cup. It was the first time Clyde had ever qualified for Europe and the club have never qualified since.

Rangers' 3-2 victory over Dynamo Moscow in the 1972 European Cup Winners Cup Final was marred by a pitch invasion and crowd trouble following the final whistle. As a consequence of the disturbances, Rangers' captain, John Greig, had the trophy handed to him by a UEFA official in a spare room at the Nou Camp stadium. That done, the official informed Greig, 'Right, you can go now.' As a result of the crowd trouble, Rangers were banned from defending their title the following season.

Rangers' success in the European Cup Winners Cup of 1972 is also unique for the fact, they won the competition having been knocked out of the competition in an earlier round. On 20 October 1971, Rangers beat Sporting Lisbon 3-2 at Ibrox in Round Two and lost the second leg in Portugal 4-3. Referee, Peter van Ravens of the Netherlands, misinterpreted the competition rules, noting the teams were level on aggregate he ordered a penalty shoot-out, which Sporting won to progress. Rangers subsequently protested to UEFA, citing they should have won the tie on the away goals rule. UEFA agreed and awarded the tie to Rangers.

In 1971-72, Chelsea, were eliminated from the European Cup Winners Cup by FC Atvidabergs on away goals. Atvidabergs is a Swedish town whose population at the time was less than 5,000.

The 2019-20 and 2020-21 finals apart, which had attendance restrictions due to Covid, the smallest attendance for a final of the European Cup/Champions League occurred on 17 May 1974 for the replayed final between Bayern Munich and Atletico Madrid, which attracted 23,283 spectators to the Heysel Stadium in Brussels. The original tie resulted in a 1-1 draw, the replay, a 4-0 victory for Bayern Munich. The historically low attendance for a European Cup final had much to do with the fact the replay took place just two days after the original final, with many supporters of both clubs unable to make travel and accommodation arrangements at such short notice. The 1974 final remains the only European Cup/Champions League final to have involved a replay.

The agony and the, well, more agony. In 1982-83, Real Madrid finished as runners-up in La Liga, La Copa, the Spanish Super Cup, the Spanish League Cup and the UEFA Cup Winners Cup.

The only English team to have beaten Bayern Munich over 90 minutes in a European competition at either their former home, Olympiastadion or current venue, Allianz Arena, is Norwich City. On 19 October 1993, Norwich beat Bayern Munich 2-1 at the Olympiastadion in the second round, first leg of the UEFA Cup. Norwich City won the tie 3-2 on aggregate. Bayern lost to Chelsea in the 2012 Champions League final staged at the Allianz Arena, this being 4-3 on penalties (after 1-1).

In 1996-97, five clubs from the same city competed in European competitions. Moscow provided CSKA Moscow, Torpedo Moscow, Spartak Moscow and Dynamo Moscow for the UEFA Cup and Lokomotiv Moscow for the Cup Winners Cup. A feat equalled in 2004-05 by Athens which provided two clubs for the Champions League (Olympiakos and Panathinaikos) and three for the UEFA Cup (AEK Athens, Egaleo and Panionios).

Champions scored fewer goals than any other team in league. In 1998, AIK won the Swedish Allsvenskan (Premier League) despite having scored fewer goals than they played matches (25 from 26 matches), furthermore, AIK's tally of 25 goals was less than any other club in the 14-team league. AIK also won fewer matches (11) than runners-up Helsingborgs and fourth-placed Halmstads BK.

At various stages of the 2000-01 Champions League, Leeds United played four teams from the same country (Spain), Barcelona, Real Madrid, Deportivo La Coruna and Valencia.

Dundee United have played Barcelona on four occasions in European competitions and won every game, scoring seven goals and conceding two.

The only player to have played in a Champions League Final and not be capped by his country is Jermaine Pennant, who played for Liverpool in their 2-1 defeat to AC Milan in the 2007 Final.

Up like a rocket, down like a stick. Sporting Fingal was formed in 2007 and between 2008 and 2010 played in the League of Ireland. In their second season, the club won promotion to the League of Ireland Premier League. The following season, Sporting Fingal finished fourth, which qualified them for the Europa League, the shortest period between a club being formed and playing in a major European competition. Sporting Fingal lost 6-4 on aggregate to Maritimo (Portugal) in July 2010. In February of the following year, the club folded. The club had only been in existence for 965 days.

Chelsea are the only team to simultaneously be holders of the Champions League and Europa League cups. Chelsea won the Champions League in 2011-12. The following season, Chelsea won the Europa League, beating Benfica 2-1 on 15 May 2013. As the 2012-13 Champions League Final between Bayern Munich and Borussia Dortmund did not take place until 25 May, Chelsea simultaneously held both cups/titles for ten days.

In 2016-17, Leicester City became the first club in the Champions League to win their opening four matches when debuting in the competition.

Zlatan Ibrahimovic played in six Champions League Finals and was on the losing side every time - Ajax, Inter Milan, Barcelona, Juventus, AC Milan and Manchester United.

On 7 December 2021, Liverpool defeated AC Milan 2-1 in the San Siro stadium in the Champions League Group B. Liverpool's victory made them the first English club to win all six games in a Champions League group. Liverpool finished eleven points ahead of group runners-up Atletico Madrid.

Family Affair

On 12 September 1896, Nottingham Forest fielded two sets of brothers in their team against a Stoke City side which included one set of brothers. Frank and Fred Foreman and Arthur and Adrian Capes for Forest, the latter being former Stoke City players; Billy and Arthur Maxwell for Stoke City.

The Clapton Orient team of 1922-23 included three sets of brothers - Sam and John Toner, Tom and Owen Davies and John and Robert Duffus.

Dick Ray was manager of Doncaster Rovers between 1923-1927, during which time he signed the Keetley brothers, Tom, Harold, Joe and Frank. In 1927, Ray was appointed manager of Leeds United, his first signing was the one Keetley brother he did not sign for Doncaster, Charlie, who went on to score 108 League goals in 160 appearances for Leeds.

England International Jack Rutherford's career as a player ended with Clapton Orient at the end of 1926-27, at the time his son, John, was playing for Arsenal having made his debut for the Gunners two years previously.

The first brothers to play in a World Cup match were Manuel and Filipe Rosas, who lined up together for Mexico in their 6-3 defeat to Argentina on 19 July 1930, in the inaugural World Cup. Manuel Rosas became the first player to score from a penalty in a World Cup match, doing so in the aforementioned game against Argentina.

Between 1929 and 1948, the five Wallbanks brothers all enjoyed careers as professional footballers. James Wallbanks (Millwall and Norwich City); John (Chester and Bradford Park Avenue); Fred (Nottingham Forest and Bradford City); Horace (Grimsby Town and Luton Town) and Harold (Barnsley).

The Aston Villa team of 1947-48 contained five players whose fathers had also played for the club - Amos and Frank Moss, Eddie and Reg Lowe and Tom Wood.

Keen to make an impression. On 24 August 1953, the left-side of the Barrow team that faced Port Vale comprised three Keen brothers. Jack at left-back, Alan (inside-left) and Bert (outside-left).

The Swansea Town team of 1953-54 included four sets of brothers - Cyril and Gilbert Beech, Ivor and Len Allchurch, Alan and Colin Hole, Cliff and Bryn Jones.

On 20 April 1955, Wales included brothers Ivor and Len Allchurch and John and Mel Charles for their Home International Championship match against Northern Ireland at Windsor Park.

Mel Charles, white shirt, centre, in action for Swansea Town against Sunderland in the FA Cup 5th round on 19 February 1955 (2-2). The Vetch Field pitch looking every inch a field, rutted and strewn with snow. Mel, like his brother, John, was eminently capable of playing either centre-half or centre-forward for club or country.

The only known instance of father and son both playing for two clubs in the same provincial city is that of Bob Walker and his son, Geoff. Bob played for Bradford City and Bradford Park Avenue prior to WW2 whereas son, Geoff, played for both Bradford clubs in the 1950s.

In July 1959, four brothers signed for the same League club on the same day - Tony, Billy, Peter and Roy Leighton for Doncaster Rovers.

Brothers in arms. Notts County fielded two sets of brothers in their Third Division match against Portsmouth on 24 February 1962, Peter and John Butler, and Tony and Peter Bircumshaw. In the same season, Chelsea also had two sets of brothers, John and Peter Sillett; Ron and Alan Harris.

Father and son who managed the same club. Harry and Joe Bradshaw - Fulham. Bill Dodgin senior and Bill Dodgin junior - Brentford, the Dodgins also both managed Fulham. John and Kevin Bond - Bournemouth. Brian and Nigel Clough - Derby County. Gary and Lee Johnson - Bristol City.

In the 1960s/70s, five Clarke brothers played professional football and with considerable success. Frank (Shrewsbury Town, QPR, Ipswich Town and Carlisle United); Derek (Walsall, Oxford United, Leyton Orient); Kelvin (Walsall); Wayne (Walsall, Wolverhampton Wanderers, Birmingham City and Everton), and, Allan (Walsall, Fulham, Leicester City, Leeds United and Barnsley.) Allan also won 19 caps with England.

Worthy of a mention. Frank Worthington (clubs included Huddersfield Town, Leicester City, Bolton Wanderers, Birmingham City and Sunderland) had two brothers and a nephew who all enjoyed fruitful football careers. Dave, with Grimsby Town (over 300 senior appearances), Southend United, Halifax Town and Barrow; Bob with Notts County (over 250 senior appearances), Halifax Town, Middlesbrough and Southend United; and, nephew, Gary, whose clubs included Darlington, Wigan Athletic, Wrexham and Exeter City.

Three Wallace brothers played together in the same Southampton team. On 22 October 1988, Danny, Ray and Rodney Wallace played together for Southampton against Sheffield Wednesday.

The only instance of brothers being sent off for the same team in the same match occurred on 26 April 1986 - Colchester United's Tom and Tony English were dismissed during the Division Four game at Crewe Alexandra.

In 1990-91, four Linighan brothers were playing for Football League clubs - Andy (Arsenal), David (Ipswich Town) and twins Brian and John (both Sheffield Wednesday).

Three generations of Hateley's enjoyed fruitful careers. Tony (clubs included Notts County, Aston Villa, Chelsea, Liverpool, Coventry City and Birmingham City). Tony's son, Mark, (clubs included Coventry City, Portsmouth, AC Milan, Monaco, Rangers and QPR), and Mark's son, Tom, whose clubs include Motherwell, Tranmere Rovers, Dundee and who, in 2021-22, was playing in the Ekstraklasa (Polish Premier League) for Piast Gliwice. Tom Hateley is possibly the only English footballer to have been born in Monte Carlo, during Mark's spell with AS Monaco.

On 13 January 1990, Bury goalkeeper, Gary Kelly, faced his brother, Alan Kelly junior (Preston North End), in a Division Three match watched by their father, former Preston goalkeeper, Alan Kelly.

Wright on. Ian Wright and his son, Shaun Wright-Phillips both have Premier League Champions medals, Ian with Arsenal and Shaun with Chelsea. Ian's son, Bradley, played for Manchester City, Southampton, Plymouth Argyle and Charlton Athletic. Shaun's son, D'Margio Wright-Phillips plays for Stoke City (2021-22).

The only known instance of father and son facing one another in an FA Cup tie is Bobby Scaife, aged 41, who was playing for Bishop Auckland in an FA Cup qualifying tie against Pickering Town, whose line-up included Bobby's son, Nick. Bishop Auckland won 3-1.

The first brothers to play against one another in the Finals of a World Cup were Jerome Boateng (Germany) and Kevin Prince Boateng (Ghana) in the 2010 World Cup in South Africa.

Brothers who played for the same team in an FA Cup Final: Jack and Bill Smith (Portsmouth, 1934); Frank and Hugh O'Donnell (Preston North End, 1937); Denis and Leslie Compton (Arsenal, 1951); Allan and Ron Harris (Chelsea, 1967); Brian and Jimmy Greenhoff (Manchester United, 1977); Gary and Phil Neville (Manchester United, 1996 - Gary came on as a substitute for David Beckham), also in the 1999 Final.

Paul Ince is the father of Tom Ince (clubs include Stoke City, Blackpool, Derby County), uncle of singer Rochelle Humes (The Saturdays) and cousin of Clayton Ince (Crewe and Walsall).

Uncle and nephew in same teams. Gary Speed, who spent his entire professional career at Leeds United (531 appearances), played in the same Leeds United team as his nephew, Ian Harte. The pair were also part of The Republic of Ireland's 2002 World Cup squad.

On 18 September 2010, twins faced one another in an English league game. Dean Holdsworth for Newport County faced his twin brother, David, of Mansfield Town.

Karl Darlow (Nottingham Forest and Newcastle United) is the grandson of former Welsh International, Ken Leek (Northampton Town, Leicester City, Newcastle United, Birmingham City and Bradford City).

All three of Lou Macari's (Celtic and Manchester United) sons played professional football as does his grandson. Lou's son, Michael, played for Stoke City; Paul for Stoke City and Huddersfield Town; Jonathan for Nottingham Forest (without making a first team appearance), whilst grandson, Lewis, graduated to the professional ranks with Stoke City in 2021-22.

FOOTBALL ASSOCIATION CHALLENGE CUP.
Final Tie, 1881-82.

OLD ETONIANS v. BLACKBURN ROVERS

KENNINGTON OVAL,
SATURDAY, MARCH 25, 1882.

BLACKBURN ROVERS.
(white).

Goal.
ROGER HOWARTH.

Backs.
H. McINTYRE.   F. SUTER.

Half Backs.
H. SHARPLES.   F. W. HARGREAVES, Capt.

Forwards.
J. DUCKWORTH.   J. DOUGLAS.   J. BROWN.   T. STRAHAN.   G. AVERY.   J. HARGREAVES.

—O—

Forwards.
P.C. NOVELLI.   A. T. B. DUNN.   R. H. MACAULAY.   H. C. GOODHART.   J. CHEVALLIER.   W. J. ANDERSON.

Half Backs.
C. W. FOLEY.   Hon. A. F KINNAIRD. Capt.

Backs.
P. J. DE PARAVICINI.   T. H. FRENCH.

Goal.
J. F. P. RAWLINSON.

OLD ETONIANS.
(light blue and white).

SCORE—BLACKBURN ROVERS............   OLD ETONIANS............

Umpire—C. H. WOLLASTON (Wanderers);
C. CRUMP (President Birmingham Association.)
Referee—J. C. CLEGG (vice-President Sheffield Association).

PREVIOUS WINNERS—1872, Wanderers; '73, Wanderers; '74, Oxford; '75 Royal Engineers '76 Wanderers; '77 Wanderers; '78 Wanderers; '79 Old Etonians; '80, Clapham Rovers '81 Old Carthusians.

At Oval—Saturday, April 1st—For London Charities—

Old Etonians v. Old Carthusiaus.

Printed by Cricket Press, 17, Paternoster Square, E.C.

FA Cup

Port Vale, then known as Burslem Port Vale, are the only club to have reached the Fifth Round of the FA Cup, remain unbeaten in the competition yet not win it. In 1885-86, Vale defeated Chirk, Welsh Druids and Leek, were given a bye in Round Four and drawn at home against Brentwood in Round Five. Vale won the original tie against Brentwood 2-1 but the FA ordered the tie to be replayed on a neutral ground as Vale's home ground had not met FA requirements. The 'replayed' home tie was played at the County Ground, Derby. The tie ended 3-3 which necessitated a replay at Brentwood in Essex. Vale could not afford the cost of travel and hotels and withdrew from the competition.

Blackburn Rovers remained unbeaten in the FA Cup for three seasons (winners 1884-1886) a total of 24 ties. Blackburn's unbeaten run came to an end on 4 December 1886 when they were beaten at home by Scottish club Renton (now defunct) in a second round replay.

Oddest FA Cup result? In the early years of the FA Cup it was common for Scottish and Irish clubs to be admitted to the competition, on 4 December 1886, Partick Thistle won 11-0 at Cliftonville.

An administrative error resulted in Burton Swifts having a Second Division match against Crewe Alexandra and a Preliminary Round FA Cup tie against Coventry Singers (later to become Coventry City) on the same day (10 October 1892). The cup tie was moved to the previous Wednesday and given an 8am kick-off, the earliest kick-off of any FA Cup tie. Coventry won 3-0.

Mad rush for tickets? In 1892-93, Everton required three attempts to defeat Preston North End in their semi-final tie. The second replay took place on Monday 20 March, later in the week, on Saturday 25 March, Everton met Wolves in the FA Cup Final, Wolves triumphed 1-0.

Tykes swinging fortunes. Second Division Barnsley lost to Newcastle United in the 1909-10 Final. The following season, Barnsley finished second from bottom in Division Two and had to apply for re-election to the Football League. The following season, Barnsley beat West Bromwich Albion after a replay in the 1911-12 Cup Final.

Utley fantastic. George Utley appeared in five FA Cup Finals in six seasons on four different grounds. Utley appeared for Barnsley in the 1910 Final at Crystal Palace and replay at Goodison Park. In 1912 Utley was in the Barnsley team that drew with West Bromwich Albion at Crystal Palace and won the subsequent replay at Bramall Lane. In 1914-15, Utley was in the Sheffield United side that defeated Chelsea at Old Trafford.

Didn't make a spectacle of himself. The FA Cup Final between Huddersfield Town and Preston North End at Stamford Bridge in 1922 was not only the last final before finals switched to Wembley, it is the only final in which a player, Preston goalkeeper Jim Smith, wore spectacles. Billy Smith scored the only goal of the game for Huddersfield from the penalty spot.

West Bromwich Albion won the FA Cup and promotion from Division Two in 1930-31, the only club to have achieved this feat.

On 23 January 1932, in Round Three, Newcastle United drew 1-1 against Southport at St.James' Park. The replay at Southport also ended in a draw, 1-1. The second replay was played at neutral Hillsborough, where Newcastle triumphed 9-0, the largest victory in an FA Cup tie by a team that failed to win their home tie.

Prior to the 1932-33 Final between Everton and Manchester City, Wembley authorities issued the following statement - 'People in the south of England favour sandwiches, but those from the north prefer meat pies. As the north will predominate at this year's FA Cup Final, the number of meat pies ordered for the Final has been increased from 14,000 to 17,000 and the order of sandwiches reduced in proportion'. Even at Wembley prices, one should imagine it was still not enough. Everton beat Manchester City 2-0 in a final notable for innovations. This was the first final in which teams wore numbered shirts, Everton 1 to 11 and Manchester City 12 to 22. When the teams took to the pitch, they did so side-by-side led by their respective managers.

On 29 April 1939, Stan Burton played in the 1939 FA Cup Final for

Wolverhampton Wanderers in their 4-1 defeat to Portsmouth. Five days later, on 4 May, Burton was transferred to West Ham United, becoming the first player to play in an FA Cup Final, then play in the Football League for another club in the same season. Stan Burton was partially deaf and so did not play to the referee's whistle, during matches he responded to hand signals given by team-mates.

Leicester City twice scored five goals in an FA Cup tie without winning the game. In 1913-14, Leicester drew 5-5 with Spurs only to lose 2-0 in the replay at White Hart Lane. In 1948-49, Leicester drew 5-5 with Luton Town in the Fifth Round, albeit the Foxes did win the replay 5-3.

On 22 November 1922 in a 4th Qualifying Round replay, St. Albans' Wilf Minter scored seven goals against Dulwich Hamlet but was on the losing side. The replay took place on a Wednesday afternoon at Hamlet's Champion Hill ground before a crowd of 4,060. St Albans were without their number one and reserve goalkeepers due to work commitments and had to play Alf Fearn, a reserve team full-back, in goal. With the match deep into injury time of extra time and the score-line 7-7, Hamlet scored the decisive goal with less than a minute remaining. Even then, the drama was not over. From the restart, St. Albans won a free-kick from which seven-goal Minter rose above the Hamlet defence only to see his header clip the top of the Dulwich Hamlet crossbar. Wilf Minter died in December 1984 and his body placed in an unmarked grave. Years later, when St.Albans' supporters heard of this, they raised £2,700 to ensure a suitable headstone be placed above Minter's grave.

The only player to have scored five goals in two successive FA Cup ties is Harry Brooks who did so for Aldershot in 1945-46. Brooks scored five against Reading in Round One and five against Newport (Isle of Wight) in Round Two.

In 1947-48, Liverpool were drawn away to Manchester United in Round Four. At the time, United shared Maine Road, as their Old Trafford home was out of action due to bomb damage in WW2. As Manchester City were at home to Chelsea in Round Four, United's tie against Liverpool was switched to Everton's Goodison Park. The only instance in the FA Cup of a team, Liverpool, playing an away tie much nearer to home than the designated home team.

Everton played four FA Cup Ties on successive Saturdays in January and

February 1948 without playing a League game during that period. On January 24, Everton drew 1-1 with Wolves in Round Four, the following Saturday (31st) they triumphed 3-1 in the replay. On 7 February, Everton drew 1-1 at Fulham only to lose the replay the following Saturday (14th).

Shrewsbury Town refused to play in the FA Cup in 1950-51. Shrewsbury had been elected to the Football League in the summer of 1950, but the FA refused them exemption until the First Round proper as they had been a non-league club the previous season. Shrewsbury refused to play in the qualifying rounds of the competition and subsequently withdrew from the FA Cup.

Non-League Wigan Athletic drew an attendance of 27,100 for their Second-round tie against fellow non-leaguers Hereford United on 12 December 1953. In Round Three, Wigan were drawn at home to Newcastle United on 13 January, the attendance was 26,500.

On 6 January 1954, 15 of the 32 ties in the third round of the FA Cup were drawn, the highest number of drawn matches in a single round in the history of the competition.

Doncaster Rovers met Aston Villa five times in Round Four in 1954-55. Having drawn three times, the sides met again on 14 February only to draw again after extra time. With the Fifth Round scheduled for 19 February, the clubs were ordered to play again the following day (15 February) for a fifth time, a tie which Doncaster won 3-1.

The first ever FA Cup tie to take place under floodlights involved non-league clubs. On 14 September 1955, Kidderminster Harriers defeated Brierley Hill Alliance 4-2 in a Preliminary Round replay at their Aggborough stadium.

Nat Lofthouse (Bolton Wanderers) twice scored within the opening two and a half minutes of FA Cup Finals. After one minute thirty-seconds against Blackpool in 1953 and after two minutes twenty-nine seconds against Manchester United in 1958.

Since World War Two, four amateur clubs have reached the Third Round proper. Finchley in 1952-53; Bishop Auckland, 1954-55 (reached Round Four); Tooting and Mitcham, 1958-59; Barnet, 1964-65. In the case of Finchley and Bishop Auckland, both beat Crystal Palace along the way.

The only amateur player to score five goals for a Football League club in the FA Cup is George Bromilow in Southport's 6-1 defeat of Ashton United, First Round, 19 November 1955.

There'll be bluebirds over the white cliffs of Beeston. Leeds United were drawn at home to Cardiff City in the Third Round in three successive seasons 1955-56 to 1957-58, on each occasion Cardiff City won 2-1.

Bill Spurdle missed Manchester City's 3-1 victory over Birmingham City in the 1956 Final due to a severe attack of boils.

A curious aspect to the FA Cup being when two teams from the same division meet, often the team that loses the league matches, will win the FA Cup tie. This was the case in 1955-56; in the League, Newcastle United beat Sunderland 6-1 at Roker Park and 3-1 at St.James' Park. The two were drawn together in the sixth round at St.James', Sunderland winning 2-0. Such was the interest in the tie, the turnstiles were closed an hour before kick-off as St. James' had already reached the capacity of 62,000…

Amazing queues of supporters for the sixth-round tie between Newcastle United and Sunderland in 1956. Stretched another 900 yards! And not a policeman in sight.

The 1956 Final was refereed by Alf Bond who only had one arm. At the age of 19, Bond lost his right arm in an industrial accident when working in a rubber factory. For years, Alf Bond ran a newsagent's near Fulham's Craven Cottage, popular with Fulham fans.

Arsenal programmes of the 1950s very sportingly devoted a page to a player from another club who, in the estimation of the editor, was the outstanding 'Player of the Week'. Arsenal's programme for their Division One game against Portsmouth on 12 January 1957 selected 'Wee Willie' Windle of New Brighton. The Lancashire Combination club, having previously beaten Stockport County and Derby County, beat Torquay United 2-1 in Round Three. Windle scored both New Brighton goals. The tie was noteworthy for Windle's 'party trick'. With a minute remaining and New Brighton hanging-on to a single goal lead, Windle received the ball in the Torquay half of the field, wound his way to the corner quadrant and flicked the ball-up, balancing it on top of what was then the rectangular wooden corner flag.

PLAYER OF THE WEEK

WILLIE WINDLE

Wee Willie Windle, ex-Chester and now New Brighton's outside-left whose two goals against Torquay took the non-League club into the 4th round of the F.A. Cup.

The page from the Arsenal programme celebrating Wee Willie Windle, the exponent of the corner flag ball balancing act and whose two goals eliminated Torquay United. Wee Willie Windle, Gordon 'Twinkle-Toes' Turner (Luton Town), 'Cup-Tie' Mackay (Aberdeen) - you don't get players with such names in the modern game - more's the pity.

Three players have scored hat-tricks in FA Cup ties against teams they previously played for. Geoff Hazeldine for Boston United v Derby County in 1955-56; Bert Llewelyn for Port Vale v Northampton Town, 1961-62 and Denis Law for Manchester United against Huddersfield Town, in 1962-63.

The third round of 1962-63, is the longest lasting round in the history of the FA Cup. The third round began on 5 January, however, due to the 'Big Freeze' during the winter of 1962-63, was not completed until 11 March, there were 261 postponements with Lincoln City's tie against Coventry City postponed 15 times.

In the late 1950s to mid 1960s, Bolton Wanderers and Preston North End met eight times in seven seasons in the FA Cup. Once in 1957-58; and, including replays, three times in 1958-59; twice in 1963-64 and twice in 1964-65.

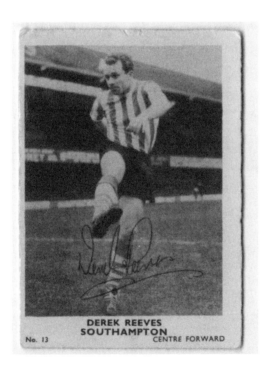

DEREK REEVES
SOUTHAMPTON
No. 13   CENTRE FORWARD

Southampton's Derek Reeves twice scored four goals in FA Cup ties away from home, against Walthamstow Avenue 1957-58 and at Manchester City, 1959-60.

The 1959 finalists, Luton Town and Nottingham Forest fielded unchanged teams from Round Three to the Final, including replays. The only instance of this occurring in the history of the FA Cup.

West Ham United are the only club to have won the FA Cup scoring three times in every round. In 1963-4, West Ham beat Charlton Athletic 3-0; Leyton Orient 3-0; Swindon Town 3-1; Burnley 3-0; Manchester United 3-1 (semi-final) and Preston North End 3-2 (Final).

Three members of the Everton team which lost 1-0 to West Bromwich Albion in the 1967-68 Final, went on to manage the club in FA Cup Finals. Howard Kendall, 1983-84, 84-85 and 85-86; Colin Harvey 1988-89 and Joe Royle in 1994-95. Every member of Everton's 1968 Final team plus substitute Roger Kenyon was English, as was manager, Harry Catterick.

And so, to Ted. On 25 November 1970, Ted McDougall scored six for Bournemouth in their FA Cup tie against Oxford City. On 20 November 1971, McDougall scored nine in Bournemouth's 11-0 First Round win against Margate. McDougall's nine against Margate is a record for an individual player in an FA Cup tie proper.

Second Division Sunderland beat Leeds United in the 1973 Final. Of the Sunderland team - and unused substitute, David Young, only one player, Richie Pitt, had ever been to Wembley before and he for an England Schools international. The two captains, Bobby Kerr (Sunderland) and Billy Bremner (Leeds United) were both 5'4" tall.

Sunderland were the last team to win the FA Cup (see above) with a team that did not include a single international player.

In 1973-74, Bideford, then of the Southern League, played 13 FA Cup ties yet only reached Round One. In the third qualifying round, Bideford were involved in five ties (four replays) against Falmouth Town and four matches (three replays) against Trowbridge Town in the fourth qualifying round. Bideford then lost 2-0 to Bristol Rovers in the first round proper.

Wrexham's away support for their 1973-74 quarter-final tie against Burnley at Turf Moor was officially recorded as being 20,018, from an overall attendance of 35,500. Burnley won 1-0.

1973-74, was the fifth and final season of the FA's idea of replacing a Cup

Sunderland's Dick Malone clears following, goalkeeper, Jim Montgomery's famous 'double-save' during the 1973 FA Cup Final against Leeds United. Also featured, l to r, Trevor Cherry, Richie Pitt, Dave Watson and Montgomery. Only one of Sunderland's victorious team had ever been to Wembley before, Richie Pitt, for a schoolboy international, furthermore, Sunderland's winning team did not contain a single international player.

Final eve fixture between England and Young England with a third place play-off match. Burnley secured 'third place' in 1974 by beating Leicester City 1-0 at Filbert Street before just 4,432 spectators, fewer than had attended four First Round matches involving non-league clubs in home ties - Banbury United (4,800 v Northampton Town), Walton and Hersham (6,502 v Brighton), Willington (4,505 v Blackburn Rovers), Wycombe Wanderers (6,888 v Newport County).

Dixie McNeill is the only player to have scored in eight successive rounds of the FA Cup. Whilst playing for Wrexham, McNeill scored 11 goals in Rounds One to Six in 1977-78, the following season he scored four times in Rounds Three and Four.

The longest semi-final was that between Arsenal and Liverpool in 1979-80. The original tie at Hillsborough ended goalless; the replay at Villa Park ended 1-1 after extra time; the second replay, again at Villa Park also ended 1-1 after extra time; the third replay at Coventry City's Highfield Road was won by Arsenal with a goal from Brian Talbot - the only instance of an FA Cup semi-final being staged at Highfield Road.

Alan Davies played for Manchester United in the 1983 FA Cup Final against Brighton, both the original final tie and replay. The original final tie on 21 May 1983, was Davies' first ever appearance for Manchester United in the FA Cup.

Blackpool and Bolton Wanderers famously contested the 1953 FA Cup Final, the two clubs met again in 1989-90, in Round One, two former opposing finalists meeting again in the competition, on this occasion with a gap of eight rounds to the Final.

Only four clubs have won the FA Cup with a team comprising entirely of English players. Aston Villa (1919-20), West Bromwich Albion (1930-31), Bolton Wanderers (1957-58) and West Ham United (1963-64).

Steve Hodge is the only player to have played in two FA Cup Finals and lose them both to own goals. In 1987, Hodge was in the Spurs team which lost 3-2 to Coventry City, Coventry's winning goal being an own goal by Gary Mabbutt. In 1991, Hodge was in the Nottingham Forest team which lost 2-1 (aet) against his former club, Spurs, whose winning goal was an own goal by Forest's Des Walker.

David O'Leary won the FA Cup with Arsenal in 1979 and again, fourteen-years later, in 1993. Ray Clemence made his first appearance in an FA Cup Final in 1971, for Liverpool against Arsenal; 16-years later, Clemence was in the Spurs team which lost the 1987 Final to Coventry City.

The last Scottish team to appear in the FA Cup proper was Gretna, in the First Round,1991-92 and 1993-94, first as a Northern League club, secondly as a Northern Premier League club.

The 1992 FA Cup Final broke with tradition. It was the first FA Cup Final in which the losing team ascended the Wembley steps first to collect their medals.

The only losing FA Cup finalists to be presented with winners' medals are Sunderland. In 1992, Sunderland were erroneously presented with winners' medals having lost 2-0 to Liverpool. When the mistake was spotted it was too late to change the presentation ceremony. Liverpool received runners-up medals and the two teams exchanged their medals once back in the Wembley dressing rooms.

Sunderland's appearance in the 1992 Final was that of the second lowest placed club to appear in an FA Cup Final. Sunderland had finished in 18th place in Division Two. The lowest placed Finalists being Leicester City who finished 19th in Division Two in 1948-49.

The only team to appear in an FA Cup Final wearing sponsored shirts of a company which did not exist is Chelsea, who did so in the 1993-94 FA Cup Final against Manchester United. Chelsea wore shirts with the sponsors name 'Amiga', a company which had folded earlier in the season but whose shirts Chelsea were contractually still obligated to wear.

Not so (Billy) smart cup tie. On 8 January 2000, the 4th Round tie between Tranmere Rovers and Sunderland ended in highly controversial fashion. With minutes remaining and Tranmere leading 1-0, Tranmere's Clint Hill was sent off for a second bookable offence. As Hill left the field amidst protests from the home players, Tranmere sent on substitute Stephen Frail whose entry to the field went unnoticed by referee Rob Harris and his assistants. No player was called to the bench, hence Tranmere, having had a man sent off, resumed play with eleven men. When play resumed, the Tranmere trainer was still walking across the pitch, having had administered medical attention to one of the Tranmere players. Tranmere held-out to win 1-0. In a TV interview after the game, Sunderland manager, Peter Reid was asked what he made of the final minutes of the game. Reid replied, 'It was like Billy Smart's circus out there.' Sunderland subsequently lodged an appeal to the FA to have the game replayed. The appeal was rejected, albeit the FA stated the referee had 'less than proficiently applied the rules of the game.' The one person to be reprimanded by the FA was Peter Reid for his post-match comments.

Chelsea were the last team to win the FA Cup at the old Wembley, beating Aston Villa in 2000, and the first to win it at the new Wembley, 2007 against Manchester United.

In 2007-08, Portsmouth were the only Premier League club to reach the FA Cup semi-finals, the other teams being Championship sides Barnsley, Cardiff City and West Bromwich Albion. This was also the first time that a team from the top seven of top-flight football in England had not appeared in the semi-finals.

The 2008 Final between Cardiff City and Portsmouth was the first Final not to feature a club from London, Liverpool or Manchester since the 1973 Final between Leeds United and Sunderland.

On 7 December 2010, Leyton Orient found themselves trailing 2-0 and down to ten men in their 2nd round replay at Brisbane Road against non-league Droylsden. Ben Chorley pulled a goal back for Orient from the penalty spot on 77 minutes and Jonathan Tehoue equalised on 89 minutes to send the tie into extra time. Orient then scored six in time added to win the tie 8-2. There were two hat-tricks, Tehoue and Scott McGleish for Orient and five red cards - Terrell Forbes and Ben Chorley for Orient; Natt Kerr, Lee Roche and manager Dave Pace for Droylsden.

When Portsmouth contested the 2010 FA Cup Final against Chelsea, they had already been relegated from the Premier League.

Wigan Athletic beat Manchester City 1-0 in the 2013 Final, Wigan became the first club to win the FA Cup and be relegated in the same season.

In 2016-17, Lincoln City, then of the National League, reached the quarter-finals of the FA Cup, the first non-league club to reach this stage of the competition for 103-years, since Queens Park Rangers (then of the Southern League) in 1914.

Manchester City's 6-0 victory over Watford in the 2019 Final equalled the joint-highest winning margin in an FA Cup Final, equalling Bury's 6-0 victory over Derby County in 1903. City's success followed their winning of the Premier League and League Cup enabling them to become the first club in English football to win the domestic treble.

Should one adhere to the FA line that the extra-preliminary round of the FA Cup forms part of the Preliminary round, Jamie Vardy's appearance for Leicester City in the 2020-21 FA Cup Final made Vardy the first ever player, at some point, to have appeared, in every round of the FA Cup from Preliminary Round (when with Stocksbridge Park Steels) to the Final.

On 2 November 2021, Northern Premier League club Buxton sacked manager Gary Hayward and his assistant, Mark Ward, just days before the club's biggest game in some forty years, a First Round FA Cup tie at York City. The sacking followed assistant manager Ward informing the club he would be unavailable for the tie at York City due to a long standing commitment to a family holiday. Steve Cunningham was appointed manager, Buxton won the tie 1-0.

The First Round tie between Yate Town (Southern League) and Yeovil Town (National League) on 6 November 2021 is the most extreme fixture alphabetically in the history of the FA Cup.

Bolton Wanderers 5-3 extra time defeat to Stockport County (National League) in a First Round replay on 17 November 2021, was the first time Bolton had lost an FA Cup tie to a non-league club since having become a Football League club in 1888, a period of 133 years.

On 4 December 2021, Yeovil Town's (National League) 1-0 victory over Stevenage in Round Two was the 21st occasion on which Yeovil, as a non-league club, had defeated League opposition in the FA Cup. No other non-league club has enjoyed so many FA Cup victories against League opposition.

Firsts

The first football cup competition in the world was the Youdan Cup in 1867, the final was contested at Bramall Lane where Hallam beat Norfolk 2-0 on 9 March 1867. The competition took its name from a local theatre owner, Thomas Youdan, who sponsored the competition and paid for the trophy. The trophy was 'lost' and did not resurface again until 1997, when a Scottish antiques dealer contacted Hallam FC to tell them he had come across it. Hallam FC bought the trophy back for £1,600. The trophy has since been valued at in excess of £150,000, although Hallam FC insist it will never again be for sale. The Youdan Trophy, a Sheffield-based International Youth Tournament founded in 2014, takes its name from the Youdan Cup.

The first football club in London to turn professional was Fulham - 1898.

The first league game to be played on Christmas Day was Preston North End v Aston Villa in 1889. Preston won 3-2 before a crowd of 9,250 at Deepdale. Preston's previous home game against Everton had attracted a crowd of 7,202.

The first international match played in South America took place on 16 May 1901 - Uruguay 2 Argentina 3. It was the first international match to take place outside Great Britain.

The first player to score in a World Cup match was Lucien Laurent who netted after 19 minutes in France's 4-1 victory over Mexico on 13 July 1930, in what was the first ever World Cup match. Laurent was the only surviving member of France's team at the 1930 World Cup to see France win the World Cup on home soil in 1998.

The first and, to date, only Second Division club to win the Scottish FA Cup are East Fife who beat Kilmarnock 4-2 in a replay in 1938, after a 1-1 draw.

Bolton's thirst for firsts. Bolton Wanderers were one of the twelve first members of the Football League (1888); Bolton's Ken Davenport scored the first ever goal in the Football League, against Derby County on 8 September 1888; Bolton were the first winners of the FA Cup at Wembley, beating West Ham United 2-0 on 28 April 1923, in what was the first football match at Wembley. In this game, David Jack, scored for Bolton after two minutes, thus becoming the first player to score a goal at Wembley. Following World War Two, Bolton were the first FA Cup holders to win the Charity Shield, defeating Wolves 4-1 on 6 October 1958; Bolton also participated in the first Football League match to be broadcast 'live' on national television, winning 1-0 at Blackpool on 10 September 1960. As this game kicked-off in the evening, Bolton also participated in the first English League match to have taken place on a Saturday night. Finally, Bolton were the first team to come from behind and win a Premier League match at Old Trafford, defeating Manchester United 2-1 on 20 October 2001.

The first Football League club to install floodlights on a permanent basis was Swindon Town. Swindon played their first match under lights on 2 April 1951, a friendly against Bristol City, Swindon won 2-1. Swindon Town preceded Wolverhampton Wanderers in playing prestigious friendlies against foreign opposition, in October 1953, a crowd of over 7,000 at the County Ground saw Swindon beat Fenerbache (Turkey) 5-1, this was followed by a floodlit match against SK Admira Wien (Austria).

The first floodlit match involving League clubs was a First Round FA Cup tie, second replay between Carlisle United and Darlington which took place at neutral St. James' Park, Newcastle on 28 November 1955.

The first League match played under floodlights took place at Fratton Park on 22 February 1956, a First Division match between Portsmouth and Newcastle United.

Chelsea were the first club to fly to a domestic away match. Chelsea travelled by air for their First Division game against Newcastle United on 19 April 1957.

The first player of African heritage to play professionally on Merseyside was Elkanah Onyeali who played for Tranmere Rovers during the 1960-61 season whilst studying at Birkenhead Technical College. A centre-forward,

Onyeali averaged better than a goal every other game for Tranmere in the Third Division, scoring twice on his debut in a 4-3 win over Bournemouth. He also played for Nigeria scoring 11 goals in as many internationals. Whilst studying at Liverpool University, Onyeali could not combine full-time football and university studies, he signed as a part-time professional for Prescot Cables where he was top scorer in 1961-62. Upon graduation from university Onyeali returned to Nigeria.

The first player to score in an FA Cup Final and League Cup Final at Wembley was Jeff Astle. He scored the only goal of the 1968 FA Cup Final for West Bromwich Albion against Everton, also in Albion's 2-1 defeat against Manchester City in the 1970 League Cup Final. Astle had previously scored in the first leg of the 1966 League Cup Final for West Brom' at West Ham United.

The First Division match between Stoke City and Chelsea at the Victoria Ground on 21 January 1974, was the first top-flight game in English football to take place on a Sunday. Stoke won 1-0 courtesy of a penalty from Geoff Hurst before an attendance of 31,985.

Wales recorded their first ever victory over England (1-0) at Wembley on 31 May 1977.

The first player-manager of an FA Cup Final team was Kenny Dalglish who led Liverpool to a 3-1 victory over Everton in 1985-86. Liverpool were the first club to win the FA Cup with a team which did not include an English player, comprising four Scots, three Irishmen and one each from Wales, Denmark, Zimbabwe and Australia. The only Englishman in the squad was substitute Steve McMahon.

'Shots gave it their best shot. Aldershot were the first ever team to win a Football League play-off final, defeating Wolverhampton Wanderers 3-0 on aggregate in the Division Four play-off final of 1986-87.

The original lumbering striker. The Faroe Islands' first ever international match resulted in a 1-0 victory over Austria in a European Championship qualification game on 12 September 1990. The match took place in Landskrona, Sweden, as none of the pitches in the Faroes at the time met UEFA standards. The first Faroe Island goal at international level was scored by Torkil Nielsen, who worked in a timber and lumber shop.

Is there anybody out there? The first club to have a website was Ipswich Town in 1990, albeit few people had internet until 1998. The club's website was set up by Ipswich fan, Phil Clarke, who worked for BT.

In the days when clubs were allowed but two substitutes, the first time all four substitutes scored in a league game occurred in the Division Three match between Barnet and Torquay United at Underhill on 28 December 1992. Substitutes Nicky Evans and Mark Carter scored for Barnet, whilst Duane Derby and Paul Trollope scored for Torquay. Barnet won 5-4, the only game in English league football in which all substitutes called-upon scored in the game.

Danny Bergara, born in Montevideo, Uruguay, was the first foreign manager to lead out an English club at Wembley when he guided Stockport County to the 1992 Autoglass Trophy final.

The first player to have been awarded a goal in English football by goal-line technology is Edin Dzeko for Manchester City v Cardiff City, Premier League, 18 January 2014.

In 2017, Arsene Wenger became the first manager to guide a club to seven FA Cup Final victories.

In 2020-21, Salford City became the first League club to hold a senior trophy for just twenty four hours. On 13 March 2021, Salford beat Portsmouth (0-0, 4-2 on penalties) at Wembley in the 2019-20 Papa John Trophy Final held over from the previous season due to Covid - 342 days after the original date. The following day, Salford handed the Trophy back to competition organisers for presentation to Sunderland who, that afternoon, triumphed over Tranmere Rovers (1-0) in the 2020-21 Final.

Games

You couldn't make it up. On 12 September 1885, Dundee Harp beat Aberdeen Rovers 35-0. That night the Dundee Harp officials and players held a party to celebrate their record winning score in a British first-class match. Just after 9pm they received news that on the same day, Arbroath had beaten Bon Accord 36-0 in the First Round of the Scottish FA Cup.

So good they could play him in his overcoat. On 12 November 1894, Aston Villa's Division One game against Sheffield United at Wellington Road was played in driving, freezing rain and sleet. At half-time, the Villa players changed into a dry strip and were given hot tea, a courtesy not extended to the Sheffield United players. In the second-half, with conditions having worsened, Villa's Jack Devey played in his overcoat whilst winger Charlie Athersmith borrowed an umbrella from a spectator. Sheffield United players left the field one-by-one suffering from exposure, until only six remained. With the rules stating a team must have a minimum of seven players on the field, the referee abandoned the game minutes from the end with Aston Villa leading 5-0. The Football League ordered the result to stand. The story that Athersmith scored a goal whilst holding the umbrella, is apocryphal.

There has been a festive programme of three games in three consecutive days on five occasions, 1902, 1913, 1919, 1924 and 1930.

The tradition of players eating half an orange at half-time started in 1918-19 and continued with most clubs until the 1960s. Eating oranges at half time was introduced as a source of Vitamin C in response to the Spanish Flu' pandemic which reached the UK in 1918. It is thought 'Spanish Flu' came to these shores via soldiers returning from WW1. Once the pandemic had subsided, having claimed 228,000 lives in the UK, clubs continued providing oranges as an alternative or accompaniment to tea at half time.

The 1961-62 League Cup Final between Norwich City and Rochdale was the last final of a senior cup competition in English football to be contested by two clubs who, at the time, were not in the top tier of English football. Norwich triumphed 4-0 on aggregate.

The term 'derby' match dates back to the late Victorian age when working men wore flat cloth caps. On special occasions, however, such as weddings, funerals and anniversaries, men would don their 'Sunday best' suits and wear a derby hat of the bowler variety. As the meeting of two local clubs was deemed a special occasion in the fixture list, such games began to be referred to as 'derby' matches, the insinuation being such games merited the wearing of Sunday best and a derby hat as opposed to everyday clothing and a flat cap, albeit this never happened.

A game of three halves. On 1 September 1894, Sunderland and Derby County met on the opening day of the Division One season. Referee Mr. R. Kirkham from Darwen missed his connecting train at York so, sent a telegram to Sunderland, informing the club he would not be arriving much before 5pm. The match was scheduled to kick-off at 3.30pm. With over 9,000 spectators in the ground, Sunderland officials did not want the fans to have a ninety-minute wait. A local referee, Mr Conqueror from Southwick, was located and both clubs agreed to start the game with Mr Conqueror in charge. At half-time, with Sunderland leading 3-0, the designated referee, Mr Kirkham, arrived and ordered the game to re-start with him in charge. The game kicked-off again at 4.30pm, with Sunderland again leading 3-0 at half-time and eventually winning 8-0. A game of three-halves, two referees, two-hours fifteen minutes of football and 11 goals of which 8 counted. Who wouldn't pay good money to watch that?

In 1896-97, Darwen did not register a single draw in their 30 matches in Division Two (Won 14 Lost 16). Darwen are the last team to complete a full season in English senior football without drawing a single game.

On 5 December 1931, Newcastle United were held to a goalless draw by Portsmouth in front of 27,901 spectators at St. James' Park, a game in which not one corner was awarded to either side.

On Boxing Day 1935, Tranmere Rovers led Oldham Athletic 8-1 at half-time. Rovers went on to win 13-4 with Bunny Bell scoring nine, missing a penalty and hitting the woodwork twice. The result is the highest aggregate score for a league match in English football.

Home alone. On Christmas Day 1936, not one of the 11 matches in Division One was won by the away team. The fixtures were reversed for Boxing Day and again, not one game was won by the away team.

Played them home and away on the same day. In 1940-41, Huddersfield Town and Bradford City met home and away on Christmas Day in the War League North. The morning match was played at Huddersfield and the two teams met again at Bradford City's Valley Parade in the afternoon. Huddersfield's Billy Price scored twice in the first meeting and once in the second, there was just nigh-on three hours between his second and third goals. The following season (1941-42) Huddersfield played Leeds United at Elland Road on Christmas morning and at Bradford Park Avenue in the afternoon.

Never the twain shall meet. Tom Sawyer never missed a game of any type at Wembley from 1946 to 1970, yet never saw one either. He was commissionaire at Wembley's main entrance.

From pre-WW1 to the early sixties, the traditional first match of the season for many clubs was the internal Blues v Reds, sometimes billed as, Possibles v Probables. These games were staged prior to pre-season friendlies and often comprised three matches in one afternoon. A twenty-minute game of teams comprising youth and amateur players on the club's books, and trialists. The second, a thirty-minute game between youth and reserve team players. Finally, an 80-minute game, Reds v Blues, comprising the first team squad and fringe players from the reserves. Starved of any football for over three months, supporters would attend such games in healthy numbers with the attendance increasing as the afternoon unfolded. Such games disappeared from the football calendar in the early sixties, clubs preferring to arrange friendlies against other clubs, especially from the Continent, which drew larger attendances and provided more competitive football.

In 1956-57, the two-legged German Floodlit Cup Final between Eintracht Frankfurt and Schalke ended level on aggregate. Frankfurt won 8-6 on corners, the only top-flight match to have been decided on the number of corners awarded.

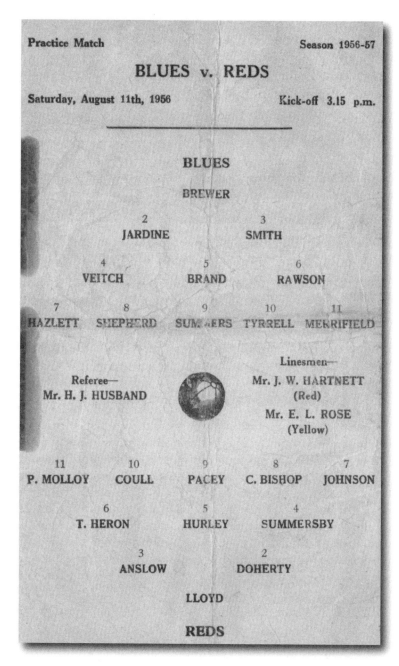

BLUES v. REDS

Saturday, August 11th, 1956

Kick-off 3.15 p.m.

BLUES

BREWER

2
JARDINE

3
SMITH

4
VEITCH

5
BRAND

6
RAWSON

7
HAZLETT

8
SHEPHERD

9
SUMMERS

10
TYRRELL

11
MERRIFIELD

Referee—
Mr. H. J. HUSBAND

Linesmen—
Mr. J. W. HARTNETT
(Red)

Mr. E. L. ROSE
(Yellow)

11
P. MOLLOY

10
COULL

9
PACEY

8
C. BISHOP

7
JOHNSON

6
T. HERON

5
HURLEY

4
SUMMERSBY

3
ANSLOW

2
DOHERTY

LLOYD

REDS

Line-ups from the team-page in the Millwall programme for the Reds v Blues practice match at the Den on 11 August 1956, attendance 9,038.

106

Two games in a day. On 26 November 1958, Danny Clapton and Jack Kelsey were on opposing sides in the England v Wales International match played in the afternoon at Villa Park. Following the game, the pair drove to London and that evening both played for Arsenal against Juventus.

In the early sixties, games between Charlton Athletic and Plymouth Argyle produced a series of extraordinary results:

1959-60	Charlton 5 Plymouth 2	Plymouth 6 Charlton 4
1960-61	Charlton 6 Plymouth 4	Plymouth 6 Charlton 4
1961-62	Charlton 3 Plymouth 1	Plymouth 2 Charlton 1
1962-63	Charlton 6 Plymouth 3	Plymouth 6 Charlton 1

What goes round comes round. Charlton Athletic's Second Division game against Huddersfield Town on 21 December 1957 is well known. With Huddersfield leading 5-1 and 27 minutes remaining, Charlton staged an amazing comeback to win 7-6. Huddersfield Town are the only team in English professional football to score six and lose. Less well known is Charlton's pre-season match against AIK (Sweden) on 7 June 1946. AIK were 7-1 down with thirty minutes remaining, only for the Swedish side to storm back to draw 7-7.

Two clubs were exempt from playing the traditional Christmas Day fixture, Hull City and Grimsby Town. The Football League gave special dispensation to both clubs as the fishing industry in both towns worked on Christmas Day.

Rowley the ringer. In the 1950s, a Football Combination Representative XI played challenge matches on the Continent either against representative teams from other national/regional reserve team leagues or, in some instances, national leagues. In October 1957, a Football Combination representative team played against a representative team from the Dutch League (Eredivisie) in Amsterdam to celebrate the founding of that league. The Football Combination team won 6-0 with Leicester City's Arthur Rowley scoring twice, albeit Rowley had never played in Leicester City's reserve team since joining the club from Fulham in 1950.

On 27 January 1962, Clyde drew 2-2 at home to Aberdeen in the 2nd round of the Scottish Cup. Four days later, Clyde travelled to Pittodrie for the replay and lost 10-3.

The last programme of English League fixtures to be held on Christmas Day took place in 1957-58, which included the Football Combination and Central reserve leagues. Blackpool, however, continued the tradition of playing at home on Christmas Day when home fixtures allowed. Blackpool's final Christmas Day game took place in 1965, a 4-2 victory in Division One over Blackburn Rovers which attracted an attendance of 20,856.

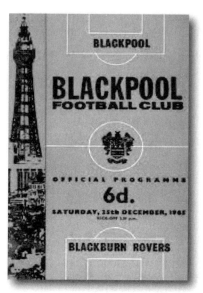

The last English League Christmas Day fixture - Blackpool v Blackburn Rovers.

The final programme of Christmas Day games in Scotland took place in 1971. A few clubs, however, continued the tradition. The final matches played on Christmas Day in Scotland took place in 1976. Clydebank drew 2-2 with First Division leaders St. Mirren, managed by Alex Ferguson, before a crowd of 7,500, Clydebank's highest attendance of the season. Also in Division One, Alloa Athletic defeated Cowdenbeath 2-1 before a crowd of 731 which was considerably below average. Alloa's previous home game against Dunfermline Athletic attracted 1,511.

In 1962-63, the Scottish Cup 1st round tie between Airdrieoneans and Stranraer, scheduled for January 12th, was postponed 33 times due to the 'Big Freeze'. No Scottish or English Cup tie has been postponed so many times. The tie was eventually played two months later on 11 March with Airdrie 3-0 victors. Airdrie were so far behind with their fixtures, having beaten Stranraer, they had to play Rangers two days later in round two, losing 6-0.

A programme from the last Christmas Day game played in Scotland, issued free to fans.

The kick-off of the Scottish League Division Two match between Queens Park and Arbroath on 26 September 1964 was brought forward from 3pm to 2.30pm in order to allow five Queens Park players to catch the ferryboat to Arran where they were going on holiday. The request was approved by both the Scottish FA and Arbroath.

Defence under pressure. On 16 January 1965, Sunderland reserves had nine successive corners awarded, all from the left wing, during their 5-1 win over Hartlepools United reserves in the North Regional League.

On 7 March 1966, Dave Clements of Queens Park Rangers played two matches against Watford on the same day. In the morning Clements appeared for Rangers' youth team against Watford youths and, in the afternoon, was called-up to play for Rangers' reserves against Watford in the Football Combination League.

The four Bolton players who played for Brazil during 1966 World Cup. In June 1966, four Bolton Wanderers' players, John Ritson, John Jackson, Les Hudson and David Lyon were invited to play for Brazil in a practice match against the 'The Rest' (of the Brazil squad) at Bolton's Bromwich Street training ground. The Bolton players, who played alongside Pele, Garrincha, Gerson and Bellini, responded to a call from Brazil to 'help out' by replacing injured players in the squad.

In 1971-72, Stoke City played eleven matches in order to reach the League Cup Final (a 2-1 victory over Chelsea). Stoke's epic journey included four games in the semi-finals against West Ham United, three ties against Manchester United and two against Oxford United. Stoke were also involved in nine ties in the FA Cup including two each against Manchester United, Arsenal and Tranmere Rovers, meaning Stoke City played Manchester United in seven competitive matches - five cup ties and two league matches. Should one include friendly matches, Stoke City played a total of 74 games, full-back, Jackie Marsh, playing in 72 of them.

Spurs skipper Dave Mackay and Celtic captain Billy McNeill about to exchange doormats prior to Celtic v Spurs at Hampden in 1967. Referee: Willie Syme

On 5 August 1967, Celtic and Tottenham Hotspur drew 3-3 at Hampden Park in a game that pitched the Scottish Champions and European Cup holders against the English FA Cup winners. The game was part of the Centenary celebrations of Queens Park FC and attracted an attendance of 91,708 to Hampden. The game was also noteworthy for the captains exchanging club doormats prior to kick-off as opposed to the traditional pennants.

Prior to Covid, the only English league game never to have been fulfilled was the Fourth Division match between Scunthorpe United and Exeter City scheduled for 2 April 1974. Exeter's small squad was ravaged by injuries, with only eight players available to face Scunthorpe. Exeter requested the game be postponed but the Football League refused. Exeter appealed against the decision, pointing out that the only way they could field the required number of players was if manager, John Newman, named unregistered players, in which case the club could be fined, have points deducted or both. The Football League dismissed Exeter's appeal and ordered the club to go ahead with the game. Exeter refused to travel; the Football League awarded two points to Scunthorpe United, fined Exeter City £5,000 and ordered the club to pay £1,334 in compensation to Scunthorpe. Exeter City had a schedule of seven other league matches in the space of 24 days in April which they managed to fulfil, including their home match against Scunthorpe United on 22 April, which Exeter won 4-0. The club and Football League records uniquely show Exeter City and Scunthorpe United as having played one another just once in the season.

On 5 October 1974, Tottenham Hotspur lost 3-2 at home to Burnley in Division One. Spurs trailed 0-2 at half-time, both Burnley goals being own goals by Spurs' John Pratt and Mike England. Pratt and England both subsequently scored in the second half for Spurs. The only instance of two players scoring for both their team and the opposition in English league football.

Mr Brown goes off to town. On 28 September 1963, Tony Brown scored on his debut for West Bromwich Albion in a 2-1 win at Ipswich Town for whom the goalkeeper was Roy Bailey. Fifteen years later, Brown scored twice in Albion's 5-3 victory at Manchester United on 30 December 1978 to create a post-war club record of 213 goals for Albion, the United goalkeeper that day being Gary Bailey, son of Roy.

Walsall defensive wall collapsed. Brighton's home Third Division match against Walsall on 5 October 1976 was goalless at half-time. The game was still goalless until the 51st minute when Ian Mellor put Brighton ahead. Brighton went on to win 7-0.

The latest abandonment of a game in English football occurred on 14 May 1983. The Division Two game between Derby County and Fulham was abandoned in the 89th minute, with only 78 seconds remaining. Derby County needed to win to avoid relegation, with the score 1-0 in favour of Derby, the referee blew his whistle for a foul, the crowd mistook this for full-time and invaded the pitch. As play could not be resumed, the referee abandoned the game. The Football League ordered the result to stand.

Hartlepool United's Victoria Park hosted two League matches on the same day (23 August 1986). Hartlepool drew 2-2 with Cardiff City in a Division Four match, a few hours later, Middlesbrough, who had been locked-out of their Ayresome Park home as a result of going into administration, drew 2-2 with Port Vale in a Division Three game.

Relegation dog fight. On 9 May 1987, the final day of the season, Torquay United were in danger of losing Football League status and being relegated to the Conference League. Torquay required a point to ensure their safety but, with only minutes remaining, were trailing 1-2 at home to Crewe Alexandra. It was then that a police dog, 'Bryn', who was patrolling the pitch perimeter with his handler, jumped-up and bit United's Jim Nichol on the thigh. The referee allowed four minutes of added time for the treatment of Nichol's injury, it was in this added time that Paul Dobson equalised for Torquay to ensure the club's safety and avoid relegation from the Football League. Much later, when 'Bryn' died, he was stuffed and put on display in the Torquay United boardroom.

Chesterfield enjoyed an excellent start to 1987-88. When they travelled to Gillingham on 5 September, Chesterfield had yet to concede a goal, but were beaten 10-0. In their previous home match, Gillingham had beaten Southend United 8-1.

Over thirty years on, the longest Cup competition in British football history has still not concluded. In 1987-88, English clubs were banned from European competition following the Heysel stadium disaster. In an attempt to fill the void, the Anglo-Scottish Challenge Cup was launched which pitted the English FA Cup holders, Coventry City, against the Scottish FA Cup holders, St. Mirren in a two-legged final. The first leg took place at

Coventry City's Highfield Road on 22 December 1987 and ended 1-1. Due to the lack of a sponsor and fixture congestion, the second-leg, due to be played in February 1988, did not take place and it was agreed the game would be rescheduled. The game has yet to be played.

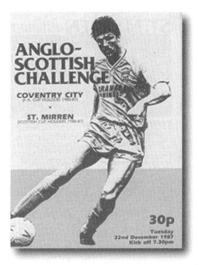

Programme from the longest running cup competition in British football, over thirty years on, the outcome is still awaited, the cup still to be presented.

Substituted though he never set foot on the pitch. On 25 April 1981, three Stockport County players, Les Bradd (travelling from Nottingham), Chris Galvin and Dave Sunley plus manager Jimmy McGuigan (all travelling from Yorkshire) were caught in a blizzard when attempting to cross the Pennines for Stockport's Division Four match at Bury. Stockport's assistant manager, Trevor Porteous, took control of team affairs but had only eight players available. Tony Coyle, who was injured and had not played for over a month, had travelled with the team to watch the game but agreed to play. Porteous, to avoid the club being fined, named eleven players on the team sheet with Bradd in the starting line-up and Dave Sunley as substitute. Stockport played the first half with nine men and at half-time there was no score. Chris Galvin and Dave Sunley arrived at Gigg Lane two minutes before the break and changed in order to take their place in the team for the second half, with substitute Sunley replacing Bradd, originally named on the team sheet but who was still stranded in the blizzard. Stockport County won the game 1-0 with a second-half goal from Martin Fowler. Les Bradd is the only player to have been substituted in an English league game who never set foot on the pitch.

On 27 March (Easter Monday) 1989, referee Kelvin Morton awarded five penalties in 27 minutes (spread across the closing minutes of the first half and opening stages of the second) during Crystal Palace's 2-1 victory over Brighton in Division Two. Four penalties were awarded to Crystal Palace and one to Brighton; Mark Bright converted one penalty for Palace but also missed one, as did Ian Wright and John Pemberton. Brighton's penalty was successfully converted by Alan Curbishley.

Conceded penalty then took over in goal to save the spot-kick. On 23 November 1991, Aberdeen's Brian Irvine conceded a penalty whilst playing against Hibernian at Easter Road. Irvine tripped Hibernian's Keith Wright, who so incensed Aberdeen 'keeper Theo Snelders for the way he went to ground, Snelders struck Wright and was red-carded by referee David Syme. Irvine took over in goal and saved the penalty he'd conceded.

The Anglo-Italian Group match between West Ham United and Bristol Rovers on 2 September 1992, ended 2-2. The two teams in this, the final group match, were contesting qualification to the next stage of the tournament against teams from Italy. West Ham and Bristol Rovers completed their group level on points and goal difference. West Ham 'won' the game and progressed to the knock-out stages courtesy of the toss of a coin. The only instance when a senior match between two English clubs has been decided in such a way.

On 9 October 1993, Reading recorded a 6-4 away win at Exeter City in Division Two, a rare game in which five players each scored two goals; Jimmy Quinn, Scott Taylor and Stuart Lovell for Reading; Ronnie Jepson and Mike Ross for Exeter City.

Cup-tie postponed due to solar eclipse. The League Cup first round tie between Torquay United and Portsmouth in 1999-2000 was postponed due to a solar eclipse which coincided with the cup-tie. Torquay police felt they could not cope with both the cup-tie and the number of visitors wanting to view the eclipse from the town's seafront, so made a request for the League Cup tie to be postponed. The request was granted and the tie re-scheduled for 17 August. Torquay never did have their moment in the sun, following a goalless draw at Plainmoor they were defeated 3-0 at Fratton Park.

Hardest earned point? On 7 April 2001, Brighton travelled for a Division Two game at FC Halifax Town only to discover on arrival at the Shay, the game had been postponed due to a waterlogged pitch. On the journey back to Brighton, the team's coach ran out of fuel. A situation which resulted in the coach company losing their contract with the club. Brighton, conveyed by a new coach company, travelled to Halifax for the rescheduled game on 24 April. The coach suffered a flat battery whilst stopping off at Warwick services on the M40, the players having to disembark and push the coach in order for it to restart. Having arrived at FC Halifax Town in a downpour, the referee postponed the game forty-five minutes before kick-off due to a waterlogged pitch. Brighton travelled to Halifax for a third time for the again rearranged fixture on 3 May, a game in which 3,979 spectators witnessed a goalless draw.

The Division One game between Sheffield United and West Bromwich Albion at Bramall Lane on 16 March 2002, saw the home side reduced to six players due to a combination of injuries and dismissals. A team can continue to play with a minimum of seven players, therefore the referee, Eddie Wolstenholme, had no option but to abandon the game after 82 minutes with West Brom' leading 3-0. The Football League ordered the result to stand.

In 2005-06, Walsall's Ishmael Demontagnac missed his team's game at Bristol City on 2 January because he thought the fixture was taking place the following day, so stayed at home in bed. Bristol City won 3-0.

Snow saved Sunderland drifting to unwanted record. On 8 April 2006, Sunderland's Premier League match against Fulham at the Stadium of Light was abandoned by referee Mike Reilly after twenty-one minutes with Fulham leading 1-0. A snowstorm hit Wearside, though snow did not lie for long on the pitch due to undersoil heating, such was the volume which fell, the pitch became waterlogged. The game was replayed in May, with relegated Sunderland winning 1-0. It was Sunderland's only home win of the season.

On 9 April 2008, in the Northern Premier League, Newcastle Blue Star were 2-0 ahead against Bamber Bridge after only 47 seconds.

Beans and jam produce nightmare journey. On 3 April 2013, Ebbsfleet United left at 10.45am for their evening game in the National League at Barrow. Initially the team coach was held-up on the M25, but further problems lay ahead when the coach reached the M6 near Newton-le-Willows. The M6 was closed due to a lorry shedding its load of baked beans and the team coach was caught up in a huge three-lane traffic jam that stretched back thirteen miles. Having telephoned ahead to warn Barrow of their situation, kick-off was put back to 9.15pm. Ebbsfleet arrived at Holker Street at 8.40pm and did well to secure a 1-1 draw in a game that did not finish until 11.03pm. Ebbsfleet travelled through the night to get back to Kent, manager, Liam Daish, finally arriving home at 8.30 in the morning. Ten hardy Ebbsfleet supporters also made the 640-mile round trip. Having left at 10am, they too endured a nightmare journey, one that should have taken 5 and a half hours to Barrow but, in fact, took them ten and three-quarter hours.

On 12 August 2014, the League Cup First Round tie between Dagenham and Redbridge and Brentford ended 6-6. The tie went to penalties, Brentford winning 4-2. A curious instance of twice as many goals having been scored from open play in a cup-tie than in the penalty shoot-out.

The most consecutive games a team has played against League opposition whose name began with the same letter is five. In 2014-15, between 16 September and 4 October, Watford played five consecutive Championship matches against Blackpool, Bournemouth, Blackburn Rovers, Brentford and Brighton. Amazingly, Watford repeated the sequence between 24 January and 14 February albeit including another team whose name begins with 'B' - Blackpool, Bournemouth, Blackburn Rovers, Brentford and Bolton Wanderers. Not involved in this record sequence were fellow Championship side Birmingham City.

Blackpool's final home game of the 2014-15 season against Huddersfield Town was halted after 48 minutes when Blackpool supporters invaded the pitch for a peaceful protest against the ownership of the club by the Oyston family. The pitch invasion included one home fan on a mobility scooter. Due to home supporters refusing to leave the pitch, the referee had no alternative but to abandon the game with score at 0-0. The Football League later ordered the result to stand.

In their Champions League match against FC Basel on 7 March 2018, Manchester City recorded 979 passes (source Perform/Opta). City lost 2-1.

Goose stops play is always worth a gander. The League Two game between Macclesfield Town and Grimsby Town on 11 August 2018 was subject to eleven minutes of added time, eight of which were taken up with the attempts by the Macclesfield ground staff to capture a Canada goose that had landed on the pitch and refused to leave. The groundsman was eventually successful.

On 16 August 2020, Bohemians beat UCD 10-1 in the League of Ireland Premier Division, three days later Bohemians lost 6-1 at Dundalk. A similar extreme results sequence was experienced by Hull City in 1938. On 27 December, Hull City lost 6-1 at New Brighton and in their following match on 31 December crashed 6-2 at Bradford City. Hull's next game took place on 14 January at home to Carlisle United, which Hull won 11-1.

On 26 September 2020, the Oxford United team had to change at their Lancashire hotel and travel to their game at Accrington Stanley in a fleet of taxis. An alcohol spray used on the team coach to protect against coronavirus left the driver unable to take the players to their game. The alcohol spray was located by a device that stops the coach driver starting the vehicle if alcohol is detected in the vicinity of the driver's seat.

On 21 August 2021, for the Premier League match against Liverpool at Anfield, Burnley players displayed a sight not seen for some years, wearing shirts numbered 1 to 11. Apart from commemorative occasions, the last instance of a team using shirts numbered 1-11 in the Premier League had been Queens Park Rangers in 1995-96.

On 18 September 2021, the Premier League Under 18 Youth Cup tie between Leicester City U18 and Newcastle United U18 was abandoned seconds before the kick-off with the teams on the pitch and ready to face one another. Whilst conducting his pre-kick-off check, the referee noticed there were no paramedics present, a contravention of Premier League rules. The referee abandoned the game. A request by Newcastle United staff that a friendly may be played was denied as this would also be in contravention of the rules. The Newcastle team and staff had no alternative but to change and return to Tyneside, a 372 mile round trip for nothing.

Was a game of two halves..and a bit. On 30 October 2021, part of the first-half of Leyton Orient's League Two game against Hartlepool United was played after half-time. Referee Alan Young blew for half-time having failed to add four minutes of added time to the first half. After the interval, the teams played the 'lost' four minutes, after which Mr Young blew his whistle and signalled the teams to swap ends in order for the second half to commence.

On 7 December 2021, the League One match between Fleetwood Town and Bolton Wanderers involved eleven minutes of added time at the end of the first half. The added time was due to three suspensions of play. The first, when a duck landed on the pitch and, at first, refused to move of its own free will. The second delay was due to a floodlight malfunction. The third, on what was a stormy night, when part of the scoreboard was blown onto the pitch.

The Premier League game between Liverpool and Aston Villa at Anfield on 11 December 2021, was only the third time Liverpool had kicked-off at the traditional time of 3pm on a Saturday in three successive matches since May 2007, a period of fourteen years.

Perseverance of the saints. On 22 December 2021, St. Mirren attempted to have their Scottish Premiership match at home to Celtic postponed as eleven players had tested positive for Covid. The Scottish Premiership, however, ruled the game had to go ahead. In order to name the required number of players for the game, St. Mirren had to recall six Under 18 players from loan spells with Lowland League clubs, three teenagers being named in the starting line-up, along with former Burton Albion and Blackpool goalkeeper, Dean Lyness, who was making only his third start in two-and-a-half years with the club. Not one of the six players on St. Mirren's substitute bench had ever featured in the first team squad before. Despite Celtic having 83% of possession and 31 shots at goal, the game ended goalless.

On 2 January 2022, the game between Chelsea and Liverpool at Stamford Bridge was the first Premier League match to use safe standing for spectators following laws, in 1994, stipulating stadiums in England's top two tiers must be all-seater.

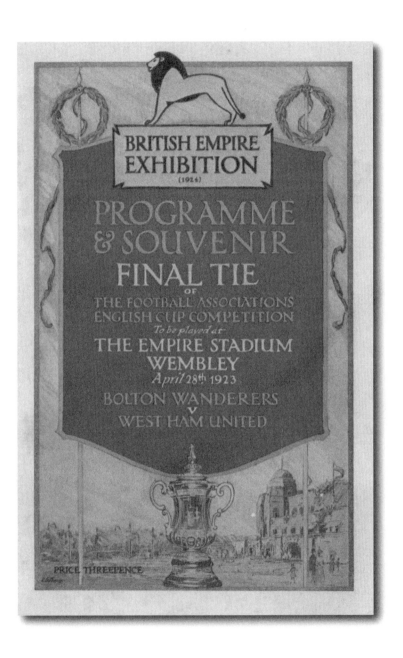

Goalkeepers

In the 1882-83, Sir Arthur Conan Doyle played in goal for amateur club Portsmouth FC under the pseudonym of A.C. Smith. The club folded in 1896.

The first goalkeeper to score from open play was Charlie Williams playing for Manchester City against Sunderland at Roker Park on 14 April 1900. A long clearance from Williams bounced over the head of advancing Sunderland 'keeper John Doig and into the net.

Arnold Birch kept goal for Chesterfield throughout 1923-24 but ended the season with five goals to his name - all from penalties.

Sagar's trial saga. Ted Sagar's career as a goalkeeper with Everton spanned four decades. Sagar joined Everton from non-league Thorne Colliery in 1929 and played his last game for the Toffees in 1953. Sagar made a total of 499 senior appearances for Everton which would have been far more but for the six-year postponement of regular football due to WW2. In 1926, at the age of sixteen, Sagar was given a trial by Hull City in City's reserve team against Scarborough in the Midland League. Hull City were suitably impressed and wished to sign Sagar but, unbeknown to him, the club had lost his address. Thinking he had not impressed in the trial, Sagar was only made aware of the truth some years later when he was informed of the club's futile attempts to locate him by Hull manager, Bill McCracken.

During 1928-29, Halifax Town fielded two goalkeepers whose aggregate age was 93 and had a combined total of 55 years as professionals in the Football League. Bob Suter was 48 years old and had made his league debut for Notts County in 1898, his League career spanned 30 years. Howard Matthews was 45 years old and had made his League debut for Port Vale in 1906. Matthews' League career spanned 25 years and, at the age of 45, he was transferred from Halifax Town to Chester.

Middleton named on the bench. In 1950, Ray Middleton, then of Chesterfield, was appointed a magistrate. Middleton remains the only active footballer to serve as a Justice of the Peace, albeit other players achieved such a distinction when their playing days were over.

On 1 June 1952, Jimmy O'Neill made his International debut for The Republic of Ireland against Spain in Madrid. O'Neill conceded twice before he touched the ball for the first time, Spain scoring after 30 seconds and one-minute and thirty seconds. Despite eventually conceding six, Ireland's defenders were deemed culpable; O'Neill retained his place in the team and went on to win a further 16 caps for the Republic.

Sheffield United 'keeper, Ted Burgin, who was a member of England's 1954 World Cup squad was only 5'7" tall. Steve Death, who played 471 league matches for Reading between 1969 and 1982, was also just 5'7". Until 31 January 2009, Death held the record of 1,074 minutes without conceding a goal. The record was subsequently broken by Edwin van der Saar of Manchester United.

The 1956-57 Charity Shield match was played between Manchester City and Manchester United at Maine Road on 24 October 1956. United goalkeeper, Ray Wood, was injured after 37 minutes and, unusually for the time, was substituted. The substitute goalkeeper was, David Gaskell, a United debutant aged sixteen years and nineteen days, who helped United to a 1-0 win. Gaskell remains the youngest player ever to have appeared in a Charity (Community) Shield match.

In 1958-59, Accrington Stanley's three goalkeepers all simultaneously succumbed to injury. Stanley manager, George Eastham senior, was forced to play full-back, Bob McNicholl, in goal for three League games. McNicholl did so well, he kept his place as Stanley's goalkeeper even when the three recognised 'keepers were again fit. McNicoll's run as the Stanley goalkeeper ended when he broke a toe, an injury which also ended 147 consecutive appearances in League and Cup since joining the club. In 1959, McNicholl was transferred to Brighton & Hove Albion, his transfer form stating his position to be that of 'full-back/goalkeeper.'

George Yardley initially signed as an amateur for East Fife in 1959 and whilst with the club was capped as a goalkeeper by the Scotland amateur team. Yardley signed as a semi-professional with East Fife who continued to play him in goal, only to then switch him to centre-forward. Yardley went on to score 17 league goals for East Fife. After a brief spell at Luton Town, Yardley eventually signed for Tranmere Rovers. In four seasons between 1966 and 1970, he played 123 League matches for Tranmere and three as a goalkeeper for the reserves. Yardley scored 68 goals for Rovers and was the club's leading goalscorer on four separate occasions.

Gordon Morritt signed for Rotherham United in 1961 and in five years at the club competed with Roy Ironside for the number one jersey. Often in training, Morritt would play as a forward and so impressed manager Danny Williams he selected Morritt as centre-forward for Rotherham's League Cup 3rd round tie against Swansea Town on 14 October 1964. The tie ended 2-2 with Morritt failing to score.

Lightening exit. Goalkeeper Arthur Lightening made 150 league appearances for Coventry City (1958-62) and was then transferred to Middlesbrough. Lightening had made fifteen appearances for Middlesbrough when he asked manager, Bob Dennison, for 'leave of absence' to attend a wedding in South Africa. Dennison granted permission, Lightening travelled to South Africa but never returned to Teesside. Subsequent efforts by Middlesbrough to contact Lightening came to no avail. In 1964, Middlesbrough learned Lightening had settled in South Africa and was playing for Durban United.

On 19 September 1964, Sunderland reserves and Darlington reserves drew 2-2 in the North Regional League. The combined age of the two goalkeepers was 30. Darlington goalkeeper, John Hope, and Sunderland 'keeper, Derek Foster, both being 15 years of age.

In 1973-74, Manchester United's joint leading goalscorer after 20 matches, was goalkeeper, Alex Stepney with two goals. Both Stepney's goals came from the penalty spot; in a 2-1 home defeat to Leicester City (12 September 1973) and in United's 1-0 victory over Birmingham City (20 October 1973). On 22 December 1973, Stepney tied as United's leading goalscorer alongside George Best, Brian Kidd and Sammy McIlroy.

On 18 September 1976, Dundee United goalkeeper, Hamish McAlpine, missed two penalties against Ayr United at Somerton Park. Dundee United won 4-1.

Jimmy Montgomery's performance for Sunderland in the 1973 FA Cup Final is well known. In addition to his FA Cup winners medal, Montgomery also has a European Cup winners medal, he was substitute goalkeeper for Nottingham Forest in the 1980 European Cup Final. Prior to 1960-61 season commencing, whilst playing for Sunderland Youth team, Montgomery saved six penalties during an International Youth Tournament in Holland, won by Sunderland.

Jimmy Rimmer won two European Cup winners medals, fourteen years apart. Rimmer was a named substitute for Manchester United for the 1968 European Cup Final and was in the Aston Villa team for their 1982 Final against Bayern Munich but was injured after only nine minutes and replaced by Nigel Spink. Rimmer was the second player to win a European Cup winners medal at two different clubs, the first being Saul Malatrasi (Inter and AC Milan).

On 18 December 1979, Bruce Grobbelaar joined Crewe Alexandra on loan from Vancouver Whitecaps. Crewe were rooted to the bottom of Division Four, but subsequently contrived to lose only seven of their remaining 23 league matches, during which the ever-present Grobbelaar kept eight clean sheets. An unbeaten run of six matches at the end of the season culminated in a 2-0 win against York City, in which Grobbelaar scored Crewe's second goal from the penalty spot. It was during this final run-in that Grobbelaar's performances came to the attention of Liverpool's chief scout, Tom Saunders.

On 25 November 1986, Hull City goalkeeper, Tony Norman, was taken ill prior to the club's Full Members Cup 2nd round tie at Southampton. Regular central-defender, Peter Skipper, took over in goal for the whole of the game. Hull lost 2-1.

Phil Parkes is the only player in English football to have played in excess of 350 league and cup matches for two different clubs - Queens Park Rangers (1970-79) and West Ham United (1979 - 1990). Coincidentally, Parkes made the same number of league appearances for Queens Park Rangers as he did West Ham United - 344.

Peter Shilton played in excess of 100 matches for five different clubs - Leicester City, Stoke City, Nottingham Forest, Southampton and Derby County. Shilton made his full England debut on 25 November 1970, against East Germany, when 21 years old, but did not appear in the finals of a World Cup (Spain '82) until three months short of his 33rd birthday. Even so, Shilton jointly holds the record, 10, (along with Fabien Barthez, France) for the most clean sheets in World Cup finals matches.

Pegguy Arphexad's career as a goalkeeper spanned sixteen years, 1989 to 2005. In that period, Arphexad only played 39 league matches, his most prolific period being 1997-2000 when he made 21 appearances for Leicester City. Thus, the rest of Arphexad's playing career in England comprised 18 senior matches over 15 years.

Made in Chelsea. Kevin Hitchcock spent thirteen years at Chelsea (1988-2001) and subsequently became a much travelled goalkeeping coach. Every club Hitchcock has been connected with as a coach, there was a Chelsea connection regarding his appointment. Hitchcock left Chelsea in 2001 to become goalkeeping coach at Watford, at the request of Watford manager/coach, Gianluca Vialli, former Chelsea player and manager. In 2004, Hitchcock joined Blackburn Rovers, appointed by former Chelsea player, Mark Hughes. When Hughes was appointed manager of Manchester City, Hughes, in turn, appointed Hitchcock as his goalkeeping coach. In March 2010, Hitchcock accepted the post of goalkeeping coach at West Ham United, appointed by former Chelsea manager, Avran Grant. Hitchcock then moved to Fulham, appointed by Mark Hughes. In January 2012, Hitchcock joined Queens Park Rangers, again, appointed by Hughes. In December 2016, Hitchcock joined Birmingham City, appointed by former Chelsea player, Gianfranco Zola. In April 2019, Hitchcock then moved to the USA, becoming the goalkeeping coach of MLS club, New England Revolution, appointed by head coach, Bruce Arena, on the recommendation of Avran Grant.

Ben Foster signed for Stoke City in April 2001 but did not play a first team game. Foster was loaned-out to Tiverton Town, Stafford Rangers, Kidderminster Harriers and Wrexham. It was whilst playing for Wrexham that he was spotted by Alex Ferguson who, on 15 July 2005, signed Foster for Manchester United for a fee of £1million. Foster went on to win two League Cup winners medals with Manchester United.

On 8 February 2006, prior to Everton's Premier League match against Chelsea at Stamford Bridge, Everton goalkeeper, Richard Wright, injured himself during the warm-up when he collided with a sign bearing the message, 'Goalkeepers must use temporary goals for their warm-ups.'

Boxing Day 1970, Gordon Banks punches clear from Liverpool's, Chris Lawler, during the goalless festive encounter between Liverpool and Stoke City at Anfield. Also featured, Stoke City's Eric Skeels and Alan Bloor. An ever present in England's 1966 World Cup winning team, Banks is considered a pioneer of modern goalkeeping, turning the art of goalkeeping into a science. Banks was FWA Footballer of the Year in 1972, named FIFA Goalkeeper of the Year on six occasions and voted goalkeeper in the PFA Team of the Century (1907-2007).

Former Manchester United goalkeeper, Fabien Barthez, represented France in three World Cups and three European Championships. Following his retirement as a player, in 2007, Barthez became a racing driver competing in a number of motor sport series such as the French GT Championship and Sigma Cup, as well as the Le Mans 24 Hours. Of superstitious character, Barthez always insisted his goalkeeper jerseys bore the number 16 as opposed to the traditional number one.

In January 2007, in order to gain first team experience, Wayne Hennessey joined Stockport County on loan from Wolverhampton Wanderers. Hennessey kept nine clean sheets in his first nine matches for Stockport, the longest period without conceding a goal in English senior football. Hennessey finally conceded on 10 March 2007 when he was beaten by a second-half effort from Barnet's Oliver Allen, so, one could say Hennessey did not concede for nine-and-a-half matches.

For all there is a 45-year age gap, Wayne Hennessey is a cousin of Terry Hennessey (Birmingham City, Nottingham Forest, Derby County and Wales).

Matt added gloss. On 24 February 2007, Huddersfield Town 'keeper, Matt Glennon, saved three penalties against Crewe Alexandra during their League One encounter at the Galpharm Stadium. Glennon's first save was at the expense of Ryan Lowe. Glennon then saved a penalty from Gary Roberts, when the spot-kick was ordered to be retaken due to encroachment, the retake was hit by Julien Baudet only for Glennon to save again. Glennon finished the game playing upfront as Huddersfield desperately tried to salvage something from the game via a last-minute corner. Crewe won 2-1, both their goals were Huddersfield own goals, from David Mirfin and Frank Sinclair.

Goalkeeper wins his side a penalty. On 19 November 2011, Blackburn Rovers were trailing Wigan Athletic 2-3 when Rovers' goalkeeper Paul Robinson went up-field in the dying seconds for a Blackburn corner. In attempting to connect with the ball, Robinson was fouled by Wigan's David Jones. Referee Andre Marriner awarded Rovers a penalty, subsequently converted by Yakubu Ayebeni to make the score 3-3.

John Burridge was 43 years and four months old when he played for Manchester City against Newcastle United on 29 April 1995. The oldest player to have played in the Premier League and the oldest Premier League debutant. 'Budgie' played for thirty different clubs, some more than once. Burridge began his career at Workington in 1966, making his debut in 1969. His final club was Blyth Spartans in 1997. On 14 May 1983, as the result of a £100 bet with Newcastle manager Kevin Keegan, Burridge announced he would keep goal for Wolves against Newcastle United dressed as superman. Wolves biggest crowd of the season (22,446) duly witnessed the sight.

A page from Wolverhampton Wanderers' programme showing goalkeeper, John Burridge, in the previous home match in which, for the start, Burridge wore a superman outfit. The game against Newcastle United ended 2-2.

Named substitute over 600 times. Steve Harper spent twenty years at Newcastle United and is the longest serving player in the club's history. Harper made 157 league appearances and spent much of his time as substitute goalkeeper. Given Harper had six loan spells, the most prolific at Huddersfield Town in 1997-98 (24 league appearances) it is estimated Harper's appearances on the substitute bench for Newcastle totalled 613.

Rogerio Ceni made 1,257 senior appearances for Sao Paulo (1993-2015) and 17 for Brazil, being part of the Brazil squad which won the 2002 World Cup and competed in the 2006 World Cup. During his time with Sao Paulo, with whom he won 20 major titles, Ceni scored 131 goals, most from direct free-kicks and penalties with one coming from open play.

In 2015-16, when Leicester City won the Premier League, goalkeeper Kasper Schmeichel and father, Peter (Manchester United) became the first father and son goalkeepers to play in teams that were English champions.

On 2 February 2016, goalkeeper Paddy Roche scored his first ever goal, in what was his 492nd game, when playing for Morecambe in their 1-1 draw with Portsmouth. Roche's goal, a header, came in the 94th minute when he had gone up-field to help his forwards.

Bruges and former Sunderland and Liverpool goalkeeper, Simon Mignolet, is fluent in four languages (French, Dutch, English and German) and has a degree in Political Science.

Andy Lonergan made 231 appearances for Preston North End (2000-2011) and subsequently played for Leeds United (two spells), Bolton Wanderers, Fulham and Wolverhampton Wanderers. In 2018, following his second spell with Leeds United, Lonergan signed for Middlesbrough. Lonergan never made a first team appearance for Middlesbrough, nor for any of his four subsequent clubs, Liverpool, Stoke City, West Bromwich Albion and Everton, becoming something of a highly regarded 'back-up' goalkeeper.

To rival Jimmy Glass, Mart Poom and Allisson. Torquay United goalkeeper, Lucas Covolan equalised for Torquay United with a header five minutes into added time against Hartlepool United in the National League Play-off Final on 20 June 2021. The Final went to penalties, Covan saved two, only for Hartlepool to triumph 5-4 on penalties. (after 1-1 in normal time).

Goals

Boxing Day is the date which has produced more high scores than any other date in the football calendar. There have been five instances of games played on December 26th in which teams have scored ten goals or more, and seven instances of teams scoring nine goals. Notable Boxing Day results include Darwen 12 Walsall 0 (1896), Hull City 10 Halifax Town 0 (1930), Tranmere Rovers 13 Oldham Athletic 4 (1935), Oldham Athletic 11 Southport 0 (1962), Fulham 10 Ipswich Town 1, West Ham United 2 Blackburn Rovers 8, Manchester City 8 Scunthorpe United 1 (all 1963). The Boxing Day fixtures in Division One in 1963 produced 66 goals in ten games, a record for a single day in English top-flight football eclipsing the 52 goals scored in the First Division on the opening day of 1926-27.

The second most 'popular' date for producing high score-lines is a club's first away game of the season. Stoke City, Burnley, Rotherham United and Northampton Town have all, at one time, conceded ten goals in their first away match of a new season. Torquay United have shipped ten goals in their second away game of a season on two occasions.

Birmingham City have had the most double figure victories in League football - five. 17 December 1892, 12-0 v Walsall; 17 March 1898, 10-2 v Manchester City; 2 March 1901, 10-1 v Blackpool; 11 April 1903, 12-0 v Doncaster Rovers; 6 January 1915, 11-1 v Glossop - all in the Second Division.

Derby's January yin and yang. Within a week in January 1891, Derby County suffered their record league defeat and achieved their record league victory, both of which stand as at 2022. On 3 January 1891, Derby County lost 8-0 at Blackburn Rovers, seven days later, Derby won 9-0 at home to Wolverhampton Wanderers. Derby County's record defeat in all competitions occurred the previous season, also in January, when Everton defeated Derby 11-2 in a first round FA Cup tie on 18 January 1890.

In 1927-28, George Camsell of Middlesbrough scored nine hat-tricks, a feat no other player has since equalled in a single season. Camsell scored at least 30 goals in each of his first five seasons at Middlesbrough, a feat he repeated in his tenth season at the club. Between 1925 and 1939, Camsell scored 345 goals in 453 games for Middlesbrough. He also scored 18 goals in nine appearances for England, the highest goals-to-games ratio of any England player.

Between 1925 and 1929, David Halliday scored 156 goals in 166 league matches for Sunderland. Halliday is the only player to score at least 30 goals per season in four consecutive seasons in English top flight football and reached 100 league goals in only 101 matches. Halliday also scored 47 league goals in 76 appearances for Manchester City and 90 league goals for Dundee in 125 appearances. He is the most recent of only two players to be top goal-scorer in both English and Scottish football's top divisions - 38 for Dundee (1923-24) and 43 for Sunderland (1928-29). Despite his prolific goalscoring, Halliday was never capped by his home country, Scotland. Halliday is one of only two players to score in excess of 200 goals in English top flight football and never win an International cap, the other being Arthur Chandler (Leicester City). As former Sunderland and Arsenal player turned football journalist, Charles Buchan, is reported as saying, 'For reasons best known to themselves, the stuffed-shirted Scottish selectors never liked Davie Halliday. He was a grand lad and if there was a better Scottish goalscorer around in his time, I didn't see him, nor, I suspect, did anyone else.'

The most goals scored in English top-flight football is 128, by Aston Villa 1930-31.

In 1930-31, eight teams, spanning all four divisions of the Football League, scored in excess of 100 league goals. Arsenal, Aston Villa and Sheffield Wednesday (First Division); Everton (Second Division); Chesterfield, Lincoln City and Tranmere Rovers (Third Division North); and Crystal Palace (Third Division South).

Between 24 October 1931 and 1 January 1932, Sheffield United's, Jimmy Dunne, scored 18 goals in 12 First Division league matches.

On 24 September 1932, Stewart Littlewood scored six for Port Vale against his former club Chesterfield. Port Vale won 9-1 and, in their following match, lost 7-0 to Bradford City.

In 1933-34, Albert Dawes won an award for being leading goalscorer in Division Three South with 27 goals yet he was not the leading scorer at the club he played for. Dawes netted 11 for Northampton Town who, during the season, transferred him to Crystal Palace, for whom he scored 16.

The most goals scored on a single day of Football League fixtures is 209 in the 44 League games played on1 February 1936. The day also saw nine hat-tricks scored. The only match to end goalless was the Third Division South game between Aldershot and Bristol City.

In February 1936, Chester scored 20 goals in two successive home matches. On 1 February, Chester beat York City 12-0; in their following home game on 15 February, they defeated New Brighton 8-2. Sandwiched in between was a 4-2 victory away to Barrow. Following their 8-2 demolition of New Brighton, Chester then won two consecutive away games, at Rotherham United 2-1 and Oldham Athletic 3-1. Unbelievably, following such a run of form and free-scoring, Chester's attendance for their next home match against Carlisle United on 29 February (won 3-2) was lower than that for their game against York City.

Jimmy Lindsay (Bury 1905-06), Jim Evans (Southend United 1921-22) and Will Imrie (Newcastle United 1937-38) were all defenders who ended the season as their club's leading goalscorer.

During 1937-38, Brechin City suffered three double-figure defeats; 10-0 at Cowdenbeath (5 November 1937); 10-0 at Albion Rovers (15 January 1938) and 10-0 at Airdrieonians (12 February 1938). That same season, Brechin also lost 8-2 at home to Raith Rovers (28 August 1937); 7-2 at home and 6-1 away to Edinburgh City; 7-0 at Dumbarton (4 December 1937); 5-0 at Stenhousemuir (29 January 1938) and 6-5 at home to Alloa Athletic (19 March 1938). In all, Brechin City conceded 139 goals in 34 league matches, an average of 4.08 conceded per game. The following season (1938-39) Brechin City finished comfortably in mid-table in the Scottish Second Division but still conceded 106 goals.

Six players all reached double figures in league goals for Stockport County in Third Division North in 1938-39, Alf Lythgoe, Charlie Sergeant, Duggie Reid, John Essex, George Sherwood and Tom Bagley.

The Derby County side of 1945-46 included Sam Crooks, Raich Carter, Dave McCulloch, Peter Doherty and Dally Duncan, all of whom had scored in excess of 100 career goals.

In May 1946, Davey Walsh signed for West Bromwich Albion from Walsall for a fee of £3,500 and scored in each of his first six matches for West Brom'.

Frayed net? Duggie Reid signed for Portsmouth from Stockport County in 1946. Pompey fans nicknamed Reid, 'Thunderboots', following a penalty kick taken at Fratton Park against Manchester City when the ball ripped through the centre of the net and parted the crowd standing behind the goal.

What's the time? Twenty to two. In 1946-47, Newport County conceded a total of 20 goals in two successive matches in the Second Division. County lost 7-2 at home to West Bromwich Albion and, in their next game, were beaten 13-0 at Newcastle United. In the return fixture at Somerton Park, Newport beat Newcastle United 4-2.

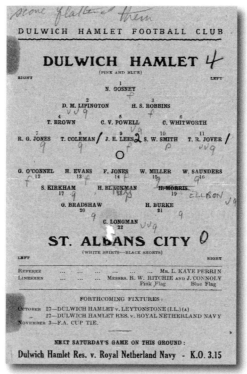

The programme for the match between Dulwich Hamlet and St Albans City during which Tommy Jover headed in his own cross.

By Jover, headed goal from his own cross. On 20 October 1945, Tommy Jover, scored a goal, thought to be unique in football, when he headed a goal from his own cross when playing for Dulwich Hamlet against St Albans City in the Isthmian League. Jover, also a Great Britain sprinter, chasing a bouncing pass down the left wing, managed to hook and sky the ball just into the St.Albans City penalty area. Chasing the ball as it descended, Jover won an aerial challenge against a defender, heading the ball further into the St Albans penalty box. The ball looped over defenders and attackers before nesting in the far corner of the net. Jover, who played one game for Luton Town (1941-42) whilst stationed at nearby RSF Henlow, was associated with Dulwich Hamlet all his adult life. He died in 2008 at the age of 91. The main stand at Dulwich Hamlet's Champion Hill ground is named in his honour.

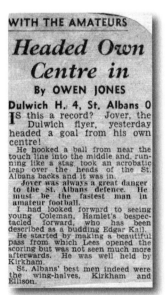

Press match report of the goal thought to be unique in football, scored by Tommy Jover, 'the Dulwich Flyer' who served Dulwich Hamlet in a variety of roles for seventy-six years.

Left it late. With less than a minute left, the Division Three South match between Norwich City and Brighton on 27 December 1950, looked to be heading for a goalless draw. Both teams however, scored within the last thirty seconds of the game. Ken Bennett looked to have won the game for Brighton when he scored with only thirty seconds remaining, only for Johnny Gavin to equalise for Norwich with the last kick of the game.

In 1951-52, Jack Lewis, playing as a half-back/defender, scored 15 League goals for Reading in Division Three South, in addition to which Lewis also scored six in cup and friendly matches, a total of 21 for the season.

Leicester City scored 89 League goals in 1952-53, of which 85 were scored by their forwards, of the remaining four goals, two were own goals.

The only player to have scored more goals than he made appearances in a career in excess of fifty matches, is Derek Dooley. Playing for Sheffield Wednesday 1947 to 1953, Dooley scored 62 goals in 61 League matches. His career was cut short when a leg infected with gangrene had to be amputated following a serious fracture sustained whilst playing against Preston North End.

In seasons 1952-53 and 1953-54, five Sheffield Wednesday players scored own goals, all when playing against West Bromwich Albion. Vince Kenny, Norman Curtis and Eddie Gannon in a 5-4 home defeat to Albion on 26 December 1952; Tom McAnearney in a 3-2 defeat at Hillsborough on 26 September 1953; and, Barry Butler in a 4-2 defeat at The Hawthorns on 13 February 1954.

There have only been two instances when the champions of every division in English and Scottish football scored more than 100 goals, 1927-28 and 1931-32. In 1960-61, the champions of each division in England scored in excess of 100 but the feat was not equalled in either Scottish division. 1960-61 First Division - Tottenham Hotspur, 115 (Wolves scored 103 and Burnley 102); Second Division - Ipswich Town, 100; Third Division - Bury 108; Fourth Division - Peterborough United 134 (runners-up Crystal Palace scored 110).

The youngest player to score more than four goals in a top-flight game in England is Jimmy Greaves, who was 18 years old when he scored five against Wolverhampton Wanderers on 30 August 1958.

During the period 24th October to 26th December 1959, Hibernian scored 71 goals in thirteen matches. The sequence began with Hibs beating Airdrie 11-1. On the same day, Hibs reserves beat Airdrie reserves 8-0.

The fabulous Baker boys. On 30 January 1960, Gerry Baker scored ten goals in St. Mirren's 15-0 victory over Glasgow University in the first round of the Scottish Cup. The following season, on 11 February 1961, Gerry's brother, Joe, scored nine in Hibernian's 15-1 victory over Peeble Rovers in the second round of the Scottish Cup.

Since World War Two, only two clubs have twice been involved in matches in which both sides scored at least five goals. On 16 October 1954, Chelsea lost 6-5 at home to Manchester United and on 10 September 1958, also at home, beat Newcastle United 6-5. On 21 December 1957, Charlton Athletic beat Huddersfield Town 7-6 and, on 22 October 1960, drew 6-6 with Middlesbrough.

Matters came to a head. On 5 November 1960, Chelsea defeated Newcastle United 4-2 at Stamford Bridge, all six goals coming from headers - Ron Tindall (3) and Peter Brabrook for Chelsea; Len White (2) for Newcastle United.

Posh accent on goals. Peterborough United's tally of 134 goals in Division Four in 1960-61, is the most ever scored in a single league season in English football.

The opium of the Peeble. East of Scotland League club, Peeble Rovers, qualified for the Scottish FA Cup First Round proper in each of the seasons 1955-56 to 1960-61. In 1955-56, Peeble were defeated 6-2 by Brechin City in a fourth round replay; in 1956-57, Peeble lost 6-0 to Albion Rovers in a second round replay; in 1957-58, they were defeated 4-0 by Raith Rovers in the first round; in 1958-59, Peeble lost 10-0 at St Mirren in round two; in 1959-60, there was a 6-1 home defeat to Ayr United in round two; in 1960-61, in round two, Peeble lost 15-1 at Hibernian. In 1961-62, Peeble Rovers failed to qualify for the first round proper.

On 21 January 1961, Sheffield Wednesday took the lead against Fulham at Craven Cottage without a Wednesday player having touched the ball. From the Fulham kick-off, the ball was played back to Alan Mullery who, in turn, played it back to goalkeeper Tony Macedo, only for the Fulham 'keeper to misjudge the bounce, the ball travelling under Macedo's boot and into the net. Sheffield Wednesday won 6-1.

Three players of promoted clubs who ended as leading goalscorer in the Second Division became the top-flight's leading goalscorer the following season; Jimmy Trotter (Sheffield Wednesday) 1925-26 and 26-27; Dixie Dean (Everton) 1930-31 and 31-32 and Ray Crawford (Ipswich Town) 1960-61 and 1961-62.

The last team to score double figures in top-flight English football were Fulham who, on Boxing Day 1963, defeated Ipswich Town 10-1. Two days later, Ipswich won the return fixture 4-2.

Weller never! Referee scored. On 12 September 1964, during Newport County's Division Four match against Southport, Newport's Jimmy Singer hit a hard, low cross into the Southport penalty area. The ball hit referee A.R.C. Weller and ricocheted past Southport 'keeper Bert Harris. The referee ordered the goal to stand, Newport won 5-0.

In 1964-65, Chester scored 141 goals in league (119) and cup (22) matches. Five Chester players scored in excess of twenty goals - Mike Metcalf (38), Gary Talbot (37), Elfed Morris (28), Jimmy Hulmes (22) and Hugh Ryden (22).

In October 1965, Neil Martin was transferred from Hibernian to Sunderland. Martin finished the 1965-66 season as leading goalscorer for both clubs, Hibs (12) and Sunderland (8).

Shared them out. In 1966-67, Celtic scored 111 league goals. Celtic's leading goalscorer was Stevie Chalmers, with a relatively modest 21 goals.

On 18 September 1968, Luton Town's Graham French scored a solo goal at Kenilworth Road following a mazy run through the Mansfield Town defence. From receiving the ball to shooting into goal, French was timed as having the ball at his feet for a total of 18 seconds.

In 1971-72, Francis Lee scored 15 penalties for Manchester City, eight of which were awarded for fouls on himself.

On 2 February 1974, only 18 goals were scored in eleven First Division matches which included Ipswich Town's 7-0 victory over Southampton. Other than Ipswich, no team scored more than a single goal. Of the other ten matches, three were goalless, three were single-goal victories and four ended 1-1.

Derek McKay was a winger who seemed to reserve his best performances for the Scottish FA Cup. McKay was transferred from Dundee to Aberdeen in 1969. In the 1969-70 Scottish Cup he scored the winning goal in Aberdeen's 1-0 quarter-final victory at Falkirk; the winning goal in Aberdeen's 1-0 semi-final victory over Kilmarnock, and, two in the 3-1 victory over Celtic in the Final, in which he was awarded 'Man of the Match'. After which, Mackay disappeared from football.

Derek McKay's exploits and goals in the
Scottish FA Cup earned him the nickname 'Cup-tie Mackay'.

On 17 September 1974, nine different players scored in Liverpool's 11-0 victory over Stromsgodset (Norway) in the first round first leg of the European Cup Winners cup. Liverpool's scorers were Phil Boersma (two), Phil Thompson (two), Alec Lindsay, Steve Heighway, Peter Cormack, Emlyn Hughes, Ian Callaghan, Ray Kennedy and Tommy Smith. The only Liverpool players not to score were goalkeeper Ray Clemence and Brian Hall. Not previously, nor since, has a team registered nine different goalscorers in a senior game in British football.

The only 'Match of the Day' without any goals. In the days when BBC TV's 'Match of the Day' was only allowed to broadcast the highlights of two matches, the programme on 22 April 1978 didn't feature a single goal. MOTD showed highlights of the First Division games between Coventry City and Nottingham Forest, and, Middlesbrough against Everton, both ended 0-0.

Like a bull in a china shop. The last player to score greater than 100 goals across two consecutive seasons was Steve Bull (Wolverhampton Wanderers). In 1987-88, in all competitions, Bull scored 52 goals and, in 1988-89, 50 goals.

On 12 September 1989, eight different players scored for Liverpool in their 9-0 defeat of Crystal Palace in Division One, the highest number of players to score for a team in a single game in the history of English league football.

Liverpool's goalscorers were Steve Nichol (two), Ian Rush, Peter Beardsley, John Barnes, John Aldridge, Steve McMahon, Glen Hysen and Gary Gillespie.

In 1991, Barnet were promoted from the Conference League to the Football League. In 1991-92, Barnet scored nine goals in their first two matches as a League club but did not win either game. On 17 August, Barnet lost their opening league game 4-7 at home to Crewe Alexandra. On 20 August, in their second match, Barnet drew 5-5 with Brentford in the first round of the League Cup. A few weeks later, on 4 September, Barnet achieved what still stands as their highest away win as a league club, winning 6-0 at Lincoln City.

The only player born in the 1950s to score a Premier League hat-trick is Gordon Strachan. Born 9 February 1957, Strachan scored a hat-trick in Leeds United's 5-2 win over Blackburn Rovers in the Premier League on 10 April 1993.

In 1993-94, Arsenal scored 53 goals in 42 league matches and 'boasted' just six different goalscorers - Ian Wright, Kevin Campbell, Paul Merson, Alan Smith, Ray Parlour and Steve Bould.

On 2 April 2000, Celtic had four goals disallowed within 17 minutes of their Scottish Premier League match against Kilmarnock, including what would have been a hat-trick for Tommy Johnson. Celtic won 4-2 with Johnson scoring a legitimate goal.

On 2 January 2001, Glyn Hurst scored five goals in Ayr United's 6-0 victory against Morton in Scottish Division One and never scored for Ayr again. Later in the season, Hurst joined Stockport County for a fee of £175,000.

Kevin Phillips is the only Englishman to win the European Golden Boot, the award for the leading goalscorer in league matches from the top division of every European national league. Phillips won the award in 1999-2000, having scored 30 Premier League goals for Sunderland. One Scot and two Welshmen have also won the Golden Boot. Ally McCoist (Scotland) won the Golden Boot twice when he played for Rangers, in 1991-92 and again in 1992-93, on both occasions scoring 34 league goals. Ian Rush (Wales) won the award in 1983-84, scoring 32 league goals for Liverpool. The other Welshman to win the Golden Boot is, David Taylor, who, in

1993-94, scored 43 goals for Porthmadog in the League of Wales. Taylor is the only non senior league player to win the award and did so as a part-time professional.

Wycombe Wanderers scored twice without the opposition having touched the ball. This unusual feat occurred during Wycombe's Division Two match at Adams Park against Peterborough United on 23 September 2000. When Jamie Bates opened the scoring for Wycombe, referee John Brandwood immediately blew his whistle for half-time, signalling there was no time for Peterborough to restart. Wycombe kicked-off the second half and immediately went on an attack which culminated in Jermaine McSporran scoring a second for Wycombe. The goals were nine seconds apart and occurred without a Peterborough player having touched the ball.

Arsenal scored in 55 consecutive matches in the Premier League 19 May 2001 to 30 November 2002.

They all count. On 1 May 2002, during the Second Division Play-Off semi-final second leg between Cardiff City and Stoke City, Stoke introduced substitute Souleymane Oulare for Chris Iwelumo after 71 minutes. The game went into extra time during which a free-kick by Stoke's James O'Connor hit Oulare on the backside, the ball ricocheting past Cardiff 'keeper Neil Alexander. The goal enabled Stoke to win 3-2 on aggregate and eventually win promotion.

Plymouth Argyle scored five goals in the opening 17 minutes of their Division Two match against Chesterfield on 3 January 2004. Argyle's goals came from Lee Hodges (4), Tony Capaldi (11), Nathan Lowndes (12), David Frid (16) and Nathan Lowndes (17). Plymouth won 7-0. That season Plymouth kept 21 clean sheets.

In 2007-08, Reading were involved in the first Premier League game to produce ten goals when losing 6-4 at Tottenham; Reading were also involved in the first Premier League game to produce 11 goals when losing 7-4 at Portsmouth.

Ryan McCann had two spells at Queen of the South (2007-08 and 2009-10) during which time he only scored one goal - but what a goal. On 8th March 2008, when playing for Queen of the South in the quarter-finals of the Scottish Cup against Dundee, Queens led 1-0 with the game into added time when Dundee goalkeeper, Craig Samson, came up-field for a corner-kick. Following the corner, the ball fell to McCann who drove the ball from 74 yards into the empty Dundee net. When the Palmerston Park pitch was relaid in 2013, the turf from which McCann had taken his shot was auctioned, along with the four corner plots and two penalty spots.

Nominative determinism. On 2 February 2013, Hartlepool United beat Notts County 2-1 in League One. The Hartlepool goalscorers were Peter Hartley and James Poole.

He did a Stirling job. Andy Stirling scored for two clubs that bear his name. Across seasons 2011-12 and 2012-13, Stirling scored 9 goals for East Stirling in the Scottish Third Division; in 2014-15 (whilst on loan from Dunfermline Athletic), Stirling scored twice for Stirling Albion in Scottish League One.

Of the 22 players who started the Hibernian v Hearts Scottish Premier League match of 12 April 2015, 21 had scored a league goal for their club that season, the exception being Hearts goalkeeper, Neil Alexander. Each of the four substitutes named by Hibernian and Hearts had also scored for their club, hence 25 of the 26 players named on the team-sheet had all scored for their respective club that season.

In 2015-16, Formartine United of the Highland League scored 137 goals in their 34 league matches, an average of 4.02 goals per game. Formartine conceded 35 goals which gave them a goal difference of +102. Formartine finished as runners-up to Cove Rangers. Rothes finished bottom of the league having conceded 165 goals with a goal difference of - 149.

In 2015-16, West Ham United recorded a positive goal difference of plus 14, the first time West Ham had recorded a positive goal difference in the top-flight since 1985-86.

On 15 October 2016, Sheffield United had four goals disallowed for offside in their League One match against Port Vale. United also scored four legitimate goals without reply.

Frank Lampard (Chelsea and Manchester City) is the only midfield player to have scored more than 150 goals in the Premier League.

The highest number of goals scored in a Premier League season is 106, Manchester City in 2017-18. The following season, City scored 169 goals in all competitions.

Keith scores for Keith. On 23 March 2019, Cammy Keith scored five goals for Highland League club Keith in their 11-0 victory over Fort William.

Three clubs have scored nine in a Premier League match. Manchester United v Ipswich Town on 4 March 1995; Spurs v Wigan Athletic on 22 November 2009 and Leicester City at Southampton on 25 October 2019.

Josh Maja was transferred from Sunderland to Bordeaux in January 2019 but still finished the season as Sunderland's leading goalscorer with 15 goals.

In 2019-20, Wycombe Wanderers' leading goalscorer in all competitions was defender Joe Jacobson with 12 goals.

When Leon Clarke scored for Shrewsbury Town against Walsall on 17 October 2020, it was the 18th different League club Clarke had scored for. No other player had scored for so many different League clubs. Having joined Bristol Rovers in August 2021, Clarke made it 19 different league clubs, scoring on his Rovers' debut in a 1-0 victory over Crawley Town.

Not often you see this. On 23 January 2021, during Swansea City's Fourth Round FA Cup tie against Nottingham Forest, Swansea's Matt Grimes' 25-yard drive whizzed past Forest 'keeper, Jordan Smith, and, Forest striker, Lyle Taylor, who was lying injured in the back of Smith's net as play continued unabated.

Sharing them out. On 10 April 2021, Oxford United won 6-0 at Crewe Alexandra, and three days later, in their following game, on 13 April, Oxford beat Shrewsbury Town 4-1. The ten goals Oxford scored were scored by ten different players. Against Crewe - Josh Ruffels, James Henry, Elliott Moore, Brandon Barker, Cameron Brannagan and Sam Winnall; against Shrewsbury - Rob Atkinson, Elliot Lee, Matt Taylor and Sam Long.

Fulham scored just nine goals at home in 2020-21, a paltry record equalled by Manchester City (2006-07) and Huddersfield Town (2018-19).

Cheap at half the price, oh, wait a minute….Paul Mullin was given a free transfer by Tranmere Rovers in May 2020 and signed for Cambridge United on 20 July. Mullin scored 32 league goals for Cambridge in 2020-21, creating a new club record for goals scored in a single season. Mullin's goals helped Cambridge United achieve promotion from League Two and won him the League Two 'Golden Boot'. He was also Cambridge United and League Two 'Player of the Season'. In the 2021 close season, Mullin refused to sign a new contract at Cambridge and dropped into non-league football, joining National League club, Wrexham.

Shaun Rooney scored the only goal of the 2020-21 Scottish League Cup Final enabling St. Johnstone to defeat Livingston. Later in the season, Rooney also scored the only goal of the Scottish Cup Final in which St. Johnstone defeated Hibernian. Coincidentally, both of Rooney's goals were timed at 32 minutes, 20 seconds.

124 penalties were awarded in the Premier League during 2020-21 - a record. Of those awarded, 102 were converted. Leicester City were awarded the most penalties (12) followed by Manchester United (11). In 1992-93, the inaugural season of the Premier League, 61 penalties were awarded, of which 57 were converted. Simply put, twice as many penalties in the Premier League in 2020-21 as in the past.

Only two players are thought to have scored in every one of the ninety minutes of a football game, Lionel Messi and Cristiano Ronaldo.

No one profligate, no one prolific. On 30 October 2021, Chelsea defeated Newcastle United 3-0 at St. James' Park. The 3-0 victory brought the total number of Premier League goals scored by Chelsea to 26, with Chelsea's leading goalscorer being right/wing back, Reece James, with four goals.

On 1 December 2021, Liverpool defeated Everton 4-1 at Goodison Park. Liverpool's four goal tally meant they had scored two or more goals in 18 successive matches in all competitions, the first team to accomplish such a feat in English senior football.

John Egan began his career with Sunderland in 2011. As at 1 January 2022, Egan, of Sheffield United, had scored 22 goals in ten years and was the only player at the time to have scored in all four leagues - Leagues One and Two, Championship and Premier League. Egan scored for Southend United against Scunthorpe United in League Two (11 March 2014); in League One for Gillingham v Port Vale (29 November 2014); for Brentford in the Championship v Ipswich Town (13 August 2016) and for Sheffield United in the Premier League against Burnley (5 July 2020).

Secured Brannagan rights on penalties. On 29 January 2022, Oxford United's, Cameron Brannagan, became the first player in the history of

English League football to score four penalties in a single game. Brannagan bagged his four penalties in Oxford United's 7-2 victory at Gillingham in League One. Ironically, the previous player to have scored a hat-trick of penalties in a league game was Gillingham's, Josh Wright, who did so on 11 March 2017 in Gillingham's 3-2 victory over Scunthorpe United.

Craving goals at Craven Cottage. On 18 January 2022, having beaten Birmingham City 6-2 at Craven Cottage, Fulham became the first team since Chester in 1933-34 to score six or more goals in three successive matches. In their two previous league matches, Fulham had beaten Bristol City 6-2 (also at Craven Cottage) and won 7-0 at Reading. Everton scored six or more in three successive league matches in Division Two in 1953-54, however, sandwiched between a 6-2 win at Derby County and a 6-1 victory over Brentford at Goodison Park, Everton suffered a 3-1 defeat at Sheffield Wednesday in the FA Cup.

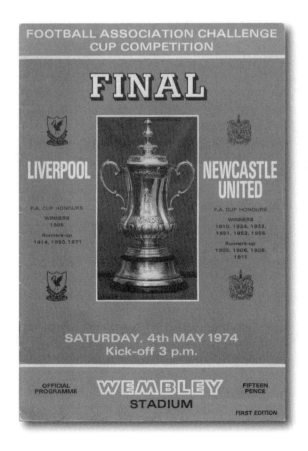

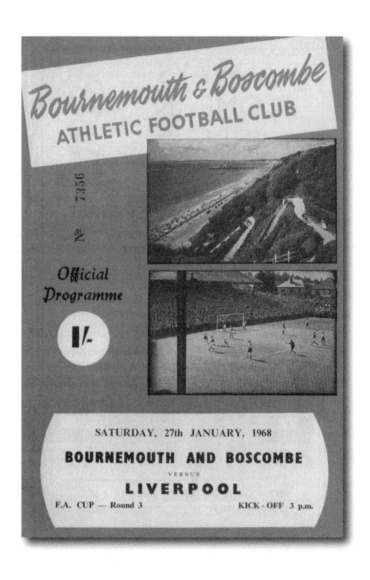

Bournemouth & Boscombe
ATHLETIC FOOTBALL CLUB

№ 7356

Official Programme

1/-

SATURDAY, 27th JANUARY, 1968

BOURNEMOUTH AND BOSCOMBE
VERSUS
LIVERPOOL

F.A. CUP — Round 3   KICK - OFF 3 p.m.

Grounds

The oldest ground in English senior football is Sheffield United's Bramall Lane, built in 1855, albeit to accommodate cricket. The first football match staged at Bramall Lane was between Sheffield FC and Hallam on 29 December 1862.

The oldest ground in Scottish senior football is Dundee United's Tannadice Park, built in 1870.

The first permanent grandstand with footings was built by Scottish club Queen's Park at the original Hampden Park in 1876 at a cost of £237.

Sheffield United's, Bramall Lane, is one of only two grounds (the other being the Oval) to have hosted an England international (five games prior to 1930); Test cricket (England v Australia, 1902) and an FA Cup Final, the 1912 Final replay, Barnsley 1 West Bromwich Albion 0.

Portsmouth were founded in April 1898, and some weeks later the shareholders purchased a piece of land which would later to become Fratton Park. Following the purchase, the club's shareholders were informed they must have the approval of the FA for the land as a football ground. Club representative, George Lewin Oliver, accompanied FA inspector, William Pickford, to the land which, to Pickford's surprise, was still covered with a crop of potatoes. That notwithstanding, Portsmouth received permission to build their football ground. Official blessing followed Pickford's visit to the club's founder and major shareholder, John Brickwood, owner of Brickwood's brewery who was, it was said, 'renowned for the generous refreshment hospitality of his boardroom.'

There have been three Hampden Park grounds. The first, home of Queens Park, was demolished to make way for the Cathcart Circle railway. The second, became Cathkin Park, home of Third Lanark, when Queens Park moved into the current Hampden Park in 1903. Queens Park now play their home matches at Lesser Hampden, a 2,250 capacity ground immediately beside the West Stand of Hampden Park.

Arsonists at Arsenal. In 1913, Blackburn Rovers' Ewood Park, Deepdale (Preston North End) and Arsenal's new home, Highbury, were all the subject of arsonist attacks by supporters of the Suffragette movement.

Stand the test of time. In 1916, Hartlepool United's Victoria Park was bombed by a Zeppelin which destroyed the main stand. A small wooden stand was subsequently erected as a temporary measure until funds allowed a permanent structure to be built. The 'temporary' stand was not demolished until 1987.

Cheated out of it? During 1932-33, in addition to greyhound racing, Scottish Second Division club, King's Park, held cheetah racing, until they were prohibited to do so by the Scottish FA.

Like a scene from a Norman Wisdom film. During World War Two, the main stand at St. Andrews, home of Birmingham City, was used as a temporary fire station by the National Fire Service. The stand burnt down when a fireman accidentally set it alight, mistaking a bucket of petrol for water when attempting to put out a brazier. The stand was completely destroyed, along with all of Birmingham City's records, memorabilia and kit. It begs the question, why was petrol kept in a bucket?

Coventry City's Highfield Road was bombed by the Luftwaffe during a night raid in 1940. The following morning, three cast-iron turnstiles were discovered in Gosford Park approximately a third of a mile away.

Kilmarnock's Rugby Park was requisitioned by the armed forces during WW2, and by 1945 the ground was in a bad state of disrepair. The ground was restored for public use for matches by German and Italian POW's.

Colchester United's former home, Layer Road, was unique in that at the Layer Road end, the boundary wall was indented to accommodate the back of the goal which 'extended' into the terracing.

Aston Villa's Villa Park was once the venue which held the fastest scoring records in both football and rugby union. On 3 December 1938, Bob

Iverson scored after only nine seconds in Villa's 2-0 victory against Charlton Athletic - then the fastest recorded goal in the history of the Football League. On 17 September 1947, the touring Australia rugby union team scored a try after only seven seconds of their match against the Midland Counties XV at Villa Park, at the time, the fastest recorded try in first-class rugby union in England.

Greyhound racing was staged at Stamford Bridge from 1933 to 1968. The Greyhound racing Association records show the Totalisator revenue at Stamford Bridge for 1946 to be nearly £6million (£5,749,592), this at a time when the record transfer fee in English football was £14,500.

The oak panelling in Blackpool's boardroom came from Nelson's flagship HMS Foudroyant which, during a violent storm, foundered on Blackpool sands. The ship's bell now resides in Blackpool Town Hall.

In August 1949, West Bromwich Albion's ground, The Hawthorns, became the first ground in the UK to install electronic turnstile aggregators to automatically calculate attendance.

When Cheltenham Town, then in the Southern League, first installed floodlights at their Whaddon Road ground in the 1950s it caused major disturbance. When the floodlights were turned on, they caused a power surge, which resulted in all the houses in the immediate vicinity of the ground being blacked-out. The pylons were only 20' tall, when a ball was kicked high into the air, the players lost sight of it and had to anticipate where it would re-emerge from the murky sky.

Fish box grandstand. For their first round FA Cup tie against Crystal Palace on 21 November 1953, Great Yarmouth Town created a temporary stand built from wooden fish boxes. 'The Bloaters', as Great Yarmouth are known, won 1-0, like the home defence, the fish boxes held firm.

Grimsby Town's Blundell Park is the lowest ground in English football, just two feet above sea level. The main stand was constructed in 1899 and wooden seats installed in 1901, and as at 2022, those seats were still in situ.

The Gallowgate End at Newcastle United's St. James' Park took its' name from a public execution site once situated near to the ground. The last public execution took place in 1844.

Stockport County's Edgeley Park is the closest elite level football ground to the River Mersey, closer than Goodison Park, Anfield and Tranmere Rovers' Prenton Park.

On 14 January 1958, Edgeley Park hosted two England matches in a single day. As part of assessing players for the 1958 World Cup in Sweden, England drew 2-2 with Manchester City and, later in the day, the remaining players in the squad formed an England X1 who beat England Under 23s, 1-0.

In 1962, the original floodlights from Arsenal's Highbury, erected in 1951, were shipped to Dublin and became the floodlights at Dalymount Park. Two years later, Highbury installed undersoil heating. Part of the old Highbury remains. The exteriors of the listed Art Deco East and West Stands were incorporated into new apartment developments built on the site of Highbury.

Possibly one of the longest lasting examples of graffiti at a football ground was to be found on the street facing wall of the Clock Stand at Sunderland's former home, Roker Park. In 1962, the wall was daubed with, 'No Fluoride', in protest of a plan to add fluoride to local drinking water. The graffiti was still there when the Clock Stand was demolished in 1997.

The main stand at Southport's Haig Avenue had been purchased from the Southport Flower Show. The stand burned down on 27 December 1966, the day after Southport had beaten Wrexham in a Boxing Day fixture. All that survived was the club's safe containing the cash takings from the previous day's game. During the fire, an aerosol spray can used to treat injuries exploded, the can remnant was sent hurtling though the air crashing through the bedroom window of a nearby house rudely awakening the sleeping occupants.

Until the late 1960s, West Bromwich Albion's ground was in three different towns. The Hawthorns was situated where the boundaries of Birmingham, West Bromwich and Sandwell met. It is now solely in Sandwell and is the highest English ground, 551 feet (168 metres) above sea level.

Hull City's former home, Boothferry Park, was unique in that it had six floodlight pylons, erected in 1964. Boothferry Park also hosted show jumping, basketball, the first Ashes rugby league Test; in 1971, a Leeds United 'home' game and in February 1972, the Northern Ireland v Spain International match which could not be staged in Belfast due to the troubles.

Boothferry Park also had its' own railway station, Boothferry Halt, opened in 1951 and closed in 1986.

In the days when supporters were allowed to watch training, a young Kilmarnock fan makes friends with the sheep 'employed' to keep the grass down at Rugby Park.

Swansea City's Vetch Field had three floodlight pylons and one on the roof of the East Stand.

In the summer of 1980, Stamford Bridge staged the first major day-night cricket match when Essex faced the touring West Indies team.

The floodlight pylons at Leeds United's Elland Road were situated outside the ground. The pylons were 260' in height and the tallest floodlights in British football. The floodlights were dismantled in 1993.

The Poplar side at Newcastle United's St. James' Park was so called because of the row of poplar trees across the road which were visible above the terracing.

In the 1970s, Rochdale installed velour seats from a disused local cinema in their main stand at Spotland.

Darlington's former home, Feethams backed on to Darlington CC cricket ground, also used by Durham CCC. Feethams was unique as supporters gained entrance via turnstiles at the 'Twin Towers' entrance, then had to walk around the cricket ground to gain entry to the football ground. The back of the 'Tin Shed' stand at Feethams was painted light blue and acted as a sight screen for batsmen playing cricket. It was the largest sight screen in English cricket.

The original cottage at Fulham's Craven Cottage was built in 1780 by Baron Craven in what was hunting woods once owned by Anne Boleyn. In the 19th century it was the home of writer, Edward Bulwer-Lytton, author of 'The Last Days of Pompeii' and well known phrases such as 'the great unwashed', 'the pen is mightier than the sword', the opening line, 'It was a dark and stormy night', and, somewhat prophetically regarding football, 'The pursuit of the almighty dollar'. The cottage was destroyed by fire in 1888 but rebuilt in 1894 when Fulham took up residency. Craven Cottage is a listed building.

Bristol Rovers' former home, Eastville Stadium, was the only ground in English senior football to have flower beds behind each goal.

Cardiff City's former home (for 99 years) Ninian Park was constructed on a rubbish tip purchased from Cardiff Corporation. The ground was named Ninian Park after Lieutenant-Colonel Lord Ninian Crichton-Stuart, who had acted as financial guarantor for the build.

On 18 January 1937, thieves broke into Cardiff City's Ninian Park in the mistaken belief receipts from the club's FA Cup tie against Grimsby Town, which attracted an attendance of 36,236, were still in the club safe. The explosives the thieves used to try and crack the safe, blew off the office roof and the main stand caught fire. A bobby on the beat heard the noise at 3.45am and raised the alarm but the fire brigade was unable to save the main stand, dressing rooms and club offices. There were two fatal casualties, the club's dog and cat.

Swindon Town's County Ground was commissioned by the Ministry of War in 1940. During the war, the County Ground was used as a POW camp, the POW's being accommodated in huts which were arranged in rows on the pitch. Following the end of the war, Swindon Town were paid £4,570 by way of compensation by the government.

Crewe Alexandra acquired their first floodlights from Coventry City in 1958 and mounted the bulbs on the roofs of two stands and on telegraph poles. The poles survived until 1995 when Crewe acquired pylon floodlights.

Chesterfield were the last League club to have floodlights, erected at their old Saltergate ground in 1963-64.

Charlton Athletic's The Valley held the loudest rock concert ever staged in the UK. On 31 May 1976, The Who played the Valley, the volume recorded was 126dB, measured at a distance of 32 metres (105 feet) from the speakers. Ironically, in 1967, plans to create a Charlton Speedway team at the Valley fell through due to protests from nearby residents regarding 'noise nuisance'.

The first permanent all-seater stadium in senior British football was Aberdeen's Pittodrie, converted to seating in 1978. The first English league club to have an all-seater stadium was Coventry City, at their former home, Highfield Road, albeit standing accommodation was reinstated in 1983, only for Highfield Road to return to all-seating in 1994.

Derby County's first ever game at Pride Park against Wimbledon on 13 August 1997 was abandoned when the floodlights failed.

On 3 November 1997, West Ham United's game against Crystal Palace was abandoned with the score at 2-2 due to floodlight failure. Despite repeated attempts, maintenance staff only managed to generate a brief flicker before the lights died again. On 22 December 1997, the Premier League match between Crystal Palace and Arsenal was abandoned when the floodlights failed thirteen seconds into the second half with the score 0-0. Three days before relegation threatened Charlton Athletic were due to play Liverpool on 13 February 1999, four men were arrested after police and power engineers discovered a device which would have cut off the power to the Valley's floodlights at a given time. The men, three linked with a betting syndicate in Malaysia and the Charlton Athletic security supervisor, were found guilty of 'conspiracy to cause public nuisance' and jailed.

Kilmarnock's Rugby Park, Dumbarton's former home Boghead Park and Queen of the South's Palmerston Park were used in the 2002 film 'A Shot at Glory' starring Robert Duvall, Michael Keaton, Brian Cox, Daniel Day Lewis, Kirsty Mitchell, Cole Hauser, Ally McCoist, Owen Coyle and Didier Agathe.

Field Mill, home of Mansfield Town, hosted its' first football match in 1861, albeit for a game involving two local works teams. Mansfield Town were formed in 1897 as Mansfield Wesleyans, not becoming Mansfield Town until 1910 and did not take residence at Field Mill until 1919-20.

Leeds United's Elland Road has two wells, some 70-feet deep, below the

North and West stands, together with a pumping system under the South Stand. The wells were dug in order for the club to draw water should an emergency occur to regular water supplies.

Swansea Town's Vetch Field was opposite a prison, Bury's Gigg Lane and Dunfermline's East End Park next to cemeteries and Ards' Castlereagh Park opposite an airfield.

Strike a light. Darlington first installed floodlights at their Feethams ground in 1960. The floodlights were first used on 19 September 1960, for Darlington's 5-2 victory over Millwall. That night, an electrical fault caused a fire which resulted in the West Stand burning down.

Due to the 'Big Freeze' in the winter of 1962-63, following their 2-2 draw with Crystal Palace on 15 December 1962, Halifax Town did not play a home match at the Shay until 15 March 1963 (a 2-1 defeat to Colchester United). To generate income, on Saturdays, the club opened the Shay pitch as an ice rink for skaters.

Aston Villa's, Villa Park, is mentioned in 'MCMXIV', Philip Larkin's poem about the First World War.

Cardiff City's Ninian Park is mentioned in Dannie Abse's poem, 'The Game', the Welsh poet's tribute to Cardiff City which also contains a reference to the Canton Stand.

Imagine this happening today? During the summer of 1963, Stoke City laid concrete on the paddock terracing of their main stand, and the work was carried out by the Stoke City players.

Prior to Wembley staging FA Cup semi-finals, Aston Villa's Villa Park had staged 55, more than any other ground in the country.

Cornered the market. Between 1964 and 1977, Newport County's Somerton Park was also the home of the Newport Wasps speedway team. When the seasons overlapped, in order to accommodate speedway cornering, turf had to be removed from each corner flag area, only for the turf to be then replaced for the next football game.

Were there in a flash. The front entrance and main stand of Albion Rovers' Cliftonhill Stadium featured in a TV advert for 'Flash' in 2006.

Stadium MK, home of Milton Keynes Dons, was officially opened by Her Majesty the Queen on 29 November 2007.

Palmerston Park, home of Queen of the South, has the tallest free-standing floodlights in Scottish football, at 85 feet. Furthermore, the Portland Drive terrace (capacity 3,500) is the largest area of covered standing terracing in Scottish football. This terrace is noted for the clock face mounted in the centre of the stand roof which, for many years, sported an advertisement for a local public house with the strap-line, 'Time to Visit the Hole I' the Wa'. The Portland Drive Terrace also boasts the biggest height differential from lowest to highest step of any standing terrace in Scottish football.

Rotherham United left Millmoor in May 2008 after negotiations with the owner of the ground broke down. Millmoor, however, still exists, is kept in a good state of repair and has been used by local junior football teams since 2016. Millmoor, of course, hosted the first ever League Cup final - the first leg between Rotherham United and Aston Villa on 22 August 1961 - due to fixture congestion, held-over from the previous season.

In 2010, Carlisle United's Brunton Park was used for the BBC TV 'docu-drama' 'United' telling the story of Manchester United at the time of the 1958 Munich air disaster.

A sign situated behind the goal at the London Road end of Macclesfield Town's Moss Rose, not the most flattering testimony to the shooting prowess of Macclesfield forwards.

A sign on the way to Rothamstead Park, home of Harpenden Town of the Spartan South Midland League.

Leeds United's Elland Road 'doubled' as Wembley stadium in the 2010 film 'The King's Speech'.

Carlisle United's Brunton Park is the largest football ground in England which is not all-seated - certified capacity for 2021-22 was 18,202. The Brunton Park pitch is laid with local Solway turf, as used at Wimbledon (tennis that is).

Shouldn't stand for it. Port Vale began redevelopment work on their Lorne Street stand in 1998, the last seats were finally installed in 2020.

Gone west. Oxford United played their first match at the Kassam Stadium in August 2001, albeit financial problems negated the construction of a west stand. As of 2022, the west stand had still not been built.

Fair play to Coldplay. Bolton Wanderers' University of Bolton Stadium has blue light covers in the Lofthouse Upper Stand. The covers were installed, temporarily, for a Coldplay gig in 2005 and have never been removed.

As at January 2021, Oxford United, Mansfield Town, Falkirk, Partick Thistle, East Fife, and Hamilton Academical were among a number of clubs operating a three-sided ground.

Albion Rovers' Cliftonhill Stadium is two-sided, the main stand and the terracing behind the goal at the 'Airdrie End' the only parts of the ground open to spectators. The floodlights at Cliftonhill are those once installed at Cardiff Arms Park.

Dumbarton's Dumbarton Stadium, also known as C&G Systems Stadium for sponsorship reasons, is a one-sided ground. The one grandstand backs onto Dumbarton rock, a 240 feet (73m) high volcanic plug on which Dumbarton castle is situated. Dumbarton's ground overlooks the River Leven. Dumbarton's nickname, 'The Sons', derives from 'sons of the rock', a term used for people born in Dumbarton.

The seats in the West Stand at Barnsley's Oakwell ground are the originals from 1900.

Lee posts some sort of record. Luton Town's Kenilworth Road ground encompasses two postcodes, L1 and L4, the border of which runs parallel to the half-way line. On 18 November 2017, Ollie Lee scored a goal from his own half of the field during Luton's 7-0 victory over Cambridge United, hence Lee's shot occurred in one postal district and entered the net in another.

Not content with having the first club TV station, Middlesbrough were the first club to have a half-time scoreboard, erected at their old Ayresome Park ground in 1902.

The main stand at Grimsby Town's Blundell Park was erected in 1901. Though most of the stand has been modified over the years, the centre of the stand is as it was in 1901.

Just as Grimsby Town do not play in Grimsby but in Cleethorpes, Partick Thistle do not play in the Partick district of Glasgow. Partick Thistle's Firhill Stadium is situated in Maryhill, the club having moved from Partick in 1908.

Nottingham Forest and Crystal Palace are the only two English clubs to have derived their name from the ground at which they were formed - in the case of Nottingham Forest, the Forest Recreation ground in Nottingham.

Manchester City's Etihad Stadium was originally used for the 2002 Commonwealth Games.

A Rolex clock is situated at the rear of the Stratton Bank stand at Swindon Town's County Ground. Erected next to the scoreboard in 1963 following the club's promotion to the Second Division, it is the only Rolex clock to be found at any football ground in the world.

Doncaster Rovers' former home, Belle Vue, had the largest playing surface in the UK, 110 yards (100 metres) long and 72 yards (66 metres) wide. The turf was Cumberland turf also used for the pitch at the old Wembley stadium.

Fleetwood Town's Highbury has a stand behind a stand. The new Highbury Stand was built directly in front of the old West Stand, part of which was still in situ in 2021.

Fleetwood Town's stand behind the stand.

Stranraer's Stair Park is on the same latitude as Newcastle United's St. James' Park yet nearer Northern Ireland than it is Glasgow.

Heart of Midlothian's Tynecastle and Hibernian's Easter Road are further west than Bristol City's Ashton Gate and Bristol Rovers' Memorial Stadium.

Preston North End's Deepdale is the longest continuously used ground in English league football, hosting its first football match on 5 October 1878. Deepdale was the first football ground to construct permanent terracing, the West Paddock, constructed in the early 1890s.

National League, Maidenhead United's York Street ground dates back to 1871 and is thought to be the oldest purpose-built, continuously used football ground in British football.

Peterhead never train. Peterhead's Balmoor ground (capacity 3.150) is the furthest from a railway station of any senior football ground in Great Britain. The nearest railway station is Aberdeen, 32 miles away, albeit there is a bus service every thirty minutes from Aberdeen to Peterhead on Saturday match days. Even then, it is a one mile walk from Peterhead bus station to Balmoor.

Spurs hit the bar. Tottenham Hotspur stadium has it's own bakery and micro-brewery. The Goal Line Bar, situated in the South Stand, is 213.25 feet (65 metres) in length and is the longest bar in Europe.

Match postponed due to stolen pitch. Northern Premier League club Mickleover FC, had to postpone pre-season friendlies in July 2021 when club officials turned up at their Don Amott Arena ground to find half the pitch had been stolen. Using a flatbed lorry, thieves had entered the stadium in the middle of the night and stolen rolls of artificial turf worth over £50,000. Locals rallied around the community-based club to raise the £50k required to complete the pitch for the new season. Contributions included a cheque from Derby County Former Players Association, presented by former Derby County player, Phil Waller.

It's a long shot but try Norway. In 2015-16, during a match at Scottish Junior club Bank O'Dee's Spain Park ground, the match ball was kicked over the boundary wall and into the River Dee. Over a year later the club received an email from, Johnny Mikalsen, who had found the ball on the shore of the Norwegian island of Vanna, six miles from Tromso. The ball - which had the club's name on it - had travelled 1,118 miles (1800 kilometres) north of Aberdeen.

In 2018, Abdallah Lemsagam completed a reported 97% take-over of Oldham Athletic. For reasons not made public, Boundary Park's North Stand was not part of the take-over deal. As at 2022, Oldham Athletic still did not own the North Stand, but have use of it on match days.

Burnley's Turf Moor is the only ground where supporters can purchase 'benny-and-hot' the French liqueur Benedictine topped with hot water. The drink was brought back to Burnley at the end of World War One by members of the 11th Battalion from East Lancashire and has remained popular in the area ever since. Burnley, along with Burnley Miners Club, are thought to be the largest consumers of Benedictine outside France, with some thirty bottles of Benedictine consumed at every Burnley home game.

On 11 December 2021, Inverness Caledonian Thistle threatened to boycott their Scottish Championship match at Morton amidst a row over changing facilities and toilets at Cappielow. Four days previously, Inverness had lost a Scottish Cup tie on penalties at Morton on a night they were provided with a portacabin as a changing room. The beige metal portacabin, sporting one small window, was said to be 'damp' and 'cold' with 'inadequate lighting.' After the cup game, due to a generator fault, there was no lighting at all and no shower facilities. Inverness manager, Billy Dodds described the changing facilities as 'not fit for vermin', adding, 'It was so dark, our kit man didn't know if he had packed all the kit'. Inverness' official complaint followed similar made by Ayr United and Kilmarnock. Inverness were persuaded to fulfil their league fixture at Morton, the frugal facilities did not unduly affect their performance, Caley won 6-1.

Borderline case. On 7 January 2022, National League North club, Chester, faced action by the Welsh government for allegedly breaching Covid restrictions. On 28 December and 2 January, Chester played home matches against Fylde and AFC Telford United respectively, each before an attendance in excess of 2,000 which the Welsh government stated, contravened strict rules prohibiting mass gatherings in excess of 500 people. Chester's home ground, Deva Stadium, straddles the English-Welsh border, the car park and some buildings being in England, whereas the stadium and pitch is in Wales. To complicate matters, the club and stadium has an English address and a central Chester postcode.

Hat-Tricks

The first player to score a hat-trick for England was Howard Vaughton, who scored five goals in England's 13-0 win over Ireland in Belfast on 18 February 1882. Vaughton's Aston Villa team-mate, Arthur Brown, scored four in this game, however, Vaughton's hat-trick was accomplished before Brown's.

George Camsell scored nine hat-tricks for Middlesbrough in 1926-27; he went on to score a total of 24 hat-tricks for the club. Camsell scored in every game he played for England, which included four goals against Belgium on 11 May 1929 and a hat-trick against Wales on 20 November 1929.

Between January and February 1932, Alex Haddow scored five consecutive hat-tricks for Kings Park in Scottish Division Two.

In 1931-32, Clarrie Bourton scored seven hat-tricks for Coventry City in the Third Division South. Bourton scored 49 goals that season, thus nigh-on half comprised hat-tricks.

Value for money wherever you went. On 1 February 1936, the 44 league matches produced 209 goals, an average of 4.75 per game and six hat-tricks.

Following his transfer from Bradford Park Avenue, Len Shackleton made his debut for Newcastle United on 5 October 1946 against Newport County. Newcastle won 13-0 - the last team to score 13 in a League game - with Shackleton scoring two hat-tricks, one of which was accomplished in only two and a half minutes.

Hat-trick of hat-tricks. In 1946-47, Liverpool's Jack Balmer scored a hat-trick on three successive Saturdays in Division One. Balmer's first came on 9th November in Liverpool's 3-0 victory over Portsmouth; on the 16th in a 4-1 win at Derby County and on 23rd in Liverpool's 4-2 home win over Arsenal. In 1952-53, Leicester City's Arthur Rowley scored home and away hat-tricks against Fulham, the club which had sold him to Leicester.

John Shepherd overcame polio to sign for Millwall in October 1952. On his debut, Shepherd scored all four Millwall goals in a 4-1 win at Leyton Orient on 25 October 1952. Shepherd went on to score a further four hat-tricks in his next twelve appearances for Millwall.

On 5 January 1957, Ian Lawson scored four goals on his debut for Burnley in a 7-0 victory at home to Chesterfield in the third round of the FA Cup.

On 15 August 1959, Ian St. John scored a hat-trick in two-and-a-half minutes for Motherwell against Hibernian at Easter Road in a Scottish League Cup tie. St. John signed for Liverpool on 2 May 1961, and seven days later, St. John scored a hat-trick on his Liverpool debut in his side's 4-3 defeat against Everton in the Liverpool Senior Cup final at Goodison Park (51,669).

In 1958-59, Middlesbrough's Brian Clough scored home and away hat-tricks against both Brighton and Scunthorpe United. In the first meeting with Brighton on 23 August, Clough scored five, thus fourteen of Clough's goals that season were scored against just two clubs.

Three Spurs players hit hat-tricks in their clubs' 13-2 Third Round FA Cup replay victory over Crewe Alexandra on 3 February 1960 - Bobby Smith (4), Les Allen and Cliff Jones. Spurs led 9-1 at half-time. When the Crewe Alexandra team left Crewe station for London their train departed from platform 13 and returned to Crewe on platform 2.

Cliff Holton scored hat-tricks on successive days for Watford in 1959-60. His first on Good Friday April 15th 1960, in Watford's 4-2 victory over Chester in the Fourth Division. The following day, Holton scored another hat-trick in Watford's 5-0 victory over Gateshead.

Johnny Goodchild scored a hat-trick for Sunderland against Leeds United at Elland Road on 25 February 1961. It was Goodchild's first appearance of the season for Sunderland, he never played for Sunderland again.

Between 1957-58 and 1962-63, Brian Bedford scored four hat-tricks for Bournemouth and QPR in FA Cup ties. In 1959, Bedford was signed by

QPR manager Alec Stock for just £750, he went on to score 180 goals for QPR in 291 appearances.

Denis Law scored four hat-tricks in FA Cup ties between 1961 and 1964. For Manchester City in 1960-61, for Manchester United in 1962-63 and two further hat-ticks for United in 1963-64.

On 14 November 1964, Chester's Gary Talbot scored a hat-trick in the final three minutes of Chester's 5-0 1st Round FA Cup victory over Crewe Alexandra. Talbot's goals were timed at 87, 89 and 90 minutes.

In 1966-67, several Saturday fixtures in the First Division featured eight players all of whom had scored a hat-trick for England - Jimmy Greaves (Spurs), Bobby Charlton (Manchester United), Roger Hunt (Liverpool), Fred Pickering (Everton), Johnny Byrne (West Ham United), Johnny Haynes (Fulham) and Terry Paine (Southampton).

Jimmy Greaves scored six hat-tricks for England; Gary Lineker and Harry Kane, five (the latter as at January 2022); Bobby Charlton, four.

Five players, Albert Allen (Aston Villa), Frank Bradshaw (Sheffield Wednesday), Walter Gilliat (Corinthian), John Veitch (Corinthian) and Jack Yates (Burnley) scored hat-tricks on their only international appearance for England.

On 7 September 1968, Birmingham City's, Geoff Vowden, became the first substitute to score a hat-trick in English football. Vowden came on in the second half against Huddersfield Town for injured Ron Wylie and scored in the 71st, 74th and 89th minute. Birmingham City won 5-1; it was Vowden's first appearance as a substitute in his four years at Birmingham City, having never previously been dropped from the team.

On 23 March 1986, David Speedie became the second player since Geoff Hurst in the 1966 World Cup Final to score a hat-trick at Wembley, the first being Malcolm McDonald who scored all five England goals in a 5-0 victory over Malta on 16 April 1975. Speedie's hat trick came in Chelsea's 5-4 victory over Manchester City in the Full Members Cup Final before a Wembley crowd of 67,236. Manchester City's Mark Lillis scored twice and was denied a hat-trick when his second effort which came-off Chelsea's Doug Rougvie was awarded as an own goal. Should Lillis' second effort, in the 88th minute have been awarded to him, Lillis would have scored the fastest hat-trick in

Wembley history as his first goal was timed at 85 minutes; his deflected effort awarded as an own goal at 88 minutes; and, his second legitimate goal at 89 minutes. Both Chelsea and Manchester City had played First Division matches the previous day. Chelsea in a 1-0 victory over Southampton; Manchester City a 2-2 draw with Manchester United. Ten players from each side featured in both games over weekend with neither club, or their respective manager (Chelsea - John Hollins; Manchester City - Billy McNeill), complaining about having to play two games on successive days.

Eric Cantona scored the first ever hat-trick in the Premier League, in Leeds United's 5-0 win over Tottenham on 25 August 1992.

All the hat-tricks scored in the first season of the Premier League had a connection to Leeds United. Three Leeds United players scored hat-tricks, Eric Cantona, Gordon Strachan and Rod Wallace; former Leeds striker John Hendrie scored a hat-trick for Middlesbrough; future Leeds striker Brian Deane for Sheffield United; and, Teddy Sheringham (Tottenham) and Chris Sutton (Norwich City) scored hat-tricks against Leeds United.

In 1992-93, Les Ferdinand scored two hat-tricks for Queens Park Rangers in the space of three days; On 10 April in QPR's 4-3 win over Nottingham Forest and, on 12 April, in a 5-3 win at Everton.

James Hayter scored a hat-trick in only 2 minutes and 21 seconds when playing for Bournemouth against Wrexham on 23 February 2004.

Alan Shearer scored eleven hat-tricks in the Premier League.

Teddy Sheringham was 37 years and 146 days old when he scored a hat-trick in the Premier League for Portsmouth in their 4-0 victory over Bolton Wanderers at Fratton Park on 26 August 2003.

You must be Pulling my leg. On 22 March 2004, Worthing's Mark Pulling scored a hat-trick in his club's 3-1 win at Corinthian Casuals in the Ryman League Division Two South. All Pulling's goals were scored direct from corner-kicks in a 24-minute spell in the first half.

On 13 February 2021, Sunderland defeated Doncaster Rovers 4-1 in League One. All four Sunderland goals were scored by Charlie Wyke, all headers from crosses by Aiden McGeady. Doncaster's goal was an own goal by Sunderland goalkeeper Lee Burge, who also saved two penalties in the game.

On leaving the club in May 2021, Sergio Aguero had scored 12 hat-tricks for Manchester City.

The highest number of hat-tricks scored in a single season in the Premier League is 19, in 1993-94 and 2011-12.

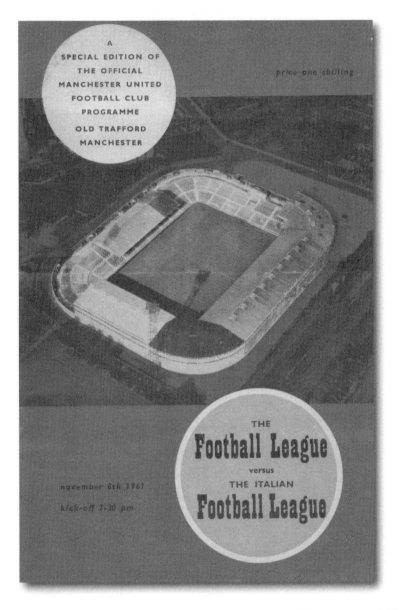

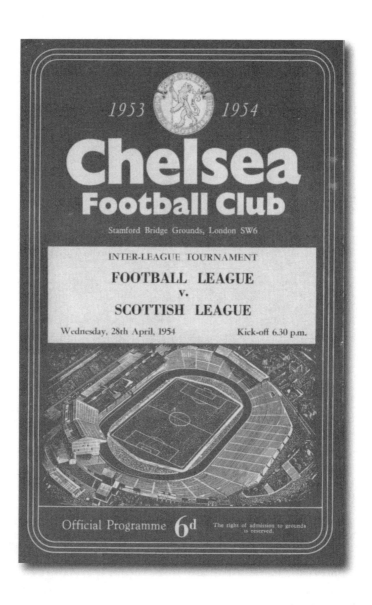

Chelsea Football Club

1953 1954

Stamford Bridge Grounds, London SW6

INTER-LEAGUE TOURNAMENT

FOOTBALL LEAGUE
v.
SCOTTISH LEAGUE

Wednesday, 28th April, 1954   Kick-off 6.30 p.m.

Official Programme **6d**   The right of admission to grounds is reserved.

Home Sweet Home

The only club to concede ten goals at home in a League match is Burslem Port Vale, who were beaten 10-0 by Sheffield United in a Second Division match on 3 December 1892.

There have been four occasions when all matches in a single division were won by the home team. First Division, 23 February 1926 and 10 December 1955. Third Division South on 23 April 1926. Third Division North on 14th March 1931, in each case 11 matches.

Spanning 1926-27, Bradford Park Avenue won 25 consecutive home matches in Third Division (North).

In 1927-28, Millwall scored 87 goals in their 21 home games in the Third Division South, ending the season with a home goal difference of +72.

Brentford won every one of their Division Three South home games in 1929-30. Brentford garnered 42 points from 21 home games, nineteen points away from home.

In 1950-51, Billingham Synthonia did not concede a single goal at home in their Northern League programme of 26 league matches in which they scored 44 goals.

In 1960-61, the Football League closed Gillingham's Priestfield Stadium for 14 days after the referee of a previous home game against Oldham Athletic was attacked by a spectator. As a consequence, Gillingham's 'home' game against Wrexham on 25 March was played at Stonebridge Road, the home of Gravesend and Northfleet. The only instance since WW2 of a Football League game being played on a ground outside the competition. Gillingham's game against Wrexham subsequently became the subject of a Football League inquiry regarding match fixing, for which both club and players were subsequently cleared.

Ipswich Town's first appearance in a major European competition was in 1962 when they defeated Floriana (Malta) 10-0 in the European Cup First Round. Since when Ipswich have remained undefeated at home in European competitions, a total of 31 games. A record for a British club and a European record until surpassed by AZ Alkmaar (Holland) in 2007.

In the late 1960s and early 70s, French club FC Scheibenhard (now of Regional 3 of the LGEF) played all their home matches in another country. FC Scheibenhard is situated in Bas-Rhin in Department Grand Est in Northern France (Alsace) on the French-German border and, at the time, did not have a football ground in the town. The club played all its home matches at the home of FC Scheibenhardt based in Rhineland Palatinate in Germany. For all they are in different countries, the two clubs/towns are separated by a tributary river that forms part of the French-German border.

In 1976-77, League Champions, Liverpool, Chelsea, promoted from Division Two, Mansfield Town, Third Division Champions and Bradford City, promoted from Division Four, all remained unbeaten at home.

Liverpool were undefeated at home from January 1978 to January 1981, a total of 85 matches - 63 in the League, 9 in League Cup, 7 in European competition and 6 in the FA Cup.

In 2000-01, Port Vale conceded home advantage of their LDV Vans Trophy tie against Stoke City on 5 March. The Vale Park pitch was waterlogged, to avoid fixture congestion, the match was switched to Stoke City's Britannia Stadium at the request of Port Vale. With the tie 1-1 after ninety minutes, Vale won in extra time on the Golden Goal rule courtesy of a penalty from Marc Bridge-Wilkinson.

Chelsea remained unbeaten at home for 86 matches, a run which began in March 2004 and ended in October 2008.

During 2015-16, Carlisle United played 'home' matches at Deepdale (Preston North End), Bloomfield Road (Blackpool) and Ewood Park (Blackburn Rovers) as Carlisle's home, Brunton Park, recovered from flood damage.

Sunderland went 364 days without a home win, a total of 20 matches.

Having beaten Watford on 17 December 2016 in the Premier League, Sunderland did not win at home again until a 1-0 victory over Fulham in the Championship on 16 December 2017.

Liverpool were undefeated in 68 home games in the Premier League. The run began on 7 May 2017 with a goalless draw against Southampton and ended on 21 January 2021 when Burnley won 1-0 at Anfield courtesy of an Ashley Barnes penalty.

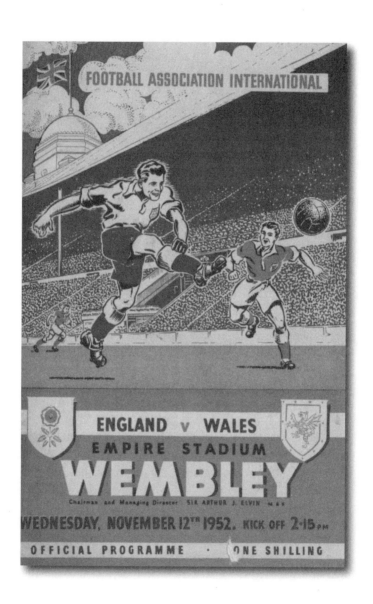

Injuries

Ted Crawford played for Clapton Orient (1933-45), during his last six-years with the club, Crawford played with a troublesome ankle. It was only when Crawford left Clapton Orient in 1945, he discovered he'd been playing with a broken ankle for six years.

On 1 November 1947, QPR's Reg Dudley broke his nose when challenging for a high ball against Bristol City. After receiving medical attention, there being no substitutes, Dudley insisted he be allowed back onto the field. Dudley had only been on the field a matter of minutes when he went into a tackle and broke his right leg.

In 1958-59, Barrow goalkeeper, Alan Coglan, suffered a broken leg whilst playing against Sunderland reserves in the North Regional League. The following season, Coglan made his comeback for Barrow reserves against Sunderland reserves, only to again suffer a broken leg. Having recovered, in 1961-62, Coglan was playing for Barrow reserves when he broke a leg for a third time - yet again against Sunderland reserves. Sadly, the injury resulted in Coglan having to retire from football.

In the summer of 1964, during England's tour of South America, Alan Mullery (Tottenham) wrenched a back muscle whilst cleaning his teeth.

Broke ankle when asleep. In 1965, Sunderland winger, George Mulhall, broke his ankle whilst asleep. Whilst at home, Mulhall had fallen asleep in his armchair with his feet up on the fireplace, his legs slipped and fell on the tiled hearth with such force he sustained a fractured ankle.

On 1 January 1966, Chester full-backs Ray and Bryn Jones, not related, both suffered broken legs in their club's 3-2 victory over Aldershot in Division Four.

On 18 March 1972, during Sheffield United's First Division match with Everton at Bramall Lane, Everton striker Bernie Wright attempted a diving header; Wright's head came into contact with the outstretched boot of United defender Eddie Colquhoun who, as a result of the collision, suffered a broken toe.

Whilst a player at Spurs, Gary Lineker pulled a back muscle whilst playing cricket for Cross Arrows CC, a team mainly made up of employees of the MCC.

In 1993, Southampton goalkeeper Dave Beasant was sidelined for two months with an injury sustained when he dropped a bottle of salad cream on his foot.

In 1996, Grimsby Town's Ivano Bonetti's jaw was broken by Town manager, Brian Laws, who took exception to Bonetti throwing food at him during a post-match team discussion.

In 1998, Leicester City goalkeeper, Kasey Keller, knocked out his two front teeth whilst attempting to extract his golf bag from the boot of his car.

In 2000, Barnsley's, Darren Barnard, sustained ligament damage when he slipped on a pool of wee deposited on his kitchen floor by his newly acquired puppy.

Portuguese man o' wor. In August 2004, Sunderland's Argentine midfield player, Julio Arca, suffered a severe allergic reaction after being stung by a jellyfish when swimming off Roker Beach in Sunderland. Arca missed part of Sunderland's pre-season preparations including two friendly matches.

In March 2008, Derek Lyle tripped and fell through a glass table at home sustaining injuries which ruled him out of Dundee's Scottish FA Cup semi-final against Queen of the South.

The striker who took a dive. In the summer of 2011, striker, Lee Hughes, missed most of Notts County's pre-season preparations after contracting decompression sickness (the bends) whilst scuba diving on his honeymoon.

On 28 August 2011, Swansea City's Alan Tate broke a leg when the golf buggy in which he was travelling overturned. As a result of the injury, Tate missed most of the season, returning as a substitute in Swansea's penultimate match of the season.

Of Hector and Crewe Alexandra, and such great names as these. On the evening of 7 December 2021, Crewe Alexandra's Chris Porter was injured in the warm-up prior to Crewe's League One home match against Lincoln City. On the same evening, Leyton Orient's Hector Kyprianou was injured during the warm-up prior to his club's League Two match against Swindon Town.

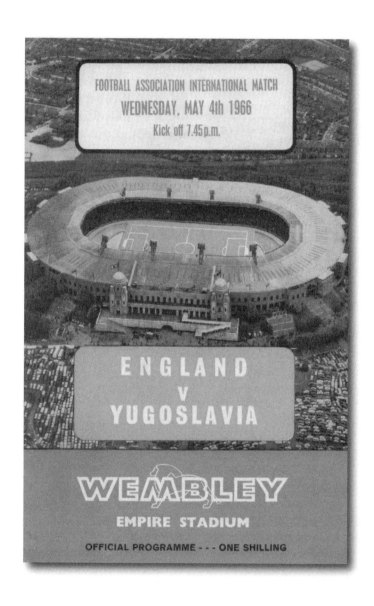

FOOTBALL ASSOCIATION INTERNATIONAL MATCH
WEDNESDAY, MAY 4th 1966
Kick off 7.45 p.m.

E N G L A N D
v
YUGOSLAVIA

WEMBLEY
EMPIRE STADIUM

OFFICIAL PROGRAMME - - - ONE SHILLING

Internationals

Johnny Arnold (Southampton, Fulham and Hampshire); Andy Ducat (Arsenal, Aston Villa, Surrey); C.B. Fry (Southampton and Hampshire); Tip Foster (Corinthians and Worcestershire); Les Gray (Corinthians and Hampshire); Billy Gunn (Notts County and Nottinghamshire); Wally Hardinge (Arsenal, Newcastle United and Kent); Alfred Lyttelton (Cambridge University and Middlesex); Harry Makepeace (Everton and Lancashire), Arthur Milton (Arsenal and Gloucestershire); Jack Sharp (Aston Villa, Everton and Lancashire); and, Willie Watson (Sunderland and Yorkshire) all represented England at both football and cricket.

The smallest goalkeeper to play for England is Teddy Davison (Sheffield Wednesday) 5'7" tall when he won his only cap against Wales on 13 March 1922.

Basil Patchitt captained England on his International debut. Patchitt, then 22, was playing for the amateur club Corinthian - later to merge with Casuals to become Corinthian Casuals - when he was selected by England for the International against Sweden in Stockholm on 21 May 1923, a game which England won 4-2. Patchitt was born in Singapore but qualified to play for England via parentage. Patchitt only played two full internationals for England yet was captain on both occasions. Curiously, though Patchitt played all his football for an amateur club, he was never chosen for the England amateur team.

The first team to contain three players who all captained England is Sheffield Wednesday in the late 1920s - Ernie Blenkinsop, Alf Strange and Jimmy Seed.

England first played Scotland at Wembley 12 April 1924; Scotland apart, England's next match against international opposition at Wembley was 27 years later on 9 May 1951 against Argentina.

Trevor Ford guides the ball 'home' in Sunderland's 5-3 defeat at Charlton Athletic on 19 August 1953, the prostrate home 'keeper is Sam Bartram. Ford scored 23 goals in 38 appearances for Wales, a record at the time before being equalled by Ivor Allchurch and eventually surpassed by Ian Rush and Gareth Bale. Ford's tally of 38 caps, however, is significantly lower than that of either Rush or Bale. Ford also represented Wales at cricket and was in the Glamorgan cricket team against whom Gary Sobers (Nottinghamshire) hit six sixes off the bowling of Malcolm Nash at St. Helen's Ground, Swansea on 31 August 1968. In an interview with the author in 1997, Ford said, 'At the start of the over I was fielding at long-on. Come the fourth ball, I was fielding outside Boots the chemists in the High Street'.

On 13 March 1928, the Scottish FA staged a trial match, Home Scots (Players based at Scottish clubs) versus Anglo Scots (those with English clubs), with a view to choosing the Scotland team to face England in a forthcoming Home International match at Wembley. The trial ended 1-1 before a Hampden Park crowd of 65,567. The England v Scotland game took place later that month (31 March) with Scotland securing a famous 5-1 victory for which the Scotland team was ascribed the nickname 'The Wembley Wizards'. Six of the Scotland team who defeated England had not been chosen for the trial match: Alex Jackson (Huddersfield Town) who scored a hat-trick; Hughie Gallacher (Newcastle United) who was selected despite not having played for two months; Tommy Law (Chelsea); Jimmy Gibson (Aston Villa); Jimmy Dunn (Hibernian) and Alan Morton (Rangers). Of the five-man Scotland forward line, hat-trick hero Alex Jackson was the tallest at 5'7" (1.70m).

Bernard Joy was the last amateur player to play for England in a full international when selected to play against Belgium on 9 May 1936. At the time, Joy was registered with Arsenal but playing for Casuals, later to become Corinthian Casuals. Joy retired from football in 1947 after 86 league appearances for Arsenal and became a journalist. He was noted for regular dinner parties held at his home in Osterley, west London, which were attended by top footballers and managers.

The forty-second international career. Tommy Brogan (Hibernian) made his international debut for Scotland against England at Hampden Park in 1945. After only forty seconds, Brogan twisted his knee when colliding with England goalkeeper Frank Swift and took no further part in the game. Brogan never played for Scotland again.

The only player to have played in England's final match before WW2, a 2-0 victory over Romania in Bucharest, and the first after the war, a 7-2 victory against Northern Ireland on 28 September 1946, was Tommy Lawton, who had been with Everton prior to the war and was with Chelsea when international football recommenced.

On 26 January 1946, Kevin O'Flanagan played rugby union as a right-wing three-quarter for Ireland against France. Seven days later, O'Flanagan played outside-right for The Republic of Ireland against Scotland at football. At various times, O'Flanagan played football for Arsenal and Brentford and rugby union for London Irish and Leinster.

Low point in his career. Aston Villa's Eddie Lowe played against Portugal in Lisbon on 27 May 1947, a game which England won 10-0, a record away win for England. Lowe was dropped for England's next international match against Belgium and never played for England again.

A fish out of water. Freddie Steele, a prolific centre-forward with Stoke City, Mansfield Town and Port Vale, was the first manager of Iceland. Steele was appointed in 1946, his first game in charge of the Iceland national team took place on 17 July 1946 against Denmark. Following the game, as a token of appreciation, the Icelandic FA presented Steele with a box of cod.

George Hardwick (Middlesbrough and Oldham Athletic) won 13 caps for England (1946-48) and was captain for every one of those matches. Hardwick is the only England player to have been captain in every game he played for the national team.

Between 1946 and 1953, Davey Walsh (West Bromwich Albion and Aston Villa) won 11 caps for Northern Ireland and 20 caps for The Republic of Ireland.

Red Laurie, World Cup Laurie. The international career of Liverpool's Laurie Hughes comprised entirely of playing in the final stages of the World Cup. Hughes played three matches for England in the 1950 World Cup held in Brazil, against Chile, USA and Spain.

Following England's historic 6-3 defeat against Hungary at Wembley in 1953, the England FA Selection committee rung the changes for England's next international against Scotland, curiously not in defence, they changed the entire five-man forward line.

Swan vistas. On 15 April 1953, the Wales team which faced Northern Ireland in Belfast contained a five-man forward line all of whom were born in Swansea and who had past or present experience with Swansea Town - Terry Medwin, John Charles, Trevor Ford, Ivor Allchurch and Jimmy Griffiths.

Debutants contrasting first touches of the ball. On 31 March 1954, Peter McParland (Aston Villa) made his debut for Northern Ireland and scored with his first touch of the ball after forty seconds of the Home International match against Wales. The Wales goalkeeper was Jack Kelsey, also making his International debut, whose first touch of the ball was to pick it out of the back of the net.

Floodlights were installed at Wembley in 1957 but it was not until 20 November 1963 that England played an entire match under the Wembley lights, an 8-3 victory over Northern Ireland.

One can't imagine it today. On 19 April 1958, England enjoyed one of their best wins against Scotland at Hampden Park, 4-0. England included four Second Division players in their team, Johnny Haynes and Jimmy Langley (Fulham) and Ronnie Clayton and Bryan Douglas of Blackburn Rovers.

Out of the mouths of (Busby) babes. Following England's 1-0 defeat to Russia on 17 June 1958 which eliminated England from the finals of the World Cup, the England party flew back into Heathrow. England manager, Walter Winterbottom, was greeted at the airport by his young son, Alan, whose first words were, 'Daddy, why didn't you play Bobby Charlton?' (related to the author by Johnny Haynes).

England have played international home matches at 52 different grounds, three of which were Derby County grounds - The Racecourse Ground, The Baseball Ground and Pride Park. England home games have also been staged at three different grounds in Blackburn - Alexandra Meadows, Leamington Road and Ewood Park.

Total football but not totally Dutch. Holland have had eleven national team managers/head coaches who were British. Edgar Chadwick, Jack Reynolds, Fred Warburton, Bob Glendenning, Billy Townley, John Bollington, Jesse Carver, George Hardwick and Denis Neville, the latter whom was manager 1964-66. (all English); Billy Hunter and Tommy Sneddon (Scots).

Wales have played home international matches at three different Swansea grounds, St Helens, Vetch Field and Liberty Stadium.

Overnight training. On 7 May 1959, Jimmy Greaves (Chelsea) and Jimmy Armfield (Blackpool) played in the England Under 23s 3-0 victory over Italy Under 23s in Milan. Greaves and Armfield had both been included in the full England squad due to fly out from Heathrow the following day for a tour of South America. Greaves and Armfield left the Under 23 party immediately after the game, travelled overnight by train to Paris and then onto Calais where the pair caught a ferry to Dover. The pair then travelled by train to London and by taxi to Heathrow to meet up with the England party in the late afternoon before flying out to Brazil.

On 8 February 1961, Johnny Byrne (Crystal Palace) became the first Division Four player to be selected for England Under 23s when he played in a 2-0 victory over Wales Under 23s at Goodison Park (Attendance - 27,235). On 22 November 1961, whilst still a Crystal Palace player but then in the

Third Division, Byrne was selected for the full England team against Northern Ireland at Wembley. Byrne is one of only five post-war Third Division players to have played for England, the others being, Tommy Lawton (Notts County), Reg Matthews (Coventry City), Peter Taylor (Crystal Palace) and Steve Bull (Wolverhampton Wanderers).

Between 8 October 1960 and 10 May 1961, England scored 40 goals in six consecutive international matches. 5-2 v Northern Ireland (in Belfast), 9-0 v Luxembourg (Luxembourg City), 4-2 v Spain (Wembley), 5-1 v Wales (Wembley), 9-3 v Scotland (Wembley) and 8-0 v Mexico (Wembley).

Alan Peacock (Middlesbrough) and Allan Clarke (Leeds United) are the only England players to make their international debuts in the finals of a World Cup. Peacock played in the 3-1 win over Argentina in Rancagua (2 June) in the 1962 World Cup in Chile. Clarke in the 1-0 victory over Czechoslovakia (11 June) in Guadalajara in the 1970 World Cup in Mexico.

England play a non-league team. On 4 June 1988, England played reigning Beazer Homes (Southern) League Champions, Aylesbury United in a warm-up game for Euro 88. A crowd of 6,031 at Aylesbury's Buckingham Road ground saw Bobby Robson's team triumph 7-0.

The Hull City Association Football Club Company Limited
(Incorporated 1946)

Members of the Football Association; Football League; North Regional League;
Northern Intermediate League

Directors:
Harold Needler (*Chairman*)
R. E. Buttery (*Vice-Chairman*)
G. H. Needler
John Needler
G. T. Rignall
S. T. Kershaw, M.B.E., J.P.

Manager:
C. S. BRITTON

Secretary:
J. B. ADAMSON

Telegrams : "TIGERS, HULL"
Telephones : 52195 & 52196

Registered Office and Ground:
BOOTHFERRY PARK,
HULL.

CSB/FC

7th October 1965.

Dear Eric,

I believe Alf Ramsey would like us to field a team against the England League Team on the Tuesday afternoon prior to Wednesdays match.

I shall be pleased to help in any way in Alf's pre-match preparations. Perhaps he will contact me on his arrival in Hull to let me know just what arrangements he would like.

I suggest that when the instructions go out to the players for the match they are asked to bring along their pumps. If the weather does happen to be bad outside they can have their workout in the training centre.

All the soccer fans here in Hull are looking forward to the match with great interest.

Shall look forward to seeing you.

Yours sincerely,

Manager.

Mr. E. Howarth,
The Football League,
Lytham St. Annes,
Lancs.

England have never beaten....Hull City. On 26th October 1965, Alf Ramsey's England lost 2-0 to Hull City in a match arranged as a warm-up game for the following day's Football League v Irish League match at Boothferry Park.

Newton gravitated to the bench. Keith Newton was the first England player to be substituted in the finals of a World Cup. The injured Everton full-back was replaced by club team-mate Tommy Wright in the 51st minute of England's match against Romania in the 1970 World Cup in Mexico.

Steve Heighway made his Liverpool debut on 22 September 1970 in a League Cup second round replay at Anfield against Mansfield Town. The following night, Heighway made his international debut for The Republic of Ireland in a 2-0 defeat against Poland at Dalymount Park. Heighway's twenty four hours is the shortest timespan between a player making his club debut and International debut.

Black cap Turner overdrive. In the early 1970s, Brentford flitted between the Fourth and Third Divisions yet possessed a player who won over 50 international caps whilst with the club. Brian Turner made a total of 102 appearances for New Zealand, winning 59 caps whilst with Brentford.

Ian Callaghan was part of the England team which defeated France 2-0 in the final group match of the 1966 World Cup on 20 July 1966. It was to be eleven years and 49 days later that Callaghan won his next England cap, in a goalless draw against Switzerland at Wembley on 7 September 1977.

Spence error traced. At the beginning of 1978-79, the Northern Ireland FA believed Derek Spence to be snubbing their invitation of a call-up to the Northern Ireland team. Spence was playing for Olympiacos (Greece) but the telegrams informing Spence of his call-up had been sent, in error, to AEK Athens. Spence won a total of 29 caps for Northern Ireland...it should have been more.

On 29 July 1985, England played West Germany in a rerun of the 1966 World Cup Final in aid of the Bradford Fire Disaster Fund. England won 6-4 with Geoff Hurst scoring a hat-trick and Martin Peters one goal.

In 2019, Hereford United of the National League North had two matches postponed due to International call-ups, the lowest level of English football for this to have occurred.

As at December 2020, San Marino's strikers, Matteo Vitaoli and Danilo Rinaldi had a total of 98 caps between them, 58 and 40 respectively, and a total of two goals, one each.

Former Crewe Alexandra manager, David Artell, born in Rotherham, was capped seven times by Gibraltar (2014-15). Artell graduated from Chester University with a degree in forensic biology.

None of the players who hold the club record number of caps for Wales' four major clubs are Welsh. Cardiff City's most capped player is Aron Gunnarsson (62 caps for Iceland); Swansea City - Ki Sung-Yueng (117 caps, South Korea); Newport County - Keanu Marsh-Brown (16 caps, Guyana); Wrexham- Dennis Lawrence (49 caps when at Wrexham for Trinidad and Tobago)

Scotland's 2-1 victory over Denmark on the 15 November 2021 in a World Cup qualifying match was Scotland's sixth consecutive victory in competitive internationals. It was the first time the Scots had achieved this feat since six consecutive victories in the Home International Championship, March 1928 to February 1930.

England's 10-0 victory over San Marino in a World Cup qualifying match on 15 November 2021, equalled England's record away win. On 25 May 1947, England beat Portugal 10-0 in Lisbon; on 27 May 1964, England beat the USA by ten clear goals in New York. In the defeat of San Marino, Harry Kane (Spurs) became only the fourth player to score a hat-trick for England in successive matches, the others being Vivian Woodward (Spurs), Dixie Dean (Everton) and Tommy Taylor (Manchester United). Kane was also the first England player to score four in an International since Ian Wright, also against San Marino, on 7 November 1993.

"At last! England have beaten Germany in a major competition!". BBC Commentator, Guy Mowbray, on hearing the final whistle signalling England's 2-0 victory over Germany in the 2020 European Championship (played 29 June 2021).

League

The world's smallest league is the Isles of Scilly Football League which has only two teams, Garrison Gunners and Woolpack Wanderers. The two teams play one another every Sunday on the archipelago's one football pitch, situated on St.Mary's island. The island's footballers and budding footballers meet in the Scillonian Club lounge bar before the start of each season to appoint two captains, who then select their two squads. This results in blended and balanced teams and an annual draft similar to those of the NFL and NBS in the USA.

In addition to the Isles of Scilly League, in which the two teams play one another 18 times a season, there are two cup competitions, the Wholesalers Cup and Foredeck Cup. A traditional Boxing Day match is also held, billed as 'Old Men v Youngsters'. A Scilly Representative team plays a team from Cornwall every year for the Lyonesse Cup, recognised by FIFA as the world's smallest football trophy as it is only six millimetres high. A replica of the trophy is on display at the FIFA Museum in Zurich.

The Lionesse Cup, the world's smallest football trophy, is six millimetres in height.

Thought you'd seen some bad games? Between 1892-93 and 1898-99, the Football League held a series of test matches between the bottom two teams in the First Division and top two sides in the Second to determine promotion and relegation. On 30 April 1898, Stoke City hosted Burnley in the penultimate match of the 'test' group with both teams knowing a draw would keep Stoke in Division One and also promote Burnley irrespective of the outcome of the other 'test' between Newcastle United and Blackburn Rovers. Stoke's game against Burnley resulted in the only English league game in which it is recorded that neither side had a shot at goal. The Football League subsequently abandoned 'tests' in favour of automatic relegation and promotion. As it happened all four teams achieved either safety or promotion as the Football League was extended the following season.

In 1907-08, Blackburn Rovers and Woolwich Arsenal finished with identical records in Division One. P38 W12 L12 D14, Goals For 51, Against 63, Points 36. The Football League decreed both would tie for 15th place.

August has not always been the month in which League football started a new season. Up to 1914-15, a new Football League season began on 1 September, unless that date fell on a Friday or Sunday.

In 1920-21, League Champions, Burnley went 30 games without defeat. Burnley, however, won just six away games; League runners-up, Manchester City won only 5 of their 21 away matches, whilst third placed Bolton Wanderers won just 4.

Imperfect perfect season. In 1922-23, Southampton finished 11th in the Second Division, their record read - Played 42, Won 14, Drew 14, Lost 14, Goals for 40, Goals Against 40, Points 42.

Not so good at Goodison. In 1927-28, League Champions, Everton, won just 11 of their 21 home matches, a figure surpassed by 13 other teams in the First Division including relegated Tottenham Hotspur.

All's well that's Oakwell. In 2021-22, Barnsley became the first club to play over 3,000 matches in the second level of English league football, in so doing, achieving the most seasons in the second level of English football than any other club.

Once a hot bed. In 1927-28, the North East boasted seven teams in the Football League - Ashington, Darlington, Durham City, Hartlepools

United, Newcastle United, Middlesbrough and Sunderland.

Home alone. On 11 April 1948, only one of the eleven games in Division Two was a home win. A feat repeated on 12 September 1949.

Shot shy City make a point. When Birmingham City won the Division Two championship in 1947-48, they won more points than they scored goals. Birmingham's goals tally from 42 matches was only 55, whereas their points tally was 59. Bury, who narrowly avoided relegation, scored more goals (58) than Champions Birmingham City.

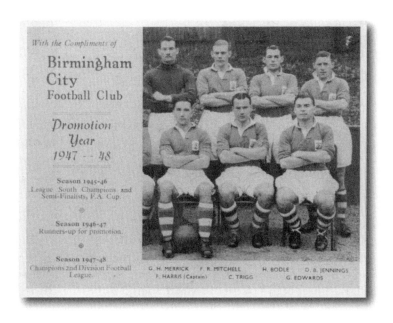

Compliments card issued by Birmingham City to commemorate winning Division Two in 1947-48, which, unusually for Divisional Champions, City achieved by securing more points than they scored goals. Equally curious, the club compliments card only features seven of the promotion winning team.

On 18 September 1948, nine of the eleven matches in Division One were drawn.

Lazarus of the league. In 1948-49, from 18 September to 12 March,

Sunderland won just five of their 23 league matches and were also famously beaten by non-league Yeovil Town in the FA Cup. With eleven matches remaining, Sunderland were in danger of being relegated from Division One for the first time in their history. Sunderland, however, staged a remarkable turn-around, were unbeaten in those remaining eleven games to finish in 8th position.

In 1952-53, Chesterfield and Tranmere Rovers concluded the season with identical records in the Third Division North. Both clubs finished with 47 points from 46 League games and with an identical goal differential, 65 scored, 63 conceded. For all Tranmere won three more matches than Chesterfield, the latter were placed above Rovers for having lost fewer games, 17 as opposed to 20.

In 1954-55, Chelsea won the League Championship for the first time in their history with the lowest points tally (52) of any champions in a 42 game season. Chelsea accumulated only 17 points more than relegated Leicester City and only eleven more than Huddersfield Town who finished in the bottom-half of the table. Chelsea qualified for the inaugural European Cup and were drawn against Djurgardens IF (Sweden) but withdrew from the competition following pressure from the Football League which opposed the new European competition.

Home run. On 10 December 1955, all eleven First Division matches resulted in wins for the home team.

Rovers poor return. Blackburn Rovers made a sensational start in the First Division in 1958-59. Rovers won their opening fixture 5-1 at Newcastle United, then beat both Leicester City and Spurs 5-0 at home. Rovers then failed to win any of their next eight matches. Come the end of October, Blackburn were three points off bottom in Division One, having registered a single win from ten matches since their opening three games of the season.

When did Charlton score for Charlton when Charlton didn't score? On 20 April 1957, during Charlton Athletic's 3-1 defeat at Arsenal. The Charlton goal was an own goal by Arsenal defender Stan Charlton.

Fans got money's worth and some. In 1957-58, Manchester City scored 104 goals in the First Division but also conceded 100, the only instance of the 'double' century occurring in English football. The total of 204 goals works-out at 4.8 per game.

At the commencement of 1959-60, in a squad of 24 professionals, Bradford Park Avenue's longest serving player was full-back, Gerry Baker, aged 20 years and four months, who had been with the club from the age of fifteen.

On 2 May 1960, Burnley beat Manchester City 2-1 at Maine Road to become First Division Champions in what was their final game of the season. When Burnley's Trevor Meredith scored after 31 minutes of play to put Burnley 2-1 ahead, it was the first time Burnley had been at the top of Division One at any stage of the season.

Due to league fixture congestion, the inaugural League Cup Final of 1960-61 between Aston Villa and Rotherham United was not played until the start of the 1961-62 season. Villa triumphed 3-2 on aggregate after losing the first-leg 0-2 at Rotherham. The second leg of the final took place at Villa Park on 5 September 1961 with Aston Villa already having been drawn away to Bradford City on 13 September in the 1961-62 competition, thus Villa began their defence of the trophy just eight days after winning it.

Dividend forecast low. On 13 October 1962, 22 matches ended in draws.

When winning the Fourth Division Championship in 1963-64, Gillingham won more points than they scored goals. Gillingham finished the season with 60 points whereas their goals tally was 59. Runners-up Carlisle United scored 113 goals. Southport, who finished in the bottom four and had to apply for re-election to the Football League, scored four more goals (63) than Champions Gillingham.

In eighteen seasons, from 1950-51 to 1967-68, Spurs were involved in only six goalless draws at White Hart Lane.

Competitive league. On 14 November 1969, Yeovil Town sat in the bottom-half of the Southern Premier League table in 14th place but only four points behind leaders Hillingdon Borough. Only one point separated the top six teams, Hillingdon, Brentwood Town, Hereford United, Wimbledon, Weymouth and Barnet. Two months later, on 14 January, Hillingdon Borough had tumbled to 10th in the league, but only three points adrift of then leaders Weymouth. Cambridge United who, at one stage in November, had sat in 14th place, ended the season as champions.

In 1971-72, Mansfield Town did not score at home until 18 December. The player to break to barren spell was John Fairbrother, in a 3-2 defeat against

Plymouth Argyle. Prior to the defeat against Plymouth, Mansfield had only won one league match, away to table topping Aston Villa before a Villa Park crowd of 28,106. Mansfield finally won a home match on 1 January, a 2-1 victory over Chesterfield. Mansfield were relegated on goal difference, what did for them was not so much their inability to score at home - Mansfield lost only two more home games than fourth placed Notts County - or the fact they scored only 19 goals in 23 home matches, moreover the number of draws - 20.

In 1973-74, Liverpool finished as runners-up in Division One and Derby County, third, both teams having scored just 52 goals from 42 league matches, the same number as Birmingham City who avoided relegation by a single point. Relegated Southampton scored 47 goals, in so doing, scoring more goals from open-play than both Liverpool and Derby County.

Also, in 1973-74, Millwall played 42 matches in Division Two and finished with 42 points; Millwall won 14 games, drew 14 and lost 14; they won 4 games 1-0 and lost four games 1-0; were awarded three penalties and conceded three penalties; scored 51 goals and conceded 51 goals.

A more competitive top flight? On 29 February 1976, Liverpool, Queens Park Rangers and Manchester United were tied at the top of Division One; Derby County were one point behind the trio, with Leeds United five points off the top but with two games in hand; there was an 8 point difference between top and 11th place.

In 1976-77, League Champions, Liverpool, scored 62 goals, the lowest total of any English League Champions in a 42-match season. Runners-up, Manchester City, scored just 60 goals. Ironically, this was the season goal difference replaced goal average in an attempt to encourage more attacking play and goals. This was also the first season in which red and yellow cards were used by referees.

On 16 October 1976, the 1975 League Champions, Derby County, recorded their first league win of the season, an 8-2 victory over Tottenham Hotspur at the Baseball Ground. Come December, Derby sacked manager, Dave Mackay and replaced him with 26 year old Colin Murphy, one of the youngest managers in the history of the Football League.

In 1985-86, Reading won their first 13 matches in Division Three, the consecutive run of victories ended with a 2-2 draw at home to Wolves on 23

October. Reading finished the season as Third Division Champions yet despite their start to the season, ended losing more matches (10) than third placed Derby County and Wigan Athletic (fourth).

Fourteen 'derby' matches for each club in the season. In 1989-90, eight teams in the First Division were London based - Arsenal, Charlton Athletic, Chelsea, Crystal Palace, Millwall, QPR, Tottenham Hotspur and Wimbledon. There had never previously been a season, nor one since, when as many London clubs competed together in English top-flight football.

Signs were there. When Brighton qualified for the Division Two play-offs in 1990-91, they did so having finished with a negative goal difference of minus 6. Brighton lost 3-1 to Notts County in the Play-Off Final before a Wembley crowd of 60,000. The following season Brighton were relegated.

On 3 October 1992, Norwich City were top of the Premier League when they travelled to play Blackburn Rovers. The Premier League leaders lost 7-1, the second biggest defeat of a table-topping team in English top-flight football. The highest being Everton's 7-0 defeat at Wolverhampton Wanderers on 22 February 1939 and West Ham United's 7-0 defeat at Sheffield Wednesday on 28 November 1959.

> Including the friendly international club fixture with Moscow Torpedo, four matches in succession have been worthily won. Enthusiasm is rising rapidly. After the sweeping 7-0 triumph over West Ham United, the 38,367 crowd really let themselves go. The roars must have been heard for miles!
>
> And no wonder. West Ham United had come as League leaders and had been removed from their pedestal in a fashion no one could have imagined. Within the first ten minutes Wednesday had scored three goals (Johnny Fantham 2, Derek Wilkinson) and the Hammers were already on their way out. They were never allowed to recover.

Extract from Sheffield Wednesday programme for home game following the historic 7-0 defeat of Division One leaders West Ham United, somewhat underplaying the achievement.

On 16 January 1993, Norwich City were top of the Premier League with a negative goal difference. Norwich finished the season in third place, but still with a negative goal difference, of minus 4.

Shrewsbury Town finished with identical records in successive seasons, 1994-95 and 1995-96. Played 46, Won 13, Drew 14, Lost 19, Points 53 and, on both occasions, finished 18th in the Division Two League table.

In 1997-98, both Cardiff City and Hartlepool United drew 23 of their 46 league matches in Division Three (now League Two). Hartlepool (17th in the league) lost just one home game, less than champions, Notts County (2) and Lincoln City (5) who were also promoted. Norwich City equalled this feat of drawn matches in 1978-79, 23 draws in 42 First Division matches, Norwich, however, were the only team in all four divisions not to record an away win.

The last club to select a team comprising 11 English players for a top-flight league match is Aston Villa, who did so on February 27, 1999 for their Premier League match against Coventry City at Villa Park. Furthermore, the three substitutes named by Villa were also English. Team - Michael Oakes, Steve Watson, Gareth Southgate, Dion Dublin, Simon Grayson, Ricky Scimeca, Alan Wright, Lee Hendrie, Paul Merson, Ian Taylor and Julian Joachim. Substitutes - Mark Draper, Gareth Barry and Stan Colleymore. The Villa manager was John Gregory.

One-nil not to the Arsenal. The most 1-0 wins in a season occurred in 2001-02, when West Bromwich Albion won 15 of their Division One matches by a single goal margin, also two FA cup matches by the same score-line. The total of 17 single goal victories included six in eight league matches between 31 October and 12 December.

In 2002, the Old Boys Football League (London) and the Southern Olympian League merged to form the Amateur Football Combination. In 2006, the London Financial Football Association coalesced with the Amateur Football Combination to form the largest adult football league in Europe and one of the largest in the world. The Amateur Football Combination has in excess of 100 clubs and over 350 teams in 31 divisions comprising more than 1% of all adult male 11-a-side football teams in England. The teams, based in and around London and the Home Counties include Old Hamptonians, the Honourable Artillery Company and the Royal Bank of Scotland. The league functions outside the pyramid system with top teams not progressing into semi-professional football.

In 2005-06, Hearts had twice as many managers as their final position in the Scottish Premier League. Hearts finished second in the League having had four managers during the season: George Burley, John McGlynn, Graham Rix and Valdas Ivanauskas.

Sunderland occupied all 24 positions in the Championship during 2006-07. Having lost their first four matches of the season and finding themselves bottom of the league, Sunderland rallied under the management of Roy Keane to finish the season as Champions.

In 2007-08, Derby County won just 11 points and a single game in what was then the Premiership. Derby County's leading goal scorer for the season was Kenny Miller, with four goals.

Prior to the commencement of 2007-08, Leeds United, about to embark upon their first season in the third tier of English football, were deducted 15 points for exiting administration without a CVA (Company Voluntary Arrangement). Despite the points deduction, Leeds finished 5th in the league and qualified for the play-offs. Leeds reached the play-off final at Wembley only to lose by a single goal to Doncaster Rovers.

Red rose days. In 2010-11, the historical county of Lancashire had eight clubs in the Premier League - Blackburn Rovers, Blackpool, Bolton Wanderers, Everton, Liverpool, Manchester City, Manchester United and Wigan Athletic.

It's all academic. In 2014-15, Hamilton Academical topped the Scottish Premier League between 5 October and 1 November. On 12 January 2015, Hamilton were fifth in the League following a 3-2 home defeat to Dundee United. Hamilton then failed to win any of their following eleven league games; come 4 April, twelve games without a win, Hamilton were still fifth in the league.

Marking time. Stoke City finished 9th in the Premier League in three successive seasons 2013-14 to 2015-16. The Stoke City manager for these three seasons being Mark Hughes.

Where did it all go wrong? In 2016-17, Tottenham Hotspur had a positive goal difference of +60, the highest of any team not to have won the English top flight title.

Clear-out pays-off. In 2016-17, Scottish Premier League Champions, Celtic, finished 30 points clear of runners-up Aberdeen. Celtic, under the management of Brendan Rogers, secured the title with a 5-0 victory at Hearts, with eight matches still to play. Celtic remained unbeaten in the league and finished with a goal difference of +81. Celtic also won the Scottish FA Cup and League Cup, thus were undefeated in 47 domestic games. Prior to, or, during the season, Celtic transferred, released or loaned-out 37 players.

In 2016-17, Premier League Champions, Manchester City, had a positive goal difference of +79. That same season, City won 18 consecutive league matches, 20 in all competitions.

Five clubs have competed in all five of the top divisions in English football, either First Division or Premier League, Second, Third and Fourth Divisions (or equivalent) and the National League - Carlisle United, Grimsby Town, Leyton Orient, Luton Town and Notts County.

During their Premier League match against Manchester United on 26 September 2020, Brighton hit the United woodwork five times. The score was 2-2 when referee Chris Kavanagh blew for time. Kavanagh was then contacted by VAR officials and, after checking VAR, eventually awarded a penalty to Manchester United for handball, some four minutes after the final whistle. The penalty was converted by Bruno Fernandes to give United a 3-2 victory. It was the first time Brighton had lost their first two home games of a season in the top division.

On 2 October 2020, Morecambe topped League Two with a negative goal difference: P5 W4 D0 L1 F8 A9 Pts 12

On 4 October 2020, Premier League Champions Liverpool were beaten 7-2 at Aston Villa. It was the first time Aston Villa had won their opening three league games since 1962-63 and the first time Liverpool had conceded seven goals since being beaten 7-2 at Tottenham Hotspur also in 1962-63. It was also the first time the reigning English League champions had conceded seven since Arsenal were beaten 7-0 at Sunderland on 12 September 1953.

In 2021-22, following eight matches in La Liga, Villarreal were the unbeaten team yet occupied 11th place.

Liverpool and Chelsea recorded exactly the same scorelines in their first five Premier League games of 2021-22 - 3-0, 2-0, 1-1, 3-0 and 3-0.

194

Managers

The first manager/coach of Real Madrid was Arthur Johnson, born in Dublin when Ireland was still part of the UK. Johnson signed as a player for Real in 1902 and scored Real's first goal in their first competitive match. Under his management Real Madrid won four regional Championships and one Copa del Rey. Johnson was manager/coach of Real for ten seasons, second only to Miguel Munoz in terms of longevity. It was Johnson who introduced the all white strip Real Madrid are famous for, mirroring the strip worn by Corinthian Casuals.

John Madden's clubs included Dumbarton, Grimsby Town, Celtic and Spurs, he also won two caps for Scotland. In 1905, against advice from friends in British football, he accepted an offer to manage Sparta Prague. Madden remained manager of Sparta for thirty years, there after serving the club as a Vice President for a further thirteen years until his death in 1948 at the age of 82.

Fred Everiss is the longest serving manager in English senior football. Everiss was appointed manager of West Bromwich Albion in 1902 and held the post until 1948 - 46 years. It is worth noting Everiss' position was that of manager-secretary and much of his time would have been spent with administrative duties. Following his role as manager, Everiss was appointed a club director, a position he held until his death, three years later in 1951.

Spottiswood spotted by Inter. Bob Spottiswood's League clubs as a player included Carlisle United, Crystal Palace and Clapham Orient. Spottiswood dropped into non-league football, playing for Aberdare Athletic, Treherbert and Sittingbourne. Following his stint at Sittingbourne, Spottiswood was appointed manager of Inter Milan in 1922.

Clem' Stephenson was manager of Huddersfield Town from 1929 to 1942, his brother, George, managed the club from 1947 to 1952.

Father and son managers at same club. Harry Bradshaw managed Fulham from 1904 to 1909, his son, Joe, managed the Cottagers from 1926-29. The Bradshaws were not the only father and son to have managed Fulham. Bill Dodgin senior managed Fulham from 1949 to 1953, his son, Bill junior - who had two spells as a Fulham player, 1949-52 and 1961-64 - was in charge at Craven Cottage from 1969 to 1972. A feat equalled by Brian and Nigel Clough (Derby County).

Only former Port Vale and Southend player to manage Real Madrid. From 1911 to 1923, Robert Firth enjoyed a playing career with Nottingham Forest, Port Vale and Southend United. In 1930, Firth entered management when appointed manager of Racing de Santander, after two successful seasons, he was then appointed manager of Real Madrid (1932-34).

Robert Firth's career as a player at Port Vale briefly overlapped that of Billy Aitken. Whilst Firth would go on to manage Real Madrid, Aitken went on to become manager of Juventus (1928-1930).

Ivor Broadis was 23 years old when he was appointed player-manager of Carlisle United in 1946. Broadis played for a number of clubs until the early 1960s, his final club being Queen of the South, scoring 20 goals in 63 appearances (1959-60 to 1960-61). Broadis, aged 39, was then offered a contract by Hearts but decided to pursue a career in football journalism.

Billy McCandless was an Irishman who played for Rangers then moved to Wales where he achieved a unique treble as a manager, guiding Newport County (1939), Cardiff City (1947) and Swansea Town (1949) to promotion from Division Three South to Division Two. When guiding Newport County to promotion in 1938-39, he called upon the services of just thirteen players throughout the season.

Theo Kelly was manager of Everton from 1939 to 1948, prior to which he had been club secretary. Kelly accused Joe Mercer of not trying when playing for England against Scotland in a wartime international, when, in truth, Mercer had sustained a cartilage injury. Even after having the injury diagnosed by an orthopaedic surgeon, Kelly refused to believe Mercer was injured, Mercer having to pay for the surgery himself. Understandably upset, Mercer jumped at the chance of joining Arsenal when the London club made a £9,000 bid for his services in November 1946. It is reported Kelly brought

Mercer's boots to the transfer negotiations so Mercer would have no reason to return to Everton to say goodbye to the other players at the club. Everton players of the time described Kelly as 'remote', 'autocratic' and 'petty'. Kelly resigned as Everton manager in September 1948 and reverted to his previous position of club secretary. On the plus side, Kelly led Everton to financial stability and devised the club motto and badge.

To be frank, unacceptable. In August 1948, Frank Hill resigned as manager of Crewe Alexandra when he discovered some of the Crewe players were earning more than him.

Quantum leap. Billy Chalmers resigned as manager of Welsh non-league club Ebbw Vale in the summer of 1948, to become manager of Juventus.

Dai Astley enjoyed a successful career as a player in the 1930s with Charlton Athletic, Aston Villa, Derby County and Blackpool, he also won 13 caps for Wales scoring 12 goals. In 1948, Astley retired as a player was appointed manager of Inter Milan. Following subsequent stints as manager of Genoa, and Swedish clubs Djurgardens and Sandvikens IF he returned to the UK to become a priest.

In 1951-52, four top Italian clubs had English managers - Jes Carver (Juventus), Ted Crawford (Bologna), Denis Neville (Atalanta) and Frankie Soo (Padova).

Manager of two teams in the same game. On 15 October 1952, York City manager, Dick Duckworth, was appointed manager of Stockport County. The clubs agreed Duckworth would manage York City for one more game, on 18 October, York's opponents that day were Stockport County.

In 1953, Bela Guttman was sacked as manager of AC Milan after 19 matches with Milan top of Serie A. During WW2, Guttman had been deported by the Nazis to a slave labour camp then to a concentration camp but had survived the Holocaust. Following his dismissal by AC Milan, for every team Guttman later managed he insisted there be a clause in his contract saying he could not be sacked should the team be top of the league. Guttman managed a total of twenty clubs (three of them twice) including Vicenza, Porto, Benfica, Penarol, Honved, Servette and Panathinaikos. He also managed the Austria national team.

Grimsby Town were the first English league club to appoint a foreign manager, Elemer Berkessey, in July 1954. Berkessey, a Hungarian, who had previously managed Ferencvarosi (Hungary), Vicenza (Italy) and Real Zaragoza (Spain) was manager of Grimsby Town for little over a year (July 1954 to September 1955).

In 1955, Bradford City narrowed down the applicants for the vacant manager's job to two candidates. The club's board interviewed both before appointing Peter Jackson. The unsuccessful applicant was Bill Shankly.

Manager Norman Dodgin was a great admirer of centre-forward, Andy Torrance, so much so Dodgin signed Torrance for two different clubs. Torrance, however, never played a game under Dodgin's managership. In the summer of 1957, Norman Dodgin, whilst manager of Yeovil Town, signed Torrance from Ayr United. Before the 1957-58 season started, however, Dodgin left Yeovil to become manager of Barrow. During 1957-58, Dodgin made two attempts to sign Torrance and was finally successful on 25 June during the close season. Six days later, Dodgin, resigned as manager of Barrow to become manager of Oldham Athletic.

From Serie A to Southern League. In 1958, Bill Dodgin senior left his post as manager of Sampdoria, the next club Dodgin senior managed was Yiewsley (Southern League).

After thirteen years as Manager, Scot Symon was sacked by Rangers in November 1967 with Rangers top of the table, a point ahead of Hibernian and three ahead of Celtic. Symon was told of his dismissal by the club's accountant. A former Rangers player, Symon played both football and cricket for Scotland.

Billy Lucas had five spells as manager of Newport County - 1953-61, 1962-1967, 1970-74 and two periods as caretaker manager. In his final spell as full-time manager (70-74) Lucas worked for the first six months without pay to help the club's dire financial situation.

Of the 92 League clubs in 1964-65, 60 were managed by managers who had played right-half during their playing careers, including First Division Champions, Manchester United (Matt Busby); Second Division Champions, Newcastle United (Joe Harvey); Third Division Champions, Carlisle United (Alan Ashman); Fourth Division Champions, Brighton (Archie Macaulay); FA Cup winners, Liverpool (Bill Shankly) and League Cup winners, Chelsea (Tommy Docherty).

When Brian Clough began his career as a manager at Hartlepool United in 1965, he did so at a club record salary for a manager, £2,500 per annum. The match programme for Clough's first home game in charge stated that during his interview, Clough told the Hartlepool board he would accept the position as manager on the condition, 'I will be in full and firm control of team matters and that decisions taken will be my decisions and no one else's.'

Not kitted-out for management. Bill Anderson was manager of Lincoln City for nigh-on 20 years (855 games, 1946-1965). Anderson's successor, Con Moulson, lasted three months. Moulson was a surprise choice as successor to Anderson, given he worked in a local factory and part-time for Lincoln City as their kit-man, albeit he had played for Lincoln City in the 1930s and 40s. Lincoln lost all eight matches in Moulson's charge, giving him what may possibly be the worst record of any permanent manager in the history of English league football. Following Moulson's dismissal, he resumed work at the factory where he had been previously employed and as Lincoln City's kit-man on a part-time basis.

Peter Hauser (who played for Blackpool and Cheltenham Town) was the second foreign manager of an English league club. Hauser, a South African, was appointed manager of Chester prior to the commencement of 1963-64. Hauser's tenure at Chester ended on 17 February 1968; he returned to South Africa to resume his career as an underground surveyor whilst playing for Addington and later, Highlands Park.

In 1965-66, three League clubs boasted managers who had also played County Cricket, Middlesbrough manager, Raich Carter (Derbyshire), Freddie Goodwin of Scunthorpe United (Lancashire) and Willie Watson of Halifax Town (Yorkshire, Leicestershire and England).

In May 1967, when Gus McClean succeeded Brian Clough as Manager of Hartlepool United, McClean bought both Clough's house and car.

On 23 May 1967, Keith Kettleborough was sacked as Manager of Doncaster Rovers and, less than an hour later, signed for the club as a player.

Eddie Firmani was a prolific striker for Charlton Athletic, Southend United and Sampdoria in the 1950s and 60s. He later went into management and, when managing in Kuwait, was taken captive in the first Gulf War. He was eventually released unharmed.

In 1968-69, Tommy Docherty managed three clubs in six weeks. On 6 November, Docherty resigned as manager of Rotherham United to become manager of Queens Park Rangers. He left Rangers after four weeks following a disagreement with chairman Jim Gregory and on 18 December was appointed manager of Aston Villa.

In 1969, Neil Warnock was transferred to Rotherham United from Chesterfield. 47 years later, in 2016, Warnock returned to Rotherham as Manager.

In 1969-70, Joe Mercer became the first manager to win the League Cup twice - with Aston Villa (1961) and Manchester City (1970).

How did he manage? Billy Bingham had two spells as Manager of Northern Ireland (1967-1971 and 1980-1993). During his first spell as Northern Ireland manager, which involved being Manager of both the full international and Under 23s team, Bingham was also Manager of first, Southport, then Plymouth Argyle.

The only instance of a manager being sacked on Christmas Day. On 25 December 1984, Felix Mourinho was serving Christmas lunch to his family when he received a telephone call informing him he had been sacked as manager of Portuguese club Rio Ave. Among those family members seated at the table was his son, Jose Mourinho, then aged 21.

Bob Stokoe managed five clubs twice. Bury (1961-65 and 1977-78), Blackpool (1970-72 and 1978-79), Carlisle United (1968-70 and 1980-85), Rochdale (1967-68 and 1979-80) and Sunderland 1972-76 and 1987 as caretaker manager.

Dario Gradi was manager of Crewe Alexandra from 1983 to 2007 and again from 2008 to 2011. He then served as Crewe's Director of Football, subsequently as Head of the Academy until October 2019, retiring aged 75. Gradi was associated with Crewe Alexandra for 36 years and was Manager for 1,359 first-team games. So highly is Gradi thought of in Crewe, he is often referred to, not as Mr Gradi, but, Mr Crewe Alexandra.

Dario Gradi is the only manager of a League club to have had a band named after him, Dario G (originally a trio led by DJ Paul Spencer) reached number two in the UK charts in 1997 with 'Sunchyme'.

Former Wrexham and Chelsea goalkeeper Eddie Niedzwiecki was a manager on four occasions but not ever permanent. In 1991, Niedzwiecki was appointed caretaker manager of Reading; in 2012 he held a similar capacity at Queens Park Rangers and, in 2018, at Stoke City. In 2019, he became caretaker boss of Reading before being appointed Assistant Manager. The period of time between Niedzwiecki first being appointed at Reading and then being appointed for second time was 28 years.

Bobby Robson was sacked as manager of Sporting Lisbon in 1993 with Sporting top of the league. Robson was not out of work long, he was immediately offered the job as manager of Porto and appointed as his assistant, the young coach/interpreter who had worked with him at Sporting, Jose Mourinho. Living in the same apartment block as Robson was a teenager whom he appointed as part of Porto's 'Sports Science and Observation' team - Andre Villas-Boas.

Clyde has provided more managers for Scotland than both Rangers and Celtic. In 1966, John Prentice left his post as Clyde manager to become the Scotland manager. In 1993, Craig Brown left Clyde to initially manage the Scotland U21 team but was then appointed manager of the national team. Though a former Rangers manager, Walter Smith, became Scotland manager after four years as manager of Everton. Jock Stein left his post as Manager of Leeds United to manage Scotland (1978) albeit Stein had a spell in charge of the national team in 1965 whilst still manager of Celtic.

How did he survive? During Jim Fallon's tenure as manager of Dumbarton, the 'Sons' went 31 games without recording a win, a period which lasted from October 1995 to September 1996.

Hardly worth putting the name on the manager's door. In 1996, Manchester City had five managers in the space of four months - Alan Ball, Asa Hartford, Steve Coppell, Phil Neal and Frank Clark.

In 2003-04, Paul Sturrock was named Division Two manager of the season even though he was, at the time, manager of Southampton in the Premier League. Sturrock joined Southampton on 3 March from Plymouth Argyle with twelve matches of the season remaining, but still won the Division Two Manager of the Season award as a result of his work at Home Park up to that point.

In 2005-06, George Burley made an excellent start to his tenure as Manager of Hearts, winning eight of his first ten matches. With Hearts top of the

Scottish Premier League, Burley was dismissed by owner Vladimir Romanov, albeit a club statement said Burley left 'by mutual consent'.

The shortest reign of a manager in English football is ten minutes. Leroy Rosenior was appointed manager of Torquay United on 17 May 2007. At the very time of his appointment, Torquay United were bought by a local consortium which installed Colin Lee as the club's new chief executive who, in turn, appointed former Torquay player, Paul Buckle as manager.

Ian Holloway won his first game as manager of Leicester City, a 2-0 defeat of Bristol City on 24 November 2007. Holloway was the first Leicester City manager to win his first game in charge of the club for over 50 years, the previous being, David Halliday, who guided Leicester to a 4-2 win over Hull City on 20 August 1955.

In December 2011, Antoine Kombouare was sacked as manager of Paris Saint-Germain with the team top of Ligue 1. PSG ended the 2010-11 season as runners-up to Montpellier.

Alan Buckley had four spells as manager of Walsall, he also had three spells as Manager of Grimsby Town, in addition to which Buckley also served the club as youth team manager. Buckley was also manager of West Bromwich Albion, Lincoln City and Rochdale. Buckley's career as a manager spanned 1978 to 2013, along with Dario Gradi (Crewe Alexandra), Alan Buckley is one of only two managers to have overseen in excess of 1,000 senior matches but not one in the Premier League or its predecessor, the First Division.

Graham Turner played 650 league matches, for Wrexham (77), Chester (218) and Shrewsbury Town (355). Turner's subsequent career as a manager spanned 36 years, during which time he was Manager of Shrewsbury Town (twice, 1978-1984 and 2010-2014), Aston Villa (1984-86), Wolverhampton Wanderers (1986-1994) and Hereford United (1995-2009 and as caretaker manager March 2010 to June 2010). Turner oversaw 1,659 matches as a manager, the most for a manager of just English clubs.

The club who had four different managers for four successive games. On 14 November 2011, Northampton Town parted company with Manager Gary Johnson. David Lee was appointed caretaker manager but was relieved of his duties following his only game in charge, a 7-2 defeat at home to Shrewsbury Town. Tim Flowers was then appointed in a caretaker capacity but having lost his only game in charge, a 4-1 defeat at Plymouth

Argyle, was replaced by Aidy Boothroyd who became Manager on a permanent basis on 30 November 2011.

Sir Alex Ferguson was has won more trophies (38) than any other manager in English football. Sir Alex oversaw 2,155 matches as a manager, 1,500 as Manager of Manchester United. He also managed East Stirling, St. Mirren, Aberdeen and Scotland. St. Mirren were the only club to sack Sir Alex, who claimed wrongful dismissal at an industrial tribunal, during which, then St. Mirren chairman, Willie Todd, described Ferguson as having 'no managerial ability'.

Sir Alex Ferguson has eight honorary degrees, from University of Salford; Robert Gordon University (Aberdeen); Glasgow Caledonian University; St. Andrews University; Manchester Metropolitan University, University of Stirling; Manchester University and Ulster University.

On 23 December 2017, following Middlesbrough's 2-1 victory at Sheffield Wednesday there followed a unique situation whereby both managers were sacked by their respective clubs - Gary Monk by Middlesbrough, Carlos Carvahal by Sheffield Wednesday.

I was there. On 21 August 2018, Gary Johnson was sacked as Manager of Cheltenham Town immediately following the club's 1-1 draw at Macclesfield Town. The author was among a group of football journalists awaiting a post-match interview with Johnson. When he appeared, Johnson informed the assembled journalists, 'I've been sacked.' Apart from being surprised Johnson had been dismissed only four matches into a new season and following a draw away from home, journalists were left wondering why the decision had not been taken when the Cheltenham party arrived home, or, the following day. As one journalist remarked, 'That's going to be one long and quiet coach journey home.'

On 24 March 2018, Graham Alexander was sacked as manager of Scunthorpe United with the team fifth in League One and occupying one of the Play-Off places. Alexander was appointed manager of Salford City but was sacked on 12 October 2020 with the team fifth in League Two and unbeaten in the League.

Chelsea have appointed eleven former players as manager - John Tait-Robertson, Tommy Docherty, Eddie McCreadie, Ken Shellito, John Hollins, David Webb, Ray Wilkins (caretaker), Roberto Di Matteo, Gianluca

Vialli, Ruud Gullit and Frank Lampard.

Three piece suits. Tony Mowbray, Sam Allardyce, Alan Pardew, John Gregory, Terry Venables and Glenn Hoddle all managed three teams or more that they used to play for. Mowbray - Middlesbrough, Celtic and Ipswich Town; Allardyce - Preston, Bolton Wanderers and Sunderland; Pardew - Charlton Athletic, Crystal Palace and Reading; John Gregory - Aston Villa, QPR, Derby County and Plymouth Argyle; Terry Venables - QPR, Spurs and England; Glen Hoddle - Swindon Town, Chelsea, Spurs and England.

Sam Allardyce has managed the most clubs in the Premier League (8) : Bolton Wanderers, Newcastle United, Blackburn Rovers, West Ham United, Sunderland, Crystal Palace, Everton and West Bromwich Albion.

Roy Hodgson managed 17 clubs and 4 international teams. Clubs - Halmstads BK, Bristol City, IK Oddevold, Orebro SK, Malmo, Neuchatel Xamax, Inter Milan, Blackburn Rovers, Grasshoppers Zurich, Copenhagen, Udinese, Viking FK, Fulham, Liverpool, West Bromwich Albion, Crystal Palace and Watford. International teams managed - Switzerland, United Arab Emirates, Finland, England (also England U21 as caretaker manager).

Arsene Wenger has an asteroid named after him. The main belt asteroid, 33179 Arsene Wenger, was discovered on 29 March 1998 by astrophysicist, Ian Griffin, an Arsenal supporter, who named his discovery after Wenger as a tribute to Arsenal's 'Invincible' season. The asteroid in question orbits between Mars and Jupiter. Wenger, however, is not the only football related person to have an asteroid named after him, there are also asteroids bearing the names of Johann Cruyff, Josef Bican, Ferenc Puskas and Michael Ballack.

On 11 December 2020, Vladimir Ivic was named 'Championship Manager of the Month' with Watford 5th in the Championship. Eight days later, Ivic was sacked.

On 6 February 2021, during Gillingham's League One match against Lincoln City, Gills' Manager, Steve Evans, picked up his sixth yellow card of the season, more than any of his players.

Three generations have a Ball. In 2020-21, Jimmy Ball took over as Manager of Forest Green Rovers. Jimmy's father, Alan, a member of England's 1966 World Cup winning team, managed, among others, Portsmouth,

Southampton, Manchester City and Stoke City; Jimmy's grandfather, Alan senior, managed Halifax Town, Preston North End and Djurgardens IF (Sweden).

In 2020-21, Daniel Farke, Norwich City, became the first overseas manager to win two Championship titles - both with Norwich.

Roy Hodgson and Ignacio Trelles (Mexico) are the only two managers to have overseen over 1,000 club games and in excess of 100 Internationals. Roy Hodgson - more than 1,100 club matches (plus one as Manager of England U21), 114 International matches. Ignacio Trelles - 1,083 club matches, 106 matches as manager/coach of Mexico.

On 4 August 2021, Louis Van Gaal was appointed as Coach (Manager) of the Netherlands for a third time.

On 27 September 2021, Dean Brennan was appointed manager of Barnet, becoming the club's 27th manager in ten seasons.

Crossing the great divide. Steve Bruce managed both Sheffield Wednesday and Sheffield United; Birmingham City, Aston Villa and West Bromwich Albion; Sunderland and Newcastle United.

Rallied round after managing. Former Spurs' manager, Andrea Villas-Boas competed in the 2018 Dakar Rally, he later competed in the Bajati Rally and, in 2021, the World Rally Championship.

Negative result. On 20 November 2021, Werder Bremen manager/coach Markus Anfang and his assistant, Florian Junger, parted ways with the club due to allegations that Anfang had used a forged COVID-19 vaccine certificate.

One lambasted, one lauded. Ole Gunnar Solskjær was appointed Manager of Manchester United (initially on an interim basis) on 19 December 2018 and sacked on 21 November 2021; Should one total the number of Premier League points won by Manchester United in Solskjær's last full season as United manager (2020-21) and those acquired in 2021-22 up to the point of his sacking (21 November 2021), it totals 91 points. Should one total the number of points accumulated by Liverpool under Jurgen Klopp in that same period, the total is 93, only two more than Manchester United won under Solskjær.

On 9 December 2021, Hibernian sacked Manager, Jack Ross, just over a week before he was due to lead them out in the Scottish League Cup Final against Celtic. The previous season Ross had guided Hibernian to a third place finish in the Scottish Premiership and the Scottish Cup Final.

Oldham's six appeal. On 22 January 2022, John Sheridan began what was his sixth spell as manager of Oldham Athletic, Sheridan's previous spells at Boundary Park were 2001 (caretaker manager), 2003-04 (caretaker), 2006-09; 2016 and 2017.

Match Officials

For over a century, linesmen, as they were then called, carried either a red or yellow flag. The colours denoted seniority, the senior linesman carried a red flag, his junior, yellow. The senior linesman was always assigned to the side of the pitch which contained the dug-outs and, eventually, substitute benches.

The first time a referee used a whistle was in 1878 during a friendly match between Nottingham Forest and Sheffield Norfolk. Previously referees used hand signals to indicate decisions. The FA sanctioned the use of whistles by referees in 1879 and commissioned Joseph Hudson of the Acme Whistle Company in London to manufacture all whistles for use in Football League, FA Cup and International matches.

For decades the referee of the FA Cup Final was offered the option of a fee or a medal to commemorate officiating the Final. No referee ever accepted the match fee until the ruling was changed in 1978 to provide both.

Strange combination. On 3 December 1910, two vicars officiated in the Division Two game between West Bromwich Albion and Blackpool (0-1). The referee was the Right Reverend J. Marsh and one of his linesman, Right Reverend W. Strange.

Referee sent off. On 22 September 1930, the annual challenge match between a Glasgow X1 and Sheffield X1 came to a halt when referee, Mr J. Thompson of Burnbank, was called off the field by Glasgow FA officials. Mr Thompson was wearing a white blazer and shirt and black shorts, the same colour of strip as the Sheffield X1, who complained they were constantly mistaking him for a team-mate. Mr Thompson returned later in a strip that did not clash and continued to officiate.

Arthur Bookim was a referee in the Football League from 1951 to 1957. Also, in the 1950s, one of the most popular referees in the Scottish League was Charlie Faultless. A little later, in the 1960s/70s, there was Maurice Fussey in the Football League.

Politics and football do mix. Having officiated in non-league football, Denis Howell was promoted to Football League Linesman in 1951-52 and graduated to become a first class referee from 1956 to 1966. For most of his time as a Football League official, Howell also served as a Member of Parliament, having been elected as the Labour member for Birmingham All Saints from 1955 to 1959, and, for Birmingham Small Heath from 1961 until his retirement in 1992. Whilst a Football League referee, Howell also held what was his first cabinet appointment, Minister for Sport (1964-69) in Harold Wilson's government.

On 21 November 1953, Huddersfield Town protested to the Football League following their 1-0 defeat to Tottenham Hotspur at White Hart Lane. Huddersfield claimed the Spurs' goal, scored by Len Duquemin, should never have been allowed. Spurs had won a corner, taken by Ron Baily. Baily's corner struck the referee, the ball rebounding back to Baily who advanced and crossed for Duquemin to score. Huddersfield claimed the goal should never have been allowed as Baily, in taking the corner, had touched the ball twice without it being touched by another player. The Football League rejected Huddersfield's protest and allowed the goal and result to stand.

Up until 1954, referees wore blazers when officiating matches. At the commencement of 1954-55, referees were kitted in black shirts and shorts. No British club then wore black shirts so there would never be a colour clash.

Hill tows the line. On 16 September 1972, TV commentator Jimmy Hill (a qualified referee) took over as linesman during Arsenal's First Division match against Liverpool following an injury to match official Michael Hunt. The game ended goalless.

Steve Baines' playing career lasted fifteen years during which time he played for Nottingham Forest, Huddersfield Town, Bradford City, Walsall, Bury (loan), Scunthorpe United and Chesterfield. Baines retired as a player in 1987 and took up refereeing. Baines graduated through the leagues and after less than ten years refereeing, was appointed by the Football League. Baines went on to enjoy eight seasons as a match referee. During his time on the League list, Baines took charge of matches involving most of his former clubs, bar Chesterfield, the town in which he resided.

Only two other referees have had experience as professional players in English leagues, Bob Matthewson and John Lloyd. Matthewson played for Bolton Wanderers and Lincoln City, and went on to officiate at some of the most memorable and talked-about matches of the 1970s - he was senior linesman for the 1970 FA Cup Final between Chelsea and Leeds United; referee for the 'marathon' 1972 League Cup semi-final between Chelsea and Stoke City, and, the 1974 Charity Shield match between Leeds United and Liverpool during which he sent off Leeds' Billy Bremner and Liverpool's Kevin Keegan. Matthewson was portrayed in the film 'The Damned United' by Peter Quinn, secretary of the Blackburn junior league club, Sporting Athletic.

John Lloyd played for Wrexham between 1965 and 1967, after which he took up refereeing. In addition to officiating in the Football League, Lloyd took charge of many European and International matches before being one of the first referees appointed to the newly created Premier League. On retirement, he became an assessor of referees for the Football League.

One of the most wonderfully named referees, Maurice Fussey, was due to take charge of the First Division game between Newcastle United and Liverpool on 21 August 1971. Having caught a train to Newcastle, Mr Fussey was in the process of removing his bag from the luggage rack when the bag hit him on the head. The official recoiled so quickly he damaged two vertebrae in his back. As a consequence, Mr Fussey was unable to referee the game.

Celebrated Scottish and International referee, Tiny Wharton, was 6'4" tall and weighed eighteen stone. Wharton refereed four Scottish Cup Finals, four League Cup Finals, 16 Internationals and 24 European games including the 1962 European Cup Winners Cup Final between Atletico Madrid and Fiorentina.

The International Football Association Board (IFAB) introduced the fourth official to football in 1991. Initially the remit of the fourth official was that of a substitute official, replacing any of the match officials should they be injured or ill. The remit quickly expanded to overseeing substitutions, maintaining order in the dug-outs and technical areas, keeping a record of goals and cards and indicating time added. Although not a part of the official remit, fourth officials occasionally take it upon themselves to assist the referee regarding incidents he may not have seen.

From 1891, assistant match officials were known as linesmen. This changed in 1996 to non-gender specific, referee assistants.

Referee wore shirt of home team. The Premier League match between Leeds United and Newcastle United on 18 October 1997, saw match official David Ellery refereeing the game wearing a Leeds United shirt. Ellery's green shirt clashed with Newcastle's away kit, as Ellery had no alternative referee top, he was kitted-out with one of Leeds United's blue shirts from their away kit.

In 2006, Mike Dean declined the invitation to referee the FA Cup Final as the game involved Liverpool. As Dean lived on the Wirral he did not wish to be accused of impartiality.

The first female official to referee a League game was Amy Fearn, who, following injury to the appointed referee, took charge of the final twenty minutes of the Championship game between Coventry City and Nottingham Forest on 9 February 2010.

The first female referee to be appointed to take charge of a League game was Rebecca Welch, who refereed the League Two game between Harrogate Town and Port Vale on 5 April 2021.

In 2020-21, Premier League referees were on a basic salary circa £70k per annum, plus £1,000 for each match officiated. In Leagues One and Two, referees were paid £450 for each game officiated, the fourth official, £130.

On 12 December 2020, referee John Busby booked Northampton Town's Joe Martin for time-wasting after only 25 minutes of their game against Crewe Alexandra at the Alexandra Stadium. Northampton were leading 1-0 at the time.

Own Goals

On 6 October 1923, Oldham's Sam Wynne scored four goals in Oldham Athletic's 3-2 victory over Manchester United. Wynne scored from a penalty and a direct-free kick for Oldham and twice put through his own net.

Middlesbrough's Bobby Stuart scored seven own goals in a single season - 1934-35.

On Christmas Day 1954, George Underwood, Kenny Boyle and Danny Murphy of Rochdale all scored own goals in their team's 7-2 defeat at Carlisle United in Division Three North.

The only known instance of players being credited with 'half-a-goal' occurred on 18 December 1954 during Leicester City's 3-1 defeat at Chelsea in Division One. Leicester players Stan Milburn and Jack Froggatt were adjudged to have touched the ball simultaneously whilst attempting a goal-line clearance and were credited with 'One-half-own-goal each'.

On 17 December 1955, Arsenal led Blackpool 4-0 in the dying moments at Highbury when a whistle was blown in the crowd. Thinking this was the full-time whistle, Arsenal full-back Dennis Evans, who had possession of the ball, turned and kicked it into his own net. The referee had no alternative but to award the goal. Stanley Matthews informed the author, 'In all my time in football, I never saw such a bizarre goal.'

Danny Malloy spent six seasons with Cardiff City (1955-61) playing 225 league matches. Malloy scored once for Cardiff, from the penalty spot in a 3-1 defeat against Manchester United on Boxing Day 1956. During his time with Cardiff City, Malloy scored 14 own goals, including two when playing against Liverpool on 22 August 1959.

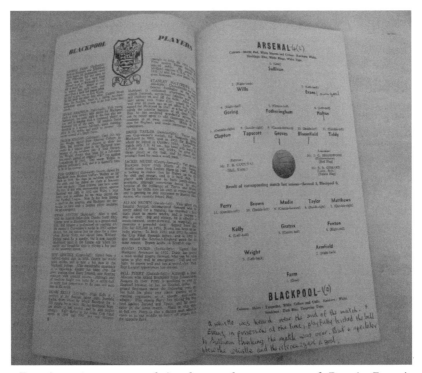

Eye-witness account noted in the match programme of Dennis Evans' extraordinary own goal when playing for Arsenal against Blackpool. Stan Matthews informed the author, 'In all my time in football, I never saw such a bizarre goal.'

On 25 September 1976, Sheffield United's Colin Franks scored both goals in United's 1-1 draw with Blackburn Rovers, on the same day, Plymouth Argyle's Paul Mariner did likewise in Argyle's 1-1 draw with Bolton Wanderers.

Aston Villa defender Chris Nichol scored all four goals in his side's 2-2 draw with Leicester City on 20 March 1976.

On 23 December 1889, George Morton of Grimsby Town scored an own goal when playing against Leicester Fosse (then a non-league club). Leicester, however, were impressed by Morton's performance and promptly signed him. On 20 March 1993, Paul Groves of Grimsby Town scored an own goal when playing against Leicester City and, days after the game, Groves signed for Leicester City.

212

On 3 January 1997, Torquay United's Pat Kruse headed into his own net after only eight seconds of the Division Four game against Cambridge United.

Leicester City scored 8 own goals in Premier League games during 2003-04.

In 2007, Northern Ireland's hopes of qualifying for the finals of the 2008 European Championship ended with two last-minute own goals in successive matches. On 8 September, Chris Baird put through his own net in the 90th minute to give Latvia a 1-0 victory. Four days later in Reykjavik, Keith Gillespie scored an 89th minute own goal to give Iceland a 2-1 victory.

On 19 March 2021, Tottenham's Sergio Reguilon scored an own goal in Spurs' 2-1 home defeat to Aston Villa. Reguilon's faux pas was the 37th Premier League own goal of the season and the 1,000th own goal since the Premier League was inaugurated in 1992-93.

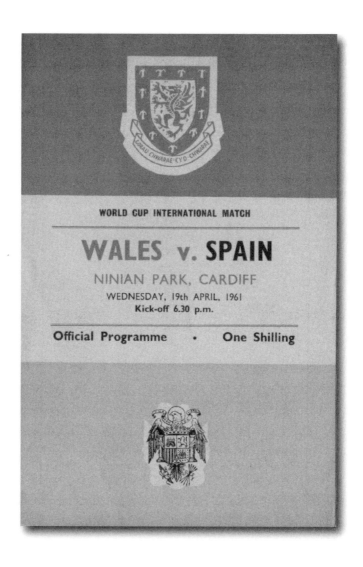

WORLD CUP INTERNATIONAL MATCH

WALES v. SPAIN

NINIAN PARK, CARDIFF

WEDNESDAY, 19th APRIL, 1961

Kick-off 6.30 p.m.

Official Programme · **One Shilling**

214

Players

Jack Devey, who scored 168 goals in 268 league matches for Aston Villa (1891-1902), also played cricket for Warwickshire and professional baseball for Aston Villa in the National Baseball League of Great Britain. Following his retirement as a player in 1902, Devey became an Aston Villa director, serving the club for a further 32 years, during which time he also worked for Villa as a scout.

Dogged Jackie became Iron legend. Jackie Brownsword, who made 791 appearances for Scunthorpe United (1947-1964), began his career with Hull City (1946-47). Brownsword made eleven first team appearances for Hull only to leave the club (initially for non-league Frickley Colliery) following an exchange of words with Hull manager, Major Frank Buckley, after accidentally sitting on Buckley's dog on the team coach when travelling to an away game.

Manchester City goalkeeper, Bert Trautman, is the only player to have been voted the Football Writer's Association 'Footballer of the Year' (1956) who was never awarded an international cap. In the case of Trautman, for West Germany.

In 1958-59, Fourth Division Gateshead had two players by the name of Ken Smith. To differentiate, the longest serving player, who served Gateshead from 1952 to 1959, was designated as being Ken Smith 1. The relatively new arrival, was ascribed, Ken Smith 2. On 29 November 1958, Gateshead defeated Northampton Town 4-1 at Redheugh in Division Four. Both Smiths scored, the longest serving player scoring twice. In the classified results, Gateshead's three scorers appeared as - K.Smith (1) 2, K.Smith (2) 1, Baldridge.

In January 2022, Nantwich Town goalkeeper, Matty Gould, was called up to the New Zealand international team for games against Jordan and Uzbekistan. Nantwich Town were in the Northern Premier League Premier Division, the seventh tier of English football. Matty Gould (on loan from Altrincham at the time), is the son of former Celtic, Coventry City and Preston goalkeeper, Jonathan Gould, and the grandson of former Arsenal, Coventry City, West Bromwich Albion and Wolves striker Bobby Gould who, as a manager, guided Wimbledon to FA Cup success over Liverpool in the Final of 1988.

Max Woosman played for Chelsea (1913-14) and Manchester City (1919-1925), captaining City in his latter three seasons. Woosman also won Olympic gold and silver medals at the 1920 Olympics in tennis (doubles and mixed doubles), that same summer he also won the doubles at Wimbledon. Woosman was also a good cricketer and scored a century (144) and 33 not out when playing for the Public Schools XI against the MCC at Lords. During a visit to Hollywood, Woosman defeated Charlie Chaplin at table tennis, playing with a butter knife instead of a bat. Woosman would have enjoyed a more prolific football career but for the First World War, in which he fought at Gallipoli and on the Western Front, the latter alongside his friend, the poet, Siegfried Sassoon. Despite his athletic prowess, Woosman was a heavy smoker all his life, he died of respiratory failure in 1965.

Spike the ad' for a club doctor. In 1919-20, Chelsea signed David Cameron and John Bell from Scottish club Queens Park, both qualified as doctors whilst at Stamford Bridge. There was a precedent, in 1909-10, Chelsea had signed Ken McKenzie for a fee of £25 from Inverness Thistle. When McKenzie left Chelsea, he completed his qualification as a doctor.

Mustafa Mansour played in goal for Egypt in the 1934 World Cup and again at the summer Olympics in Berlin in 1936. In 1937, Mansour signed for Scottish club Queens Park, the first non-British or Irish player to play in the Scottish League. Mansour remained Queens Park's regular goalkeeper until the outbreak of WW2. He subsequently became a minister in the Egyptian government.

Len Shackleton played for Bradford Park Avenue against Leeds United in the War League North on Christmas morning 1940 and, in the afternoon, as a 'guest' player for Bradford City against Huddersfield Town.

Maurice Edelston made his debut as an amateur for Fulham in 1935, he then joined Brentford as an amateur in 1937 from whom he signed for

Reading in 1939. The war intervened after which Edelston re-joined Reading signing his first professional contract in July 1947. Thus, Edelston signed his first professional contract twelve years after having made his Football League debut. Edelston played 205 League matches for Reading scoring 72 goals, he then joined Northampton Town. He retired as a player in 1953 and became a well-known football commentator for BBC radio and Southern Television.

Rochdale's Joe Hargreaves was completely deaf. Hargreaves was 30 years old when he signed for Rochdale from non-league Rossendale United in 1945-46 and went on to score 25 goals in 28 appearances including a brace in each of his first four matches.

Gentle giant of Alice Street. Undaunted by a head wound, John Charles fends off home defender, Ken Thompson, to head for goal during Cardiff City's 1-1 draw at Ipswich Town in Division Two on 12 December 1964. The grounded Ipswich 'keeper is Jim Thorburn; the Cardiff forward with his back to camera is Keith Ellis. As with Stanley Matthews and Gary Lineker, John Charles was never cautioned or sent off during his career. Former referee Clive Thomas said of John Charles, 'If you had 22 players of John's calibre, there would be no need for referees, only time-keepers'.

Play too many games? Care he not. In 1946-47, Johnny Carey played four games in a week, one in the first Division and three Internationals. On 3rd May 1947 for Manchester United v Liverpool; 4th May for The Republic of Ireland v Portugal; 6th May for Rest of Europe v Holland; 10th May for Rest of Europe v Great Britain at Hampden Park.

George Brooke, Aston Villa half-back of the late 1950s, was 5'0" tall.

Out of the left field. Les Ames (Leyton Orient), John Arnold (Fulham), Denis Compton (Arsenal), Bill Edrich (Spurs) and Laurie Fishlock (Millwall), all played at outside-left for their respective London clubs and all played Test cricket for England.

Never wandered from Bolton. Nat Lofthouse joined Bolton Wanderers in 1939 and went on to serve the club for 72 years until his death in 2011. In addition to playing over 500 senior games for Bolton, Lofthouse fulfilled a variety of roles at the club including manager, trainer, chief coach, chief scout, executive manager and president. In 1998, train operator, Virgin, named locomotive number 47807 'Lion of Vienna' in honour of Lofthouse.

Bert Trautman (Manchester City) is often referenced as a foreign player in English football after World War Two but there were several others. Among them, Marcel Gaillard, a Belgian, who, following the war, played for Tonbridge before signing for Crystal Palace in 1948 and subsequently signing for Portsmouth in 1951 for whom he made 59 appearances. Alois 'Eric' Eisentrager, like Trautman, was a POW who stayed on in England after the war. Eisentrager initially played semi-pro' for Herne Bay, then Trowbridge Town, before signing for Bristol City in 1949 for whom he went on to make 228 League appearances (57 goals). Eisentrager was a member of the Bristol City team which won promotion to the Second Division in 1955, he later played for Merthyr Tydfil and Chelmsford City, retiring as a player in 1960. Alois Eisentrager never returned to Germany, marrying a Welsh lady with whom he had four children. In the same Bristol City team as Eisentrager, was John 'Jackie' Boyd, formerly of the US air force who, after the war, played for Gloucester City before signing for Bristol City in 1950. Another German POW to try football in England was Frederik Neumann who played for Hallam in Yorkshire and signed for Blackpool in 1949-50.

Town like Alice Street. Alice Street in Cwmbwrla on the outskirts of Swansea, produced several notable footballers, all of whom signed for Swansea Town. Among them Jackie Roberts (Bolton Wanderers and Swansea Town); Ernie

Jones (Swansea Town, Tottenham Hotspur, Southampton and Bristol City); John Charles (Swansea Town, Leeds United, Juventus, Roma and Cardiff City), John's brother, Mel (Swansea Town, Arsenal and Cardiff City); and Mel Nurse (Swansea Town, Middlesbrough and Swindon Town).

Electric winger. Billy Bingham signed for Sunderland from Glentoran in October 1950 for £8,000. Sunderland arranged for Bingham to complete his apprenticeship as an electrician in the Austin and Pickersgill shipyard on the River Wear, Sunderland manager, Bill Murray, being keen for the winger to have a trade should professional football not work out for him. Bingham went on to make 419 league appearances spread across four clubs, Sunderland, Luton Town, Everton and Port Vale. Bingham also was manager of Northern Ireland and Greece international teams, as well as Southport, Plymouth Argyle, Everton and Mansfield Town. Whilst with Southport, in addition to his managerial duties, Bingham rewired the dressing rooms, office and physio room at Haigh Avenue.

Johnny Haynes first signed as an amateur for Fulham in 1950 and was to remain with the club for all his football career, retiring in 1970. Haynes made 658 senior appearances for Fulham and was capped 56 times by England, 22 of those international appearances as captain. In 1958, Haynes was a key signatory to a letter (published in 'The Times' 17 July 1958) opposing 'apartheid in world sport, in particular South Africa' and calling for, 'the principle of racial equality' to be adhered to globally. In 1952-53, Haynes made his first team debut in a 1-1 draw at home to Southampton in Division Two on Boxing Day 1952 and quickly established himself as a player of great talent and promise. On 3 April 1952, the Fulham chairman, comedian and TV star, Tommy Trinder, was appearing in an Easter show on the south coast and was invited to attend Portsmouth's home match against Wolves by the Portsmouth President, Field Marshall Viscount Montgomery of Alamein. Following the game, the two men were conversing in the Portsmouth boardroom when Trinder heard on the wireless, Fulham had won 2-1 at West Ham United, followed by a match report in which the commentator spoke in glowing terms of Johnny Haynes. 'That young Haynes is a marvellous player,' remarked Trinder, 'he's the best passer of a ball I've ever seen; has an eye for goal, fit and strong, tireless worker, mark my words, young Haynes will play for England one day.' 'How old is this Haynes?' asked Viscount Montgomery. 'Eighteen.' replied Trinder. 'Eighteen?' said Montgomery sternly, dampening Trinder's ardour, 'What about his National Service?' 'Well, that's the only sad thing about him,' replied Trinder, thinking on his feet and taking a long draw on his cigar, 'He's a cripple!' (as told to the author by Johnny Haynes).

John Hewie played in excess of 500 matches for Charlton Athletic during the 1950s and 60s, the majority as a full-back but four as goalkeeper, deputising when first-choice Mike Rose was injured. On 21 August 1965, after 11 minutes of Charlton's Second Division match at Bolton Wanderers, Hewie took over in goal from the injured Rose, who became the first player to be substituted in an English league match. It was during the aforementioned match that Hewie demonstrated the rare feat of a goalkeeper, in the space of some thirty seconds, touching the ball three times, each touch at a different end of the field, without any of his team mates ever having made contact with the ball. In the dying embers of the game, stand-in goalkeeper, Hewie sent a long kick down the field deep into Bolton's penalty area. Under pressure from Charlton forwards, the ball was put out of play for a corner by Bolton defender, Bob Napier. With Bolton leading 4-2, Hewie went upfield to lend support to his team mates for the corner. It was Hewie who met the subsequent corner, heading the ball against the Bolton crossbar only for Bolton to take possession of the loose ball and launch a swift counterattack. Hewie, having raced back downfield, arrived in his penalty box just in time to execute a save from a goal-bound shot from Bolton's Warwick Rimmer.

Ins and outs of Duff. In the early 1950s. Willie Duff played as a full-back and centre-half for Scottish junior club Slateford Athletic. Duff deputised in goal when the regular 'keeper didn't turn up for a game and was spotted by East of Scotland League side, Easthouses Lily, to whom he was subsequently transferred as a goalkeeper. In 1952, Duff signed for Hearts and, in 1958, was transferred to Charlton Athletic for whom he made 213 League appearances. In 1962-63, having lost his first team place to Peter Wakeham, Duff was appointed captain of the Charlton reserve team for whom he played both as a centre-half and centre-forward before joining Peterborough United in the summer of 1963 - as a goalkeeper.

Abe Rosenthal made 225 league appearances between 1939 and 1956 and featured in six transfer deals yet his transfers featured only three clubs, five of which featured only two clubs. At the end of 1946-47, Rosenthal was sold by Tranmere Rovers to Bradford City. In 1949-50, Bradford City then sold Rosenthal to Oldham Athletic. Rosenthal's spell with Oldham was brief and later in 1949, he was sold to Tranmere Rovers. In 1952, Tranmere sold Rosenthal to Bradford City where he remained until the end of 1953-54 when he was sold back to Tranmere Rovers, his third spell with the club. Rosenthal had a season with Tranmere but was sold at the beginning of 1955-56 for what was to be his third spell with Bradford City. Following his retirement as a player, Rosenthal began an ice cream business on Merseyside and also worked as a scout, first for Bradford City then Tranmere Rovers.

Tony McNamara played in all four divisions in 1957-58 - Everton (First Division), Liverpool (Second Division), Crewe Alexandra (Fourth Division), finally, Bury (Third Division).

On 20 September 1958, Jimmy Hill played for Fulham against Derby County in a Second Division match at Craven Cottage. Immediately after the game, Hill drove to Wimbledon, where he appeared in the Mixed-Doubles Final of the London Parks Tennis Tournament, having previously lost in the semi-finals of the Men's Singles.

In the late 1950s, Hindley Green was a small village just outside Wigan of less than 400 people yet, in that time, produced three players who went on to play for Bolton Wanderers, Syd Farrimond, Graham Cunliffe and Roy Wilkinson.

The appeal of cricketers. In 1956-57, four Charlton Athletic players were also County cricketers - Stuart Leary, Sid O'Linn and Derek Ufton (all Kent) and Mickey Stewart (Surrey).

Didn't have the heart to tell them. In 1960, as a 15-year old, Eric Stevenson signed for Hearts from Scottish junior club Edina Hearts. Stevenson continued to play for his junior club until ruled ineligible after having been registered by Hearts as a professional on his 17th birthday. Stevenson, however, maintained he'd signed no form other than his original one as a 15-year old. He returned all the weekly cheques Hearts kept sending him and was granted his release by the SFA, who also fined Hearts for submitting 'an irregular form'. Stevenson signed for Hibernian and went on to play nigh on 300 games for the Easter Road club.

Hand sewn, home grown. In 1960-61, seventeen of Notts County's 21 professional players were one-club men, having played for no other club up to that time, they included goalkeeper George Smith and Tony Hateley.

The only part-time professional player to have been voted Footballer of the Year is Bill Slater (Wolves) in 1960. Slater was also the last amateur to appear in an FA Cup Final, for Blackpool, in the 1951 Final against Newcastle United.

Sunderland pre-season photograph of 1962-63, showing Brian Clough's impish humour.

Derek Tapscott, whose clubs included Arsenal (1953-58) and Cardiff City (1958-65) and who won 14 caps for Wales, was one of sixteen children but the only one to have a career in football.

The achievements of Brian Clough as a manager are well known. Clough scored 251 league goals in 274 appearances for Middlesbrough and Sunderland before sustaining an injury whilst playing for Sunderland against Bury on Boxing Day 1962, one which effectively ended his playing career.

From avoiding the net to hitting the net. Top British tennis player and member of the GB Davis Cup team, Mike Sangster, signed for Torquay United in August 1960. Sangster scored four goals on his debut for Torquay reserves in an 11-0 victory over Barnstaple in the Western League.

Charlie Hurley (right), pictured on his Sunderland debut at Blackpool on 5 October 1957 which resulted in a 7-0 win for the Seasiders. In Hurley's second match, Sunderland lost 6-0 at Burnley. Hurley quickly overcame his inauspicious start to his Sunderland career, going on to make 401 appearances for the club. In 1964, Hurley, lost by one vote to Bobby Moore in the FWA's 'Footballer of the Year Award', the only Second Division player to have ever featured in the top three of the prestigious award. In 1980, Sunderland supporters voted Hurley the club's 'Player of the Century'.

Billy Liddell signed for Liverpool in 1938 and remained with the club for 23 years until his retirement as a player in 1961. Liddell made 534 appearances for Liverpool (228 goals) which would have been more but for WW2 in which he served as a navigator in the RAF (617 Squadron among others). Liddell also won 29 caps for Scotland. Most of Liddell's career at Liverpool was as a part-time professional as he worked for a local accountancy company and, in 1958, became a Justice of the Peace. Following his retirement, Liddell became Bursar at Liverpool University. Liddell is the oldest player to have scored for Liverpool, at 38 years and 55 days, netting in a 5-1 win over Stoke City on 5 March 1960.

Leeds United are thought to be the first club to include two players of African heritage in a League match. Gerry Francis and Albert Johanneson were in the Leeds team that played Stoke City in a Second Division match on 15 April 1961.

Cliff Lloyd, was secretary of the PFA from 1953 to 1981. Lloyd, along with Jimmy Hill, was largely responsible for the abolition of the maximum wage for footballers and the Football League's retain and transfer system in the early sixties. As a player Lloyd played for Brentford and Fulham, as did Jimmy Hill.

Harold Davis began his career with East Fife (1950-56). Davis' football career, like many others of his generation, was interrupted by his national service. Davis served with the Black Watch in the Korean War during which he was shot in both the abdomen and foot. So severe were his injuries, Davis spent two years recuperating in hospital. Undaunted, Davis returned to East Fife in 1956 determined to continue his football career. Within three months Davis joined Rangers, for whom he went on to make 272 appearances in all competitions, won seven Scottish titles, the Scottish Cup, League Cup (the latter twice) and appeared in the 1961 European Cup Winners Cup Final against Fiorentina.

In 1963-64, Alan Mullery played more League games than his club. Tottenham Hotspur played 42 League matches, whereas Mullery played 43. Mullery made 34 appearances for Fulham, from whom he was transferred to Spurs, where he subsequently made 9 appearances in the League.

To serve them all my days. John Atyeo spent almost his entire career playing for Bristol City (1951-66). Atyeo played 645 senior matches for Bristol City scoring 351 goals, he also won six caps for England scoring a highly respectable five goals. Yet for much of his career Atyeo was a part-time

John Atyeo spent almost his entire career playing for Bristol City (1951-66).

professional, training at Bristol City on Tuesday and Thursday nights. Atyeo played part-time professional football at Bristol City from 1951-58 whilst working and qualifying as a quantity surveyor. In 1963, he reverted back to part-time football in order to study and qualify as a mathematics teacher and was a member of the Bristol City team which won promotion to Division Two (Championship equivalent) in 1964-65. Following his retirement from football in 1966, Atyeo became a teacher at Kingdown School, Warminster, where he served for over 20 years rising to House Master then Deputy Headteacher.

Part-time career developed. Gary Talbot signed for Chester as a 25-year-old in 1963 after manager Peter Hauser saw him play in a charity match. Within days Talbot made his Football League debut, scoring in a 3-0 win over Newport County, he then scored both goals in a 2-2 draw with Barrow, ending the season with 23 goals. The following season, he scored 35 goals for Chester. Talbot was a prolific goalscorer in two spells with Chester and one at Crewe Alexandra. He was a part-time professional footballer as he had a successful photography business in Chester. When he retired from football, Talbot travelled the world photographing world leaders, the Royal family and Hollywood film stars. He gained international renown for his photographs of Princess Diana.

In 1964, Jim Standen won an FA Cup Winners medal as West Ham United's goalkeeper and a County Championship winners medal with Worcestershire as their wicket-keeper. When his playing days were over, Standen emigrated to the USA and became successful in business, his car registration is WHU6364.

How green was his Valley. Jim Fryatt began his career at Charlton Athletic in 1957, from where he went on to become the archetypal football journeyman. Fryatt was a prolific goalscorer in the lower divisions, establishing a Football League record when he scored after only four seconds for Bradford Park Avenue against Tranmere Rovers on 25 April 1964. Following his retirement as a player, Fryatt emigrated to the USA and worked for many years as a croupier in a Las Vegas casino before becoming a maintenance man at The Valley golf club in Vegas.

Mick Cullerton can lay claim to having been signed by three of the greatest names in British football. In the 1960s, Cullerton was signed by Jock Stein (Hibernian), Sir Stanley Matthews (Port Vale) and Brian Clough (Derby County).

Luton Town signed goalkeeper Tony Read from Peterborough United in March 1965. Read arrived at Kenilworth Road with a broken foot sustained when playing for Peterborough reserves as a forward during which time he scored six goals in seven Football Combination matches. Once fit again, Luton initially tried Read as a forward, he went on to score 12 goals in 20 starts including a hat-trick in the 5-1 win over against Notts County on 20 November 1965. Read reverted back to his accustomed position in goal for the remainder of the season in which he was Luton's third highest goalscorer behind John O'Rourke (32) and Ray Whittaker (15).

TONY READ Came to Luton in March 1965. To show his versatility he last season made 35 appearances in the forward line scoring 12 goals besides 6 appearances in goal.

GERALD KING A Welshman by birth, he played for his Country both as a Schoolboy and at Youth International level. Has played for Cardiff and Torquay, from whom he was transferred in June, 1966.

RAY WHITTAKER He gained England Youth International Caps in 1962 and 1963 and when we were in need of a left wing he was persuaded to join us in March, 1964. He went straight into the First Team and held his place ever since.

Extract of pen pictures of Luton Town players from Hartlepool United programme 1966-67 acknowledging Tony Read's versatility.

Jim Brogan made 213 league appearances for Jock Stein's highly successful Celtic teams of the late 1960s and early 70s. Brogan won seven consecutive Scottish League Championship medals, four Scottish Cups, three League Cups and was a member of the Celtic team which contested the 1970 European Cup Final. Whilst with Celtic, Brogan qualified as a chartered accountant and began what was to be a successful car sales company.

Pompey put through the Mills. In 1966, Portsmouth disbanded their Youth system - 'Principally for financial reasons, also, it is our considered opinion, none of the young players released have what it takes to progress to a meaningful career in professional football.' One of the young Portsmouth players released was Mick Mills, who was taken on by Ipswich Town and went on to play over 600 matches for Ipswich, over 100 for Southampton and captain England.

Class trio. In the late 1960s, Rodney Fern (Leicester City, Luton Town, Chesterfield and Rotherham United) and Vic Halom (an FA Cup winner with Sunderland in 1973) sat next to one another in class when at secondary school in Burton-on-Trent. For some school subjects, the boy who sat in front of the pair was Jeff Bourne, whose clubs would include Derby County, Crystal Palace, Sheffield United and Seattle Sounders.

He was a lion then a tiger. Tom Wilson was a fixture in the Millwall team between 1961 and 1967 from whom he joined Hull City (1967-1971). In July 1971, Wilson joined Northern Premier League club, Goole Town, for whom he made 350 appearances whilst studying and training to be a solicitor. Wilson left Goole Town in 1979 to focus on his legal career but returned to Hull City in 1984 as a coach. In the ensuing nine-years, Wilson served Hull City as a coach, assistant manager, company secretary and on three occasions as caretaker manager. Wilson returned to the legal profession in 1993.

Donald Ford made 254 league appearances for Heart of Midlothian between 1964 and 1976 (93 goals). In his first three seasons in the first team with Hearts, Ford was an amateur player, combining football with his studies to be a chartered accountant. Ford won nine caps (11 goals) for the Scotland Amateur team and three caps at full International level. Ford was also an accomplished cricketer, whilst at Hearts he played regularly for the West Lothian County side and continued to play cricket when his football days were over. In 1980, Ford was selected for the Scotland cricket team to become the only player to have represented Scotland at amateur level in football and full international level at both football and cricket.

Graham Schofield, who played centre-half for Oldham Athletic (1969-70) was just 5'6" tall. Schofield went on to become something of a club legend at non-league Mossley.

One minute Constable's 'The Valley Farm' the next the Valley Parade. Ces Podd made 565 league and cup appearances for Bradford City between 1970 and 1984. Podd made his City debut on 26 September 1970 in a 1-0 win at Chesterfield whilst still a student at Bradford College of Art.

Dai the Derwydd. Goalkeeper, Dai Davies, whose clubs included Swansea City, Everton, Wrexham, Tranmere Rovers and who won 52 caps for Wales was a Druid, he was initiated into the Welsh 'Gorsedd of Bards' when a player at Wrexham in 1978.

Far from his swan song. Giorgio Chinaglia, who won Serie A with Lazio, scored a total of 435 goals in 413 matches for New York Cosmos (1976-1983) and played for Italy in the 1974 World Cup Finals in Germany, began his career at Swansea Town (1962-66).

In the 1970s, Ted McDougall and Phil Boyer formed a strike partnership at four different clubs, York City, Bournemouth, Norwich City and Southampton.

Graham French, whose clubs included Luton Town (182 league appearances) and Shrewsbury Town led an off-the-pitch life atypical of a professional footballer. Whilst with Luton Town, French received a three-year prison sentence in 1970. Upon his release, French attempted to resurrect his career at Luton but prison life had taken its toll and he was released in 1973. In 1976, French signed for Southport under the assumed name of Graham Lafite but only made only two appearances before being released.

Forbes rich list of Norwich achievement. Duncan Forbes played 270 league matches for Colchester United (1961-68) before his transfer to Norwich City. Forbes was to serve Norwich City for 33 years, as a player (1968-1981) making 357 league and cup appearances, captaining Norwich to promotion to the First Division for the first time (1972) and to two League Cup Finals (1973 and 1975); he then served the club as commercial executive (seven years), followed by thirteen years as chief scout.

Turned out nice again for him. Paul Fletcher played 293 league games for Burnley (1971-80), he also played for Bolton Wanderers and Blackpool.

Following his retirement as a player (at Blackpool, 1981), Fletcher became one of Europe's leading authorities on the construction of new football stadiums, overseeing the construction of the McAlpine Stadium (Huddersfield Town), the Reebok Stadium (Bolton Wanderers) and Ricoh Arena (Coventry City). Fletcher was co-founder of the University and College of Football Business, originally located at Turf Moor (Burnley) now at the Etihad Stadium (Manchester City), and of its sister campus at Wembley Stadium. Fletcher is an active member of the George Formby Society.

And a cleaner to boot. In 1975, Craig Johnston, aged 16, arrived from Australia for a trial with Middlesbrough. Johnston's trial was extended but he had run out of money. To support himself, Johnston worked as a cleaner and slept in a converted coal-shed at the back of a nearby hotel. Johnston went on to enjoy a successful career with Middlesbrough and particularly so with Liverpool. Following retirement as a player, Johnston designed the prototype Adidas Predator football boot.

Phil Boyer is one of those rare players to have played in excess of 100 league matches for four different clubs - York City (109 games, 1968-70); Bournemouth (140 games, 1970-74); Norwich City (116 games, 1974-77) and Southampton (138 games, 1977-80).

Top-flight and tales. John Hollins began his career at Chelsea in 1961 and played his final league match, in what was his second spell at Chelsea, in 1984. Hollins played 465 league games for Chelsea, in addition to which he played 151 league games for Queens Park Rangers (1975-79) and 127 league matches for Arsenal (1979-83). In total Hollins played 939 senior games, 714 of which were in the First Division, more than any other outfield player in the history of English top flight football.

Experienced the highs and lows. Lee Dixon was in the Chester team that finished bottom of the Football League in 1983-84. The club was so strapped for cash, Dixon was among a number of Chester players who had to wash their kit themselves. Little under four years later Dixon was playing for Arsenal with whom he won two First Division Championship medals (1988-89 and 1990-91), two Premier League titles (1997-98 and 2001-02), three FA Cup winners medals (1992-93, 1997-98 and 2001-02) and a European Cup Winners Cup medal (1993-94).

Phil Sproson made 500 senior appearances for Port Vale before joining Birmingham City in 1989. Phil's uncle, Roy Sproson, made a total of 842 senior appearances for Port Vale between 1949 and 1972. A total of 1,342 senior games for a single club from just two players.

Matt Le Tissier scored 47 penalties from 48 attempts for Southampton between 1986 and 2002. The only penalty Le Tissier did not convert was an effort saved by Nottingham Forest 'keeper Mark Crossley on 24 March 1993.

Malcolm Shotton began the 1987-88 season with Oxford United. Shotton was then transferred to Portsmouth and from there to Huddersfield Town with whom he ended the season. All three clubs were relegated.

Between 1994 and 2007, Steve Claridge played for five clubs whose name begins with the letter 'B' - Birmingham City, Brighton, Brentford, Bradford City and Bournemouth; and five clubs whose name begins with the letter 'W' - Wolves, Weymouth, Wycombe Wanderers, Walsall and Worthing.

Imre Viradi played for seven clubs with the suffix 'United' - Sheffield United, Newcastle United, Leeds United, Oxford United, Rotherham United, Boston United and Scunthorpe United.

Corker of a fact. Alan Cork, whose clubs included Wimbledon (430 league appearances - 145 goals), Sheffield United and Fulham, is the only player to have scored in all four divisions of the pre-1992 Football League and the Premier League.

On 14 January 1994, Liverpool's Bruce Grobbelaar appeared in an episode of the Channel Four soap-drama 'Brookside', exactly one month before his final appearance for the club.

Ford's football fiesta. Tony Ford's career as a player totalled 27 years, spanning four decades. Ford's career began at Grimsby Town in 1975, he played his final league game in 2002, when at Rochdale. Ford's other clubs include Stoke City, West Bromwich Albion, Scunthorpe United and Mansfield Town. Ford is one of only three outfield players to have surpassed 1,000 league and cup matches (the others being Scott McGleish and Graham Alexander). Ford's league matches total 931, no other outfield player has achieved such a feat in English senior football.

Cockerill is well red. Glen Cockerill made 714 league appearances for seven league clubs and also managed two non-league clubs all but one of which play in red and white. Cockerill had two spells at Lincoln City, he also played for Sheffield United, Southampton, Brentford (all red and white stripes), Swindon Town and Leyton Orient (red shirts). The only league club Cockerill played for whose first-choice strip is not red and white was Fulham. Following his retirement as a player, Cockerill had five years as manager of non-league Woking (red and white shirts) and a spell in charge of Winchester City of the Southern League (then of red and white stripes).

The ultimate utility player. Steve Palmer is the only professional player of the modern era to have been educated at Cambridge University (Christ's College). Whilst at Cambridge he played for the University football team and also first-class cricket in the same Cambridge University team as future England cricket captain Mike Atherton. Palmer signed for Ipswich Town in 1989 (110 league matches) before making a £135,000 move to Watford, for whom he made over 250 appearances (1995-2001). Palmer enhanced his reputation as a versatile player when at Watford where, during 1997-98, he fulfilled every team position including that of goalkeeper, wearing every numbered shirt from 1 to 14, this being the season Watford won the Division Two title.

A Different Beat. In the late 1990s, when he was a youth team player with Leeds United, Harry Kewell shared a flat with United's youth team goalkeeper, Nick Byrne, who went on to become a member of Boyzone.

The one second career in the top-flight. On 22 August 1999, Manchester United's Nick Culkin came on as a substitute goalkeeper for injured Raimond van der Gouw against Arsenal. Culkin, making his debut, had only been on the field for one second when the referee blew for time. He never featured for Manchester United again. After keeping goal for a number of Football League clubs, Culkin signed for non-league FC United of Manchester in 2014, thus becoming the first player to play for Manchester United and FC United of Manchester.

Steve Finnan is the only player to have played in the top five levels of English football, Premier League (Liverpool), Championship (Birmingham City), Second Division, now League One, (Fulham), Third Division, now League Two (Notts County), Conference, now National League (Welling United). Finnan is also the only player to have played in the World Cup, European Championship, Champions League, UEFA Cup and Intertoto Cup. Steve Finnan spent the majority of the early 2010s in charity work, providing irrigation in The Gambia.

Jamie Redknapp won four cup winners medals - FA Cup 1991-92, League

Cup 1994-95, Charity Shield and European Super Cup 2001-02, yet Redknapp played in only one of those games - Liverpool's 2-1 defeat of Bolton Wanderers in League Cup Final of 1995.

Nemanja Vidic, who played for Manchester United from 2006 to 2014, is the only player to have appeared in English senior football whose surname is comprised of Roman numerals.

Richard Kell played for Middlesbrough, Torquay United, Scunthorpe United, Barnsley and Lincoln City during which time he suffered two double fractures of the leg. Lincoln City decided not to renew his contract in 2007, at which point Kell announced his retirement from the game at the age of 27. He became an airline pilot.

Rarely a dull moment. John McDermott spent over 22 years as a defender with Grimsby Town, his only club. McDermott joined Grimsby in 1985 and played his final game for the club in 2007, having played 745 senior games. During his career at Grimsby, McDermott experienced promotion or relegation nine times. He was also involved in three unsuccessful promotion battles (1988-89, 1992-93 and 2005-06, the latter in which Grimsby lost in the League Two Play-Off Final) and five successful battles to avoid relegation (1991-92, 1995-96, 1999-2000, 2000-01 and 2001-02). Thus, 17 of McDermott's 20 seasons as a Grimsby Town first team player involved either, battling for promotion, or, to avoid relegation. McDermott is one of those rare players to have been at a club for so long, he qualified for two testimonials.

James Allan played for Falkirk, Cowdenbeath (with whom he won promotion from the Scottish Third Division in 2000-01), Queens Park, Stirling Albion and Dumbarton. Whilst still a part-time professional, Allan formed the indie band Glasvegas. Having played at Hampden Park for Queens Park, with his football career over, Allan subsequently played at Hampden again, with Glasvegas, who were support band to U2 on 18 August 2009.

In 2006-07, Drogheda United, who play at the wonderfully named Head In The Game Park, formerly known as equally wonderful, Hunky Dorys Park, met IK Start (Norway) in the UEFA Cup, a tie which went to a penalty shoot-out. Graham Gatland took the first penalty for Drogheda but missed; the shoot-out turned into an epic; with all other Drogheda players having scored, Gatland again stepped up to take what was Drogheda's 12th penalty; Gatland again failed to convert, Drogheda losing the shoot-out 10-11.

Jason Scotland was born in Trinidad and signed for Welsh club Swansea City from Scottish club St. Johnstone; Scotland made his Swans debut on 11 August 2007 in England at Oldham Athletic, a match in which he scored with a shot that deflected off Irish defender John Thompson.

Iago Aspas, who made 14 appearances as a striker for Liverpool between 2013 and 2015 took more corners (21) for Liverpool than he had shots at goal (16).

Frank Lampard and John Terry played 581 games together for Chelsea. Sepp Maier and Gerd Muller played 612 matches together, for Bayern Munich and West Germany.

He's a keeper. The last footballer born in the 1960s to have played for a League club is goalkeeper Kevin Poole (born 21 July 1963). Poole's last appearance was for Burton, aged 47, in the Johnstone's Paint Trophy second round tie at home to Rotherham United on 6 October 2010, Burton lost 2-1, Rotherham's winner coming from the penalty spot. Poole's last League match, also for Burton, was in a 3-0 victory over Grimsby Town on 8 May 2010. Poole was an unused substitute for Burton Albion in their League Two match at Wycombe Wanderers on 5 October 2013, aged 50.

The last outfield player born in the 1960s to have played for a League club is Dean Windass (born 1 April 1969). Windass played for Darlington in their 2-0 League Two home defeat to Dagenham and Redbridge on 8 May 2010, aged 41 years.

Alexander the great. Graham Alexander is one of three outfield players (others Tony Ford and Scott McGleish, see entries in this section) to have played in excess of 1,000 competitive matches (833 in the league). Alexander played league football for just four clubs, Scunthorpe United, Luton Town, Burnley and Preston North End. He also won 40 caps for Scotland. Alexander is the oldest player to make his Premier League debut, two months short of his 38th birthday when he played for Burnley at Stoke City on 15 August 2009. Alexander was a penalty specialist, even so, his career total of 107 league goals is remarkable for a defender in the modern era. Alexander played his final game on 28 April 2012, coming on as a substitute for Preston North End against Charlton Athletic. With Preston losing 1-2 and the game deep into added time, Preston were awarded a free-kick some 25-yards from goal. Alexander stepped up to score with the final kick of his career.

Goalkeeper, Dave Beasant, born in the 1950s, (20 March 1959), was an unused substitute for Stevenage in their League Two Play-Off semi-final first leg against Southend United on 10 May 2015, Beasant was 56 years of age and is the oldest player to be included in a club's match day squad in the history of the Football League. Earlier in the season, Stevenage's first choice goalkeeper had been David's son, Sam Beasant.

Striker Scott McGleish began his career at non-league Edgware Town in 1993. McGleish signed for Charlton Athletic in the summer of 1994 and went on to play in excess of 800 league matches, being one of only three outfield players in English football to have played in excess of 1,000 competitive matches (see entries for Tony Ford and Graham Alexander in this section). McGleish's league clubs included Peterborough United, Colchester United, Northampton Town, Leyton Orient, Bristol Rovers and Wycombe Wanderers. McLeish's final league club was Barnet (on loan) in 2012-13 whereafter he played as a semi-professional for a variety of non-league clubs, most notably Wealdstone (2013-17) for whom he scored 44 goals in 112 league matches. As at 2021-22, aged 48, McGleish was still playing, for Leverstock Green (who play at the wonderfully named, Pancake Lane) in the Spartan South Midlands League Premier Division and also coaching at Borehamwood Youth FC.

Lucas Piazon joined Chelsea in 2011 for a fee of £5million from Brazilian club Sao Paulo. Piazon made his first Premier League appearance for Chelsea on 23 December 2012, in an 8-0 victory over Aston Villa, a game in which he had a penalty saved. Piazon joined S.C Braga (Portugal) on a permanent basis in January 2021, having made one league appearance in nine years at Chelsea.

Michael Owen is the only player to have scored for Stoke City without ever having made a starting line-up. Owen scored in Stoke City's 3-1 defeat at Swansea City on 19 January 2013, in his time at Stoke, Owen made eight appearances, all as a substitute.

At the end of 2012-13, Premier League and Football League clubs released a total of 701 players.

Bruno captained Brighton to promotion to the Premier League in 2017. In 2017-18 when Bruno made his first ever appearance in the Premier League, he was two months short of his 37th birthday. Graham Alexander was also 37 when he played his first ever Premier League game, for Burnley in August 2009.

In 2020, Brighton played Dan Burn and Tariq Lamptey as wing-backs in the Premier League. Burn is 6'7" tall and Lamptey 5'3".

Michael Hector was a member of Fulham's Premier League squad in 2020-21 having previously played at seven different levels of English football (clubs include Thurrock, Didcot Town, Oxford City, Horsham, Barnet and Bracknell Town) as well as in the Scottish League (Aberdeen), Irish League (Dundalk) and Bundesliga (Eintracht Frankfurt).

Only former Workington player to win a Premier League Champions medal. Scott Carson (aged 35), whose clubs include Workington, made one appearance on loan from Derby County for Manchester City in a 4-3 win at Newcastle United on 14 May 2021, a match in which Carson saved a penalty from Newcastle's Joe Willock. That one appearance earned Carson a Premier League Champions medal. A feat equalled by City's other cover goalkeeper, Zack Steffan, who also made one appearance during the season.

Kevin Ellison (born 23 February 1979), at 42 years of age, played for Newport County in the League Two Play-Off Final at Wembley against his former club, Morecambe on 31 May 2021. Still with Newport County in 2021-22, Ellison was the only League player that season whose career had begun in the 1990s.

As at 2021-22, Dean Lewington (Milton Keynes Dons) had the most career league appearances of any active player in League football, in excess of 700. As at 2022, Lewington was the only MK Dons player remaining at the club following Wimbledon's relocation to Milton Keynes from south London in 2003. Lewington is one of only four players in Football League history to have played in excess of 700 league matches for a single league club. The others being Roy Sproson (Port Vale), Jimmy Dickinson (Portsmouth) and John Trollope (Swindon Town). Coincidentally, all four players were left-sided defenders.

On 20 November 2021, Crewe Alexandra defender, Zac Williams, won the 'Man of the Match' award for his performance against Gillingham in a League One match at the Mornflake Stadium. Williams, however, could not receive the magnum of champagne as he was, at the time, 17 years of age. At the post-match presentation, Williams was presented with a pint of milk and a box of jaffa cakes.

Promotion

In the days when only one club was promoted from both Divisions Three North and South, Plymouth Argyle finished second in the Third Division South in six consecutive seasons (1921-22 to 1926-27), third in 1927-28, fourth in 1928-29 before finally winning promotion in 1929-30.

Sheffield Wednesday were promoted three times to the First Division within a decade - 1951-52, 1955-56 and 1958-59.

Double agony but getting nearer. In 1961-62, Sunderland required victory in their final match of the season at Swansea Town to secure promotion to Division One - Sunderland could do no better than draw 1-1, missing out on promotion by a single point. The following season, Sunderland only needed to draw their final match of the season, at home to Chelsea, to secure promotion to Division One - Sunderland lost 1-0 and missed out on promotion by what was then goal average. Sunderland achieved promotion in 1963-64.

In 1968-69, Rochdale failed to score in 17 of their 46 matches in Division Four yet finished third and were promoted. Rochdale were involved in five successive 1-1 draws (24 August to 14 September) and a total of eleven goalless draws of which four were in succession (28 September to 12 October).

Also, in 1968-69, Halifax Town finished as runners-up in Division Four and were promoted having scored just 53 goals in their 46 league matches. Only one more than Terry Bly had himself scored for Peterborough United in the same division in 1960-61.

In 1972-73, Hereford United, in their first season as a Football League club, won just two of their first 14 league matches, but, under manager Colin

Addison, turned their season around to clinch promotion as runners-up in Division Four. Coinciding with the upturn in form was the introduction of goalkeeper, David Icke, who came on loan from Coventry City and who would later make a name for himself as a sports broadcaster and later conspiracy theorist.

1980-81 Fourth Division Champions, Southend United, conceded only six goals in their 23 home matches.

In 1986-87, no club won promotion to Division One via the Play-Offs. The Play-Offs at the time involved the team finishing fourth bottom of Division One in a Play-Off with the teams finishing third, fourth and fifth in Division Two. Charlton Athletic retained their First Division status beating Leeds United 2-1 in a replay at St. Andrews after the first two legs of the Play-Off Final tied 1-1 on aggregate.

Wrexham's run-in wrecks promotion. In 1976-77, Wrexham required three points from their final four matches to be assured of promotion from the Third Division. Wrexham had lost just one of the previous ten matches but imploded on the run-in, losing three and securing one draw. Wrexham were still in with a chance of promotion on the final day, a win at home against Mansfield Town would clinch promotion to Division Two, but, before their biggest attendance of the season (22,000), Wrexham were beaten 1-0.

In 1991-92, Middlesbrough were promoted to the Premier League having scored 58 goals in their 46 league matches, only two more than relegated Brighton.

Promotion job rewards patience of Job. Stranraer were formed in 1870 and are the third oldest club in Scottish football but did not win their first promotion until 1993-94.

Reading are the only club to finish as runners-up in the Championship and not be promoted. In 1994-95, Reading finished second in what was then Division Two but due to restructuring of the leagues, only two teams were to be promoted to the top-flight, this necessitated Reading entering the Play-Offs. After beating Tranmere Rovers over two legs, Reading lost 4-3 to Bolton Wanderers after-extra time having led 2-0 within twelve minutes. One of the Bolton substitutes in the Play-Off Final was Peter Shilton, aged 46.

No strangers to promotion...or relegation. Between 2001-02 and 2008-09, Stranraer played in a different division for each of those eight seasons.

Denied promotion by a tree. In 1992-93, St. Albans City finished as runners-up in the Ryman Premier League but were denied promotion to the Conference League due to a nigh-on 150-year-old oak tree situated behind one of the goals at their Clarence Park ground. The Conference League deemed the tree 'dangerous to spectators' as it was situated to the fore of the terrace most popular with St.Albans' supporters. For all the tree was subject to a preservation order, the tree was controversially felled in August 1998 when it became diseased. There were demands for a root and branch inquiry.

The tree at the root of the problem of St. Alban's promotion.

The club who have been promoted to and relegated from the First Division/Premier League on the most occasions is Birmingham City, twelve promotions, twelve relegations.

The 2003-04 First Division Play-Off Final between Crystal Palace and West Ham United (1-0 to Crystal Palace) drew an attendance of 72,523 to the Millennium Stadium - 1,173 more than attended the FA Cup Final between Manchester United and Millwall.

Truro City won four consecutive promotions. 2005-06 from the South Western League; 2006-07 from Western League Division One; 2007-08 from Western League Premier Division; 2008-09 from Southern League Division One South and West. Arguably the most interesting thing about Truro could be, it is the only city in the UK whose name contains only letters that appear in the second half of the alphabet.

Sunderland were promoted to the Premier League as Champions of the Championship on four occasions in eleven seasons - 1995-96, 1998-99, 2004-05 and 2006-07.

Kevin Phillips was promoted from the Championship to Premier League with five different clubs: Sunderland 1998-99; West Bromwich Albion 2007-08; Birmingham City 2008-09; Crystal Palace 2012-13 and Leicester City 2013-14.

In 2014-15, the names of the promoted Champions of all the senior leagues began with the letter 'B'. Championship - Bournemouth; League One - Bristol City; League Two - Burton Albion; Conference - Barnet (Bristol Rovers also promoted); Conference North - Barrow; Conference South - Bromley (Boreham Wood also promoted).

They were top when it counted. When Portsmouth won the League Two title in 2016-17, they occupied top place, for the first time, for only the final 32 minutes of the season.

For all Wrexham have featured in several National League promotion battles, as at January 2022, Wrexham had the longest tenure of any of the current clubs in the National League, fourteen seasons, having lost Football League status in 2007-08.

Relegation

The first clubs to be relegated when automatic promotion and relegation was introduced in 1898-99 were Bolton Wanderers and Sheffield Wednesday, then known as The Wednesday.

In 1908-09, Manchester City completed their season without ever having been in the bottom two relegation places yet were relegated. City had one of the best home records in the division, only four teams won more home matches and only five teams scored more goals. City completed their fixtures with a 1-0 defeat at Bristol City, but looked safe, as the only team who could overhaul them were Liverpool, who had one match remaining, away to newly crowned champions Newcastle United. Against the odds, Liverpool won 1-0, a result which dragged City into the bottom two for the first time and subsequent relegation.

Sheffield United won only six of their 42 First Division matches in 1920-21 yet were not relegated. United finished four points ahead of Derby County and six ahead of Bradford Park Avenue, both of whom were relegated, the latter having won two more games than the Blades.

Relegation was introduced in Scotland in 1921-22 when the Scottish League was expanded to two divisions, the format prior to WW1. Three clubs were relegated from Division One - Dumbarton, Queens Park and Clydebank, with only Alloa Athletic being promoted as the First Division was cut from 22 to 20 clubs.

Notts County were relegated from Division One in 1925-26 despite having won more matches than Everton who occupied 11th position and only one less than Liverpool (7th).

The tightest relegation battle occurred in 1927-28. On the final day of the season only two points separated 13 clubs from the top-half to the bottom of Division One. Seven clubs finished on 39 points; Tottenham were relegated with 38 points along with bottom club Middlesbrough (37 points). Only seven points separated bottom club Middlesbrough from Derby County in fourth place.

FIRST DIVISION

	P	W	D	L	F	A	Pts
1 Everton	42	20	13	9	102	66	53
2 Huddersfield	42	22	7	13	91	68	51
3 Leicester	42	18	12	12	96	72	48
4 Derby	42	17	10	15	96	83	44
5 Bury	42	20	4	18	80	80	44
6 Cardiff	42	17	10	15	70	80	44
7 Bolton	42	16	11	15	81	66	43
8 Aston Villa	42	17	9	16	78	73	43
9 Newcastle	42	15	13	14	79	81	43
10 Arsenal	42	13	15	14	82	86	41
11 Birmingham	42	13	15	14	70	75	41
12 Blackburn	42	16	9	17	66	78	41
13 Sheff United	42	15	10	17	79	86	40
14 Wednesday	42	13	13	16	81	78	39
15 Sunderland	42	15	9	18	74	76	39
16 Liverpool	42	13	13	16	84	87	39
17 West Ham	42	14	11	17	81	88	39
18 Burnley	42	16	7	19	82	98	39
19 Man United	42	16	7	19	72	87	39
20 Portsmouth	42	16	7	19	66	90	39
21 Tottenham	42	15	8	19	74	86	38
22 Middlesbrough	42	11	15	16	81	88	37

The tightest relegation battle and closest League table in the history of the Football League that of the First Division 1927-28. Tottenham were relegated having won as many games as ninth placed Newcastle United.

In 1928-29, Cardiff City were the only club to concede fewer than 60 goals in Division One - 59 in 42 matches, three fewer than League Champions Sheffield Wednesday. Cardiff City also conceded the fewest goals away from home (43) than any other team in the division, yet Cardiff were relegated.

Between 1959-60 and 1963-64, Birmingham City avoided relegation from Division One in four of those five seasons by winning their final match of the season. Birmingham's luck ran-out in 1964-65 when they were relegated.

In 1960-61, Newcastle United scored 86 goals in Division One, eight more than runners-up Sheffield Wednesday, yet Newcastle were relegated.

Fulham's late show. On 25 February 1966, with thirteen matches remaining, Fulham were bottom of Division One having won just 15 points from 29 games (possible 58 points). Fulham then won nine and drew two of their remaining thirteen games to avoid relegation.

In 1967-68, Peterborough United finished in sixth place in Division Three with 50 points but were relegated when the Football League deducted 19 points as part of a punishment for offering irregular bonuses to players.

In 1969-70, Southampton and Crystal Palace avoided relegation from Division One despite both winning just six of their 42 league matches. Relegated Sunderland also won six matches, whilst the other relegated club, Sheffield Wednesday, who finished bottom, won more matches (8) than both Southampton and Palace.

Southampton's Mick Channon was the leading goalscorer in the First Division in 1973-74 with 21 goals and yet Southampton were relegated. The only instance of the season's leading goal scorer in English top flight football playing for a relegated club.

Sheffield United were relegated from Division Three in 1980-81 with a positive goal difference of +2. Champions, Rotherham United, scored fewer goals away from home (19) than relegated Sheffield United (27) and Blackpool (26).

In 1984-85, both teams who contested the League Cup Final at Wembley, Norwich City and Sunderland, were relegated from Division One.

Three clubs have suffered relegation in three successive seasons. Bristol City, First to Third Division, 1979-80, 1980-81 and 1981-82; Luton Town, Championship to League Two, 2006-07, 2007-08 and 2008-09; Wolverhampton Wanderers, First Division to Third Division, 1983-84, 1984-85 and 1985-86.

In 1991-92, Luton Town, Notts County and West Ham United were relegated from the First Division to the First Division. 1992-93 was the inaugural season of the Premier League and what had been the Second Division, was rebranded as the First Division.

In November 1995, Millwall topped Division One and looked set for promotion to the Premier League. On 9 December, Millwall lost 6-0 at Sunderland, after which they won only four of their remaining 24 league matches and ended being relegated.

In 1997-98, Doncaster Rovers won just 4 of their 46 matches in Division Three, conceded 113 goals and had a goal difference of -83. Doncaster also lost both their League Cup and FA Cup ties, conceding 13 goals in the process. Doncaster were relegated from Third Division to the Conference League.

On 3 May 1998, Stoke City met Manchester City on the final day of the season with both teams needing a win to have any hope of avoiding relegation. Manchester City won 5-2 but victories for Port Vale and Portsmouth relegated both City teams to League Two.

Iceland international Hermann Hreidarsson experienced relegation from the Premier League on five occasions with five different clubs - Crystal Palace, Ipswich Town, Wimbledon, Charlton Athletic and Portsmouth. In 2012, Hreidarsson joined Championship club Coventry City; Coventry were relegated to League One, the third tier of English football, for the first time in 48 years.

Between 1997-98 and 2001-02, Manchester City did not have a season in which they were not either promoted or relegated. 1997-98 relegated from First Division (then tier two); 1998-99, promoted from Second Division (tier three); 1999-2000, promoted from First Division (tier two) to Premier League; 2000-01 relegated from Premier League; 2001-02, promoted to Premier League from First Division.

Nathan Blake was relegated from the Premier League five times, Sheffield United, Bolton Wanderers (twice), Wolves and Blackburn Rovers. On the upside, Blake was involved in three promotions to the Premier League.

In 2007-08, Leicester City, along with Scunthorpe United and Colchester United, were relegated from the Championship to League One. Leicester conceded only 45 goals in their 46 league matches (19 at home and 26 away), only fifth placed Crystal Palace conceded fewer (42). Champions West Bromwich Albion and runners-up Stoke City both conceded ten more goals than relegated Leicester. Curiously, West Brom and Stoke both conceded the same number of goals home and away - home goals conceded

27, away goals conceded 28.

In 2009-10, when Darlington finished bottom of League Two and lost their Football League status, they called upon the services of 54 players and four managers.

In 2010-11, Walsall occupied one of the relegation places in League Two from October to March. At the beginning of March, Walsall were ten points from safety but under manager, Dean Smith, the Saddlers lost only four of their remaining 14 matches to escape relegation by a single point. In normal circumstances, Walsall would still have been relegated but for the fact Plymouth Argyle had ten points deducted for having gone into administration.

In 2012-13, Peterborough United were relegated from the Championship with 54 points which, in most previous seasons, would have seen the club finish comfortably away from the relegation places. Peterborough won only four fewer League matches than promoted Crystal Palace. A similar fate befell Southend United who were relegated from Division Three in 1988-89 with 54 points. Southend finished 17 points ahead of also relegated Aldershot.

Following Berwick Rangers' 2-0 victory against Peterhead in the Scottish Division Two on 19 March 2019, Berwick did not score another goal in their remaining nine League and Relegation Play-Off matches which resulted in the Border club losing their Scottish League status.

Sheffield United were relegated from the Premier League in 2020-21 having lost 29 league matches. Only three clubs have lost 30 matches during a season in the top flight - Leeds United 1946-47, Blackburn Rovers 1965-66 and Stoke City (31 defeats) 1984-85, these being in a 42-game season.

Steve Chalmers

SCOTTISH LEAGUE—DIVISION 1
CELTIC v. DUNDEE UNITED
Saturday, 2nd December, 1967
Kick-off 3.00 p.m.

No. 7.   PRICE · THREEPENCE

Scottish Clubs

Aberdeen were the first club to have dugouts. The dug-outs were the brainchild of trainer, Don Colman, who, in 1921-22, wanted to observe his players at close-quarters and make notes without rain smudging his inked writing. Everton played a friendly at Aberdeen, liked the idea and became the first English League club to install dugouts.

Airdrieonians were formed in 2002, initially as Airdrie United following the liquidation of the original Airdrieonians club. The new club adopted the club's traditional badge featuring a cockerel sitting atop a shield containing two lions passant and the club's initials. In March 2015, the club were informed by the Lord Lyon King of Arms (One of the Great Officers of State for Scotland) because the badge featured a shield, it constituted a heraldic device and, as such, was not allowed to carry lettering, albeit the club had used the badge from 1881 to 2000. To comply, the club removed the shield and replaced it with a chevron which was separated from the lower scroll which contains the club's name.

Unacceptable Airdrie Badge   Acceptable Airdrie Badge

Albion Rovers fielded Currie and Rice, also Sage in their 2-0 defeat against Stenhousemuir in Division Two on 9 January 1971. Bill Currie, Bert Rice and Sid Sage were not the only players of culinary essence to play for the club that season. Albion fielded a total of fourteen trialists whose number included Steve Ham and Eddie Salmon.

'alloha, another International from Alloa due soon. Alloa Athletic's most capped player is Jock Hepburn, one cap for Scotland against Wales in 1891.

Annan Athletic are holders of the Scottish Qualifying Cup in perpetuity. Annan beat Preston Athletic 3-1 in the final in November 2006. The tournament then became defunct as new criteria was introduced for entry into the Scottish FA Cup proper.

One of the 'celebrated' tickets issued by Annan Athletic for the Scottish League Two match against Queens Park in 2018. The ticket contains numerous typo errors.

Arbroath's Gayfield Park is the closest ground in Europe to the sea; the club's nickname 'The Red Lichties' comes from the red light that used to guide fishing boats back into the town's harbour from the North Sea.

Ayr United's nickname 'The Honest Men' comes from the Robbie Burns poem 'Tam O'Shanter' in which he describes Ayr as a town 'of honest men and bonnie lasses.'

Berwick Rangers' relegation to the Lowland League in 2019 robbed the club of the famous claim to be the only senior Scottish club based in England.

Technically, Berwick Rangers are still at war with Germany. When war was declared in 1914, the declaration cited 'Great Britain and Berwick-on-Tweed' as the Border was being re-drawn and it had not been officially decided if Berwick was to be in England or Scotland. When peace came, the declaration omitted Berwick as by then it had been decided the town was to be in England.

Brechin City is something of a misnomer as Brechin is a town. Brechin called itself a city due to its cathedral albeit such status is not officially recognised. In 2020, the population of Brechin was 7,460, as Brechin City's home, Glebe Park, has a capacity of 4,123, the ground is the largest in proportion to local population of any in British football. Glebe Park is also the only ground in Europe to have a hedge (beech) along one of its perimeters. Glebe Park is also unusual as the largest stand in the ground is situated behind one of the goals.

Celtic were the last senior British club to wear numbers when the SFA made it compulsory in 1960. Celtic chairman, Robert Kelly, baulked at the idea of numbers on Celtic's famous green and white hooped shirts, so the numbers appeared on the shorts. The 'tradition' of Celtic players wearing numbered shorts ended in 1994-95 when the Scottish Professional Football League instructed the club to apply numbers to the back of their shirts.

Clyde are the longest holders of the Scottish FA Cup, eight years. Clyde beat Motherwell 4-0 to win the Scottish Cup in 1938-39, but due to WW2, the competition was not held again until 1946-47.

League Champions played all their games away from home. Cove Rangers play in the Cove Bay area of Aberdeen. In 2017-18, Cove won the Highland League having played all their games away from home as Cove's Allan Park ground did not meet SPFL minimum stadia requirements. In 2018-19, Cove moved into their new home, Balmoral Stadium, and won the Highland League again. Having won the league, Cove beat Lowland League champions Edinburgh City, then East Stirling in the Play-Offs to secure a place in League Two.

Cowdenbeath won the Second Division in 1938-39, scoring 120 goals in their 34 league matches, 54 of them coming from centre-forward Rab Walls, the second highest seasonal total in Scottish League history.

Dumbarton were the first club to win the League title in each of the four tiers of the Scottish Football League system and are one of only two clubs to have achieved this feat, Rangers being the other.

Dundee is the only senior club in Scotland and England whose name does not contain any of the letters in the word 'football'.

Two teams and referee shared same name. Dundee United were formed in 1909 as Dundee Hibernian and were elected to the Scottish League in 1910. The first match was to commemorate the opening of Tannadice Park (then known as Clepington Park) on 18 August 1909, Dundee Hibernian faced Hibernian and the referee was Archie Hibernian, the game ended 1-1.

The STV drama detective series 'Taggart' was written by Stephen Hepburn, a Dunfermline fan. In one episode in 2003, Hepburn used all eleven names from Dunfermline's 1968 Scottish FA Cup winning side as names of characters.

Win, lose or draw. For decades, 'The Bluebell Polka' by Jimmy Shand and his Band has been played at the end of every Dunfermline home game at East End Park.

East Fife's Scottish Cup win of 1937-38, when they defeated Kilmarnock 4-2 after a 1-1 draw, was the last time a club from outside Scotland's top-flight won the Cup. The respective attendances for those two Finals was 80,091 and 92,716.

East Stirling, now of the Lowland League, struck a sponsorship deal with Le Coq Sportif in 1998-99. The French kit manufacturer failed to produce the strips in time for the start of the season; the company sent the club a set of Queens Park strips, with East Stirling's badge and sponsors' logo simply ironed over that of the Queens Park crest and sponsor. In 2008-09, the club's shirts were sponsored by the Chicago branch of the East Stirling Supporters club.

Edinburgh City has nothing to do with the club of the same name which played in the Scottish League in the 1930s and 1940s. Edinburgh City were formally known as Postal United. Postal United were granted permission to use the name in 1986 by Edinburgh City Football Club Ltd which had continued trading as a social club when the football club folded in 1955.

Elgin City's home ground, Borough Briggs, is the most northerly senior league ground in the UK. The main stand at Borough Briggs has 478 seats,

The most northerly ground in British senior football, Elgin City's Borough Briggs. A clean, neat and tidy ground with a capacity of 4,520. The main stand (left) has 478 seats which were purchased from Newcastle United when the Tyneside club redeveloped their Milburn Stand.

which were purchased from Newcastle United when the Tyneside club redeveloped their Milburn Stand.

Falkirk have won the second tier of Scottish football a record seven times. A record they share with St. Johnstone. Falkirk have also won the Scottish Challenge Cup a record four times. After the creation of the SPL in 1998, Falkirk were denied promotion on three occasions (another record) as their then Brockville Park home did not meet SPL minimum standards. The club shares its ground with East Stirling of the Lowland League.

Over a century of appearances on loan. In 2013-14, Forfar took Dale Hilson on loan from Dundee United. Hilson went on to make a total of 113 appearances for Forfar on loan (99 in the League and 14 in cup competitions). Hilson signed permanently for Forfar in 2014-15 and made a further 34 appearances in the league before joining Queen of the South. Hilson returned to Forfar (2018-20) playing 42 league games before joining Arbroath in 2020.

Hamilton Academical are the only senior club in British football to have originated from a school team - Hamilton Academy. On 12 October 1937, Hamilton received a letter from Mr James Grant of Glasgow citing he had attended a home match of 25 September, thinking, on seeing crowds entering Douglas Park, that it was Hamilton racecourse. Mr Grant requested the club reimburse his price of admission. The club rejected his claim.

Heart of Midlothian were the last club to have their name on the Scottish Cup. All winners since 1955-56 have had their names inscribed on the plinth.

In 1977-78, Hibernian became the first club in Scotland and British senior football to carry the name of a sponsor on their shirts, football kit manufacturer Bukta.

Inverness Caledonian Thistle were admitted to the Scottish League in 1994-95 as Caledonian Thistle. The club played two seasons as Caledonian Thistle before Inverness was added to their name at the request of the local council who had contributed funds for a new stadium, Caledonian Stadium, the club having previously played league matches at Caley's Telford Street Park.

Kelty Hearts is the only senior club in the UK based in a village. On the Fife/Kinross-shire boundary, the population in 2021 was 5,282, making Kelty Hearts the senior club with the smallest local population, narrowly beating Forest Green Rovers (based in Nailsworth, Gloucestershire) whose population in 2020 was put at 5,994.

Kilmarnock are the oldest professional club in Scotland, formed in 1869. In 1964-65, Kilmarnock travelled to Hearts on the final day of the season in a match which would decide which of the two clubs would win the Scottish League title. To be crowned champions Kilmarnock had to win 2-0, which they did, to pip Hearts on goal average of 0.042, the number of goals scored in the season divided by the number conceded. The match was played on the same afternoon as the Scottish FA Cup Final between Celtic and Dunfermline. As goal difference was introduced in 1971-72, Kilmarnock are the last club to be Scottish League champions on goal average.

Kings Park was a thriving Scottish Second Division club prior to World War Two. In 1940, the club's ground, Forthbank Park, was badly damaged in an air raid. Lacking the finances to redevelop their ground, Kings Park never played another game and folded in 1945. The club, however, was not wound-up until 1953, when the War Office settled their bomb damage claim. Football was not lost to the town. Kings Park begat Stirling Albion.

Livingston were the first British club to appoint a Brazilian coach. Marcio Maximo was appointed in June 2003 having at one time been Manager/Coach of Brazil U18s. Maximo left the club after four months.

Montrose won the League Two Championship in 2017-18, to end a period of 22 consecutive seasons in Scotland's basement division.

When Greenock Morton won the Scottish Second Division in 1963-64, they scored 135 goals in 36 league games. Centre-forward Ally McGraw scored 58 goals. Morton began the season with a goalless draw against Albion Rovers from which Morton went on to record 32 wins, two draws and one defeat, 1-3 at East Fife in October.

In 1962-63, Motherwell led Falkirk 9-0 after only thirty three minutes of their Scottish League Cup tie on 11 August 1962. Only two players scored, Bobby Russell (5) and Pat Quinn (4). Motherwell won 9-1.

Partick Thistle won the Glasgow Dental Cup in 1929 and still hold the trophy to this day. The Dental Cup was a one-off tournament to raise money for Glasgow Dental Hospital, Thistle beat Rangers 2-0 in the Final. Apparently, to commemorate winning the Dental Cup, the club failed in many attempts to install a commemorative plaque.

On 11 April 1998, Peterhead hit the woodwork twice and had two goals disallowed during their Highland League match against Fort William but still won 17-0. Strikers Colin Milne and Gary Clark both scored five goals.

Queen of the South's three Division Two league title wins in 1950-51, 2001-02 and 2012-13 were all secured when playing at Forfar's Station Park. The first two came at the expense of Forfar Athletic whereas the latter title, secured by a 6-0 win against Brechin City, was played at Forfar as Brechin's Glebe Park had been deemed unfit for play.

Queens Park was an amateur club from foundation in 1867 to November 2019. The club now plays home matches at Lesser Hampden. Queens Park's, Robert McColl, won 13 caps for Scotland scoring 13 goals. When his playing days were over, McColl, along with his brother Tom, began the newsagent chain R.S.McColl. The company took advertisements in most Scottish International, Scottish Cup and League Cup semi-final and Final match programmes, and, at some point, the programmes of most Scottish league clubs. The company logo was the signature of R.S.McColl. In the 1940s, 50s and 60s, when one could easily decipher a footballer's autograph, McColl's was thought to be the most reproduced and recognised autograph of any British footballer.

The most reprinted football autograph, that of R.S. (Robert) McColl of Queens Park, Newcastle United, Rangers and Scotland. Robert McColl scored 13 goals in 13 games for Scotland and is the only player to have scored a hat-trick against each of the home nations.

In terms of trophies won, Rangers is the most successful club in the world. As at July 2021, Rangers had won 29 more major trophies than Real Madrid. Rangers, like Celtic, have supporters' clubs in most towns in Scotland and fan bases around the world. In 2019, the Faculty of Economics at Glasgow University estimated the presence of Rangers to be worth £100million to the Scottish economy.

Raith Rovers are the only club to have been shipwrecked on their way to a match. In the close-season of 1923, Rovers were on their way to a tournament in the Canaries when their ship, Highland Loch, ran aground in a storm off the coast of Galicia. The team took to lifeboats which were towed by Spanish fishing boats to the village of Villagarcia. Rovers continued their journey the following day courtesy of a passenger liner bound for the Canaries.

Ross County had eight English players in their team in 2020-21- Connor Randall, Carl Tremarco, Ross Draper, Tom Grivosti, Jermaine Hylton, Regan Charles-Cook, Charlie Lakin and Jordan Tilson.

St. Johnstone are so called because Perth was known as 'St. John's Toun' in the Middle Ages. In 2020-21, St Johnstone won their first League Cup and

Rangers v Celtic from the halcyon 'derby' days of the 1960s. From right to left, Bobby Murdoch, Ralph Brand (Rangers), Ian Young and Captain Peacock from 'Are You Being Served'.

second Scottish FA Cup to complete a historic Cup double, becoming only the second club, Celtic and Rangers apart, to win both cups in a season, Aberdeen being the other club to achieve this feat. The club is also notable for being the only senior club in the UK to contain the letter 'J'.

In 1958-59, St. Mirren's second round Scottish FA Cup tie against Peeble Rovers was scheduled for the night of Friday 13th February to commemorate the turning-on of the floodlights at their Love Street ground. Initially, there were misgivings, as some officials in the club were of the mind playing such a prestigious game on Friday 13th would bring the team bad luck. St. Mirren won 10-0 and went on to win the Scottish Cup defeating Aberdeen 3-1 in the final.

Half of Stenhousemuir's 22-man squad in 2019-20 had names which began with the letter 'M'. The players - Aidan McIlduff, Andy Munro, Marky Munro, Scott McLaughlin, Mark McGuigan, Adam McCracken, Jamie McKernon, Kyle Marley, Abdelhak Massouaghou, Connor McBride and Connor McBrearty. The Stenhousemuir manager was Colin McMenamin.

On 8 December 1984, Stirling Albion beat Selkirk 20-0 in the Scottish Cup. In the summer of 1966, Stirling Albion accepted an invitation to tour Japan, Greece and Iran after the original team selected, Sheffield Wednesday, withdrew. Albion played to huge attendances and whilst in Japan discovered they had been invited simply because the organisers had selected another British club that began with the letter 'S'.

Stranraer were founded in 1870 and are the third oldest football club in Scotland (behind Queens Park and Kilmarnock) and the 20th oldest football club in the world. For all their history, Stranraer were the last senior British club to have floodlights installed.

Third Lanark was formed in 1872 as an offshoot of the 3rd Lanarkshire Rifle Volunteers. Third Lanark, the only senior club in British football to have a number as part of the club name, went out of business in June 1967, only six years after having finished third in the First Division. In 1960-61 the aggregate attendance for Third Lanark home and away matches was 567,501, come 1966-67, the aggregate attendance for all home matches was just 51,012. Third Lanark's former home, Cathkin Park, is still partially standing and, for all it has been over 50 years, the club's demise is still lamented by supporters far and wide.

Cathkin Park, former home of Third Lanark. Over fifty years after the club's demise a proportion of the terracing and crush barriers remain in situ and the pitch is still well maintained.

SCOTTISH LEAGUE—Nineteenth Match

OFFICIAL PROGRAMME

The RANGERS
FOOTBALL CLUB LTD

IBROX STADIUM GLASGOW

Directors: John Lawrence, J.P. (chairman), John F. Wilson (vice-chairman), Alan L. Morton, George C. P. Brown, M.A. and Matthew C. Taylor.
Secretary: J. Rogers Simpson, C.A.   *Manager:* J. Scotland Symon.

No. 366	January 9th, 1965	Price Threepence

RANGERS

Right   1   *Left*
                          RITCHIE

              2   3
          PROVAN   CALDOW

          4   5   6
      GREIG   McKINNON   WOOD

2   8   9   10   11
WILSON   MILLAR   FORREST   BECK   JOHNSTON

1873   1965

ROBERTSON   COOKE   HARLEY   PENMAN   MURRAY
11   10   9   8   7

          STUAR   EASTON   COUSIN
                      5   4

                  HAMILTON

                              Right

AITKEN'S
EXPORT & ST
Just what I

CLYDE FOOTB
BULLY WEE
NEWS

No. 9   FIRST

CIG

WELL MA

FOUR CROWN
CONVOY SHERRY
All first class
South African wines
CAPE CLUB SHERRY
BULLOCH & CO. LIMITED

THIRD LANARK A.C. LTD.
HI-HI NEWS
Official Programme
6d.

No. 14   FIRST DIVISION
THIRD LANARK v. DUNFERMLINE ATH.

AFTER THE GAME
DRYBROUGH'S
THE NAME!

The
QUE
E.C.
QFC

Strips and Kit

From 1878, ten years before becoming founder members of the Football League, Blackburn Rovers' famous blue and white halved shirts changed with every season, the club alternating the sides on which the blue and white appeared. At the commencement of 1946-47, the club opted for blue on the left and white on the right, a design which has since remained unaltered.

In 1907-08, Norwich City changed the colour of their shirts from light blue and white to yellow to match their nickname of 'The Canaries'. The club's nickname having derived from the city's history of breeding canaries, thought to have begun in the 16th century by immigrant weavers from Europe.

Numbered shirts were first worn in a league game on 25 August 1928 by both Arsenal and Chelsea. Arsenal wore numbered shirts in a 3-2 defeat at Sheffield Wednesday in Division One; Chelsea in their 4-0 victory over Swansea Town in Division Two at Stamford Bridge.

Literally short of money. In 1946-47, Clyde were so strapped for cash the club could not afford new shorts. Players wore khaki shorts bought from a local Army and Navy stores for the game on 10 August 1946 away to St. Mirren and for the home game against Celtic on 17 August. Thereafter traditional football shorts were purchased.

On 16 October 1948, Bolton Wanderers arrived at Ayresome Park for their First Division match against Middlesbrough only to discover they had not packed any shinguards. Bolton manager, Walter Rowley, sent out for 22 paperback books which the players used as temporary replacements.

On 28 February 1953, Arsenal wore a strip of black and white striped shirts, white shorts and black and white hooped socks for the sixth round FA Cup tie against Blackpool at Highbury. The only occasion on which Arsenal have worn this strip for a senior game.

On 25 March 1961, Leytonstone (Isthmian League) wore strips acquired from Tottenham Hotspur for their FA Amateur Cup semi-final against West Auckland Town (Northern League) at Roker Park, Sunderland. The strip, complete with white shirt bearing the Tottenham cockerel badge, did not bring good fortune for Leytonstone, who lost the tie 3-1.

Clyde were the first team to wear squad numbers in a senior match, rather than the traditional numbers 1 to 11. On 10 September 1966, Clyde wore squad numbers for their opening league match at home to Celtic. Clyde players, however, felt uncomfortable wearing the squad numbered shirts. At half-time, manager, Davie White, instructed the players to change into a set of traditional numbered shirts. The squad numbered shirts were relegated for use as training tops.

Sporting of Brugge. Sporting Lisbon arrived for their Inter Cities Fairs Cup tie, first leg against Club Brugge (Belgium) on 13 September 1967, only to be informed the skip containing the teams' strips and boots had been forwarded in error to Stockholm. Club Brugge loaned Sporting their second strip, whilst the Sporting players bought boots and shinguards from a local sports store.

Fulham left the skip containing their kit at Euston station when setting off for their Third Round FA Cup-tie at Sunderland on 4 January 1969. Fulham borrowed Sunderland's away strip of all light blue for the tie, which Fulham won 4-1.

From 1972 to 1974, Birmingham City's third choice kit comprised the German flag, rotated clockwise, first worn on a pre-season tour of Germany in the summer of 1972 to foster friendly relationships with their hosts.

Blackburn Rovers only wore shirts bearing a badge (the town's coat of arms) when they appeared in FA Cup Finals, a tradition carried through all eight FA Cup Finals in which Blackburn have appeared, the last being the final of 1959-60 against Wolverhampton Wanderers. Blackburn first adopted a badge permanently on their shirts in 1974-75, the original red rose and town motto design being slightly modified in 1989.

The Arsenal strip of red breast and white sleeves has inspired a number of other clubs to adopt similar. In 1906, the president of Sparta Prague (then known as Athletic Club Sparta) attended a game at Woolwich Arsenal and was so taken with the colour and design of Arsenal's shirts he purchased a set which, on his return to Prague, the club adopted as their regular strip as opposed to their previous black and white stripes. The Arsenal design has also been adopted by Sporting Braga (Portugal) in 1920, Braga's nickname being 'Os Arsenalistas'; in 1938, by Hibernian, albeit green breast and white sleeves, and, in 1941 by Sante Fe (Colombia).

Arsenal shirts also influenced Charlton Athletic's choice of strip. Due to lack of finances, the 14-15 year-old boys who founded Charlton Athletic in 1905, had to borrow strips from their local rivals, Woolwich Arsenal. When finances allowed, the embryonic Charlton Athletic, chose to have a red and white strip similar to that of Arsenal.

Players first wore their names on the back of their shirts on 18 April 1993 for the League Cup Final between Arsenal and Sheffield Wednesday (2-1 to Arsenal). A practice repeated when the two teams met again a month later in the FA Cup Final (Arsenal 2-1 in replay after 1-1). The Premier League adopted the idea the following season as a means of helping viewers identify players more readily when watching games on SkySports TV.

In 1995-96, the shirt sponsor of Carlisle United's David Currie, was The Viceroy Bangladeshi restaurant, an award winning, family-run restaurant which is involved in sponsorship of Carlisle United to this day.

On 17 April 2009, Hibernian travelled to Celtic taking their white 'away' kit. The white shirts were deemed to clash with Celtic's green and white hoops, Hibernian, however, had no alternative shirts. Hibernian played the game wearing a set of black goalkeepers' tops.

Stranraer has the longest running shirt sponsorship deal of any senior club in British football, at over 30 seasons. Stena Line have been on the front of Stranraer shirts since 1996-97, prior to which, from 1988-89 to 1996-97, Stranraer shirts were sponsored by Sealink, a company purchased by Stena Line.

Substitutes

The first substitutes deployed by England took to the field during England's friendly against Mexico in Mexico City on 24 April 1959. Warren Bradley (Manchester United) replaced Doug Holden (Bolton Wanderers) and Ron Flowers (Wolves) replaced Wilf McGuinness (Manchester United). England lost 2-1.

Bobby Knox was the first substitute to score in a Football League match. On 21 August 1965, Knox scored in Barrow's 4-2 victory over Wrexham in Division Four. Knox later went on to become the first substitute to save a penalty. On 27 December 1965, Knox took over in goal from injured goalkeeper, Lance Millard, and saved a penalty in Barrow's 2-1 victory over Doncaster Rovers.

The first substitute in Scottish football was Archie Gemmill, who replaced, Jim Clunie, during St. Mirren's League Cup tie against Clyde at Shawfield on 13 August 1966. It was the first tactical substitution in Scottish football.

The only player to be substituted because he was too cold is Ayrton Ignacio. During Clydebank's League Two game against Forfar Athletic on 12 November 1966, Brazilian, Ignacio, signalled to the Clydebank bench he could not continue playing as he was too cold. Ignacio was promptly substituted, Clydebank won 3-0. Ignacio was originally on trial with Celtic, he then played once for Albion Rovers, before joining Clydebank. Ignacio was the first Brazilian to play for a Scottish club.

Iorfa he goes. On 5 December 1998, Dominic Iorfa senior was sent off whilst waiting to come on as a substitute for Aylesbury United in their Isthmian League Premier Division match at St. Albans City. Iorfa took exception to how long the referee and his assistant were taking to allow him entry to the field of play and, before the substitution could take place, was dismissed for 'foul and abusive language to match officials'.

On 8 October 1983, Darlington's, Colin Ross, was substituted after four seconds and without having touched the ball during the Division Four game against Chester City. From kick-off, the ball was played back to Ross who, in moving towards the ball, jarred his knee. Ross was replaced by Peter Cartwright. Darlington won 2-1.

On 28 December 1992, all four substitutes scored in the Division Three match between Barnet and Torquay United. Nicky Evans and Mark Carter came on and scored for Barnet, Duane Derby and Paul Trollope did likewise as substitutes for Torquay. Barnet won 5-4.

The last Premier League match in which neither side introduced a substitute was Manchester United against Fulham on 22 March 2003. United won 3-0, Ruud Van Nistelrooy scoring a hat-trick.

On 15 May 2005, Manchester City manager, Stuart Pearce, brought on substitute goalkeeper, Nicky Weaver, for outfield player Claudio Reyna during City's Premier League match against Middlesbrough. Pearce then put Weaver in goal and played first-choice goalkeeper, David James, as a striker. The game ended 1-1. It was Nicky Weaver's only Premier League appearance for City that season.

Sheffield Wednesday manager, Gary Megson, substituted three players within seventeen minutes of Wednesday's Johnstone Paints Trophy tie at Bradford City on 30 August 2011. Goalkeeper Nick Weaver was replaced by Richard O'Donnell after only two minutes; Jose Semedo and David Prutton were replaced respectively by Giles Coke and Cecil Nyoni on seventeen minutes. It is thought Megson made the substitutions to get-around competition rules stipulating a team must play a minimum of six first team players in their starting line-up, making the early substitutions in order to rest players for forthcoming league games.

On 20 March 2016, in the Scottish Premiership game between Dundee and Dundee United at Dens Park, Dundee brought on a substitute, then substituted that substitute, only to then substitute the second substitute with a third, and all in the first-half. The sequence began with injured Kostadin Gadzhalov being replaced by Thomas Konrad. Injury then forced Konrad to leave the field and be replaced by Nick Low. Dundee goalkeeper Scott Bain was then sent off by referee Steven McLaren for bringing down United's Billy McKay. Dundee's substitute goalkeeper, David Mitchell, entered the fray which necessitated an outfield player being substituted,

which was Low. The game ended 2-2, the line-ups in the match report read
- Gadzhalov (Konrad 16, Low 40, Mitchell 42).

OFFICIAL   PROGRAMME

FOUNDED   1867

QUEEN'S PARK
FOOTBALL CLUB

SCOTTISH LEAGUE
QUEEN'S PARK
VERSUS
ARBROATH
Saturday, 12th Dec., 1970
KICK-OFF 2.30 p.m.

Next Home Game
Scottish Cup
QUEEN'S PARK
versus
MONTROSE
Sat., 19th Dec., 1970
Kick-off 3 p.m.

PRICE
6D

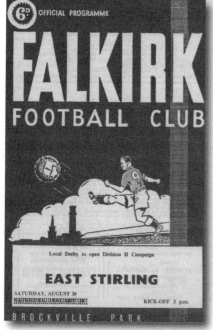

6D OFFICIAL PROGRAMME

FALKIRK
FOOTBALL CLUB

Local Derby to open Division II Campaign

EAST STIRLING

SATURDAY, AUGUST 30   KICK-OFF 3 p.m.

BROCKVILLE PARK

Teams

The Wolverhampton Wanderers team of 1912-13 included two vicars, Reverend K.R.G. Hunt and Reverend W.C. Jordan.

In 1921-22, Plymouth Argyle conceded only four goals in their 21 home matches in Division Three South. Ironically, Argyle were pipped for promotion to the Second Division by Southampton on goal average as both teams finished on 61 points.

Portsmouth did not concede a single goal in their first eight matches in Division Three South in 1922-23. The first team to score against Portsmouth were Plymouth Argyle in a 2-1 win at Fratton Park on 2 October 1922.

Sam Taylor scored for Chesterfield at Rotherham United in Division Three North on Christmas Day 1929. It was the start of a sequence of games in which Chesterfield were to score in 46 consecutive matches. The sequence came to an end the following Christmas when, on 27 December 1930, Chesterfield drew 0-0 at Carlisle United. Chesterfield's feat was finally eclipsed by Arsenal who, between 19 May 2001 and 30 November 2002, scored in 55 consecutive matches.

In 1928-29, Rangers sealed the Scottish First Division title on 16 March with eight matches of the season remaining, the earliest a title has been won in British football. Rangers' final game of the season was against Dundee at Ibrox on 27 April, for all they were champions, the match attracted an attendance of only 5,100. In 2013-14, Celtic sealed the Scottish Premier League title on 26 March, with seven matches remaining.

Manchester United lost their opening twelve matches of the season in 1930-31, a record for the English League football. United won only seven League matches and were relegated to Division Two. United's final home match of the season, a 4-4 draw with Middlesbrough, was watched by only 3,969. It wasn't United's lowest home attendance of the season, however, only 3,679 had attended a previous home game against Leicester City.

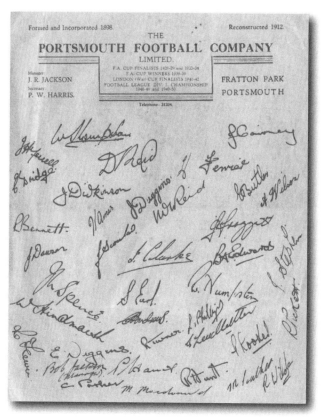

Portsmouth were English League Champions in 1948-49 and 1949-50, the first of which was accomplished without a single international player in their ranks. Come 1950-51, when the club issued this autograph sheet, despite having won two successive league titles, only two players had won international caps, Jack Froggatt and Jimmy Dickinson, both for England. Portsmouth manager, Bob Jackson, recommended Duggie Reid and Jimmy Scoular to the Scottish FA Selection committee, only to be told, 'Portsmouth is a long way for one of our selection committee to travel to view players untried at international level and who may have an off day.' (As told to the author by Tommy Docherty).

The Portsmouth team that won the League Championship in 1948-49 did not comprise a single international player.

The Cardiff City team of 1931-32 included four 'Macs' all born in different countries - Jimmy McGrath (England), Owen McNally (Scotland), Jimmy McCambridge (Northern Ireland) and Jack McJennett (Wales).

We never do well there. On 22 January 2022, Blackburn Rovers were involved in a goalless draw at Luton Town in the Championship, the draw accentuated the fact Blackburn had never won at Luton Town in 85 years of trying. Blackburn's first visit to Kenilworth Road on 6 November 1937 resulted in a 4-1 defeat, subsequently, Blackburn never secured victory at Luton in 24 visits.

In 1945-46, Rochdale called upon the services of 56 players, seventeen of whom played just one game.

Charlton Athletic were the first club to play six non-British or Irish players. During 1952-53 Charlton fielded six South Africans, Ken Chamberlain, Syd O'Linn (played Test cricket for South Africa), Stuart Leary, Eddie Firmani (capped by Italy through parentage), John Hewie (capped for Scotland through parentage) and Albert Uytenbogaardt.

In 1952-53, Plymouth Argyle scored 65 goals when finishing fourth in Division Two. The following season, Plymouth again scored 65 goals only to this time finish fourth from bottom. In 1952-53, Plymouth had four penalties awarded and scored all four, the following season, Plymouth again had four penalties awarded but missed all four.

On 6 November 1954, Middlesbrough lost 9-0 at Blackburn Rovers in Division Two. Manager Bob Dennison named an unchanged team for Middlesbrough's next game, a 4-2 victory over Fulham.

In 1954-55, Stirling Albion secured just six points from a possible 60 in Scottish Division A but were not relegated. Stirling survived due to the re-organisation of Scotland's two divisions to accommodate five new clubs. Stirling Albion, however, were relegated the following season having again finished bottom of Division A. In the 1950s, Stirling were either promoted or relegated on seven occasions.

In 1956-57, Crewe Alexandra of the Third Division North, won only one of their opening nine matches of the season. Crewe then beat Scunthorpe United 2-1, on 19 September 1956, but did not win again until they beat Bradford City 1-0 on 13 April 1957, 30 league matches and two FA Cup ties (lost replay) without a win.

In 1957-58, Wolverhampton Wanderers won the Football League Championship; the Wolves reserve team won the Central League; their third team won the Birmingham League and FA Youth Cup; the Wolves' fourth team, the Worcestershire Combination League. Manchester City achieved a similar feat in 2020-21. (see 'Champions')

From 14 December 1957 to 11 January 1958, Queens Park Rangers played eight consecutive matches in Division Three South all of which ended 1-1.

In 1957-58, Lincoln City lost only one of their first seven matches of the season, City then only managed two wins in the next 29 League matches but won their last six to avoid relegation from Division Two by a single point.

Biggest positive goal difference. Hearts won the Scottish League title in 1957-58. In 34 league matches, Hearts scored 132 goals and conceded just 29, a goal difference of +103.

From 11 February 1922 to 8 December 1958, a period of 36 years, Leeds United never had a player sent off at any level. No Spurs player was sent off in the period October 1927 to December 1965, a period of 37 years.

West Ham's B team. In 1963-64, West Ham United had a first team squad of 20 players, 12 of whom had a surname beginning with the letter B: Jim Barrett, Peter Brabrook, Peter Bennett, David Bickles, John Bond, Eddie Bovington, Ronnie Boyce, Martin Britt, Ken Brown, Dennis Burnett, Johnny Byrne and Jack Burkett. The non-B's were Jim Standen, Lawrie Leslie, Brian Dear, John Sissons, Joe Kirkup, Bobby Moore, Geoff Hurst and Martin Peters. Seven of West Ham's B's played in the team which defeated Preston North End 3-2 in the 1964 FA Cup Final - Bond, Burkett, Bovington, Brown, Brabrook, Boyce and Byrne.

In 1974-75, Forfar Athletic acquired just nine points from a possible 76 in Scottish Division Two. Forfar won only one match, at home to Raith Rovers (2-0) on 25 September, after which came a sequence of 31 League games until the end of the season without a win, a run during which Forfar only managed one goal in their last 13 matches.

In 1977-78, Benfica were unbeaten in the Primeira Divisao yet failed to win the League. Benfica finished as runners-up behind Porto, both clubs finishing with 51 points, Porto winning the title due to their superior goal difference, plus 60 as opposed to plus 45.

A similar fate befell Perugia in Serie A in 1978-79. Perugia were unbeaten in the league but finished three points behind AC Milan. Perugia's record read P30 W11 D19 L0 F 34 A16 GD plus 18 Points 41.

Leeds United were unbeaten on the opening day of the season from 1990-91 to 2009-10, a run of 19 seasons.

On 3 December 1996, Blackpool named eight players whose name begins with the letter B for their 2-2 draw at home to Plymouth Argyle in Division Two - Steve Banks, Marvin Bryan, Andy Barlow, Tony Butler, Mark Bonner, Gary Brabin, Darren Bradshaw (all started) and unused substitute, David Brightwell, who was on loan from Bradford City.

In 2003-04, East Stirling took just 8 points from a possible 108 in the Scottish Third Division. East Stirling won only two matches, one being their last match of the season, 2-1 against Elgin City. Curiously, after enduring such a torrid season, the attendance against Elgin (364), was double that of East Stirling's first home game of the season against Montrose (182) and their third highest of the season.

Wrexham included five players by the name of Williams in their squad for their Division Two (now League Two) game at Darlington on 11 August 2007, four of whom were named in the starting line-up: Tony Williams, Danny Williams, Eifion Williams, Marc Williams (all played) and Mike Williams.

On 8 December 2009, Peterborough United drew 0-0 with Ipswich Town at Portman Road. Peterborough were not involved in another goalless draw for 171 matches, when, on 9 March 2013 they drew at home to...Ipswich Town.

The last team to field five Irishmen in a single game in English top-flight football was Aston Villa in their 2-1 defeat at Newcastle United in the Premier League on 5 February 2012. The players in question being Shay Given, Richard Dunne, Ciaran Clark, Stephen Ireland and Robbie Keane.

Every time Norwich City and Sunderland meet in a league game they compete for the 'Friendship Cup'. The cup was introduced to mark the camaraderie between the two clubs, their players and supporters at the 1985 League Cup Final which Norwich won 1-0.

Double top. In seasons 2017-18 and 2018-19, Manchester City recorded 13 out of a possible 19 'doubles' against Premier League opponents. Matching a record set by Doncaster Rovers who, in Division Three North in 1946-47, achieved 13 'doubles' from a possible 21.

Having scored a penalty against Wimbledon on 23 March 1991, Sheffield United went 50 games before having another penalty awarded, against Manchester United on 15 August 1992, the first day of the Premier League. Burnley went 57 matches without being awarded a penalty. Burnley were finally awarded a spot-kick in the last minute of their Premier League game against Southampton on 2 February 2019. Ashley Barnes converted to secure a 1-1 draw.

In 2019-20, three-quarters of the teams comprising the Cymru (Welsh) Premier League had names which began with one of the first three letters of the alphabet - Aberystwyth Town, Airbus UK Broughton, Bala Town, Barry Town United, Caernarfon Town, Cardiff Metropolitan University, Carmarthen Town, Cefn Druids and Connah's Quay Nomads. The only three teams who didn't were Newtown, Pen-y-Bont and The New Saints.

Sweet Caroline! On 6 October 2020, Sunderland defeated Carlisle United 5-3 in the EFL Trophy. Included in the Sunderland team, in central midfield, were Neil and Diamond - Dan Neil and Jack Diamond.

In 2020-21, Stoke Gabriel of the Kitchen Kit South West Peninsula League Premier Division East (how that name just rolls-off the tongue), lost their first ten matches of the season, scoring two goals and conceding 122. As at December 2020, Stoke Gabriel sat bottom of the league having lost all 17 of their league games: goals scored 5, goals conceded 201, goal difference minus 197, average goals conceded per game, 11.8. Credit to Stoke Gabriel, not only did the club manage to keep fielding a team and substitutes, the club also fielded a reserve team and four teams at junior level, Under 18, 13, 12 and 11. In June 2021, Stoke Gabriel merged with Torbay Police FC to form, wait for it, Stoke Gabriel and Torbay Police FC, from which point fortunes on the field greatly improved.

The longest name of any senior professional football club is - Nooit Opgeven Altijd Doorgan Aangenaam Door Vermaaak En Nuttig Door Ontspanning Combinatie Breda, commonly known as NAC Breda who play in the Dutch Eerste Divisie, the second highest tier of football in Holland.

In 2020-21, Sheffield United endured the joint worst start to a season in the history of the four English leagues, United won just 5 points from their first 19 league matches. United also broke the Premier League record for the most consecutive games without a win from the start of the season - 17. United's first league victory did not come until 12 January 2021, a 1-0 defeat of Newcastle United. In Eddie McGoldrick (9 goals), however, United boasted a leading goalscorer who netted more than Champions League winners Chelsea's leading goalscorer for the season (Jorginho 7).

Up to 2021-22, the last time both Celtic and Rangers failed to finish in the top three in the Scottish top-flight was 1964-65 - Rangers 5th and Celtic 8th.

The only International team never to have been beaten by Brazil is Norway. From 1988 to 2022, the two countries met four times, Norway winning twice and two draws.

Hot competition for a place in the team. In 2021-22, Stoke City listed ten goalkeepers in their Under 23 squad - Jack Bonham, Paul Cooper, Jakob Glover, Xander Parke, Tommy Simkin, Nathan Broome, Adam Davies (permitted over-age player), Robbie Hemfrey, Conor Robson and Matthew Yates.

Transfers

Robertson United. At the end of 1902-03 season, Manchester United signed Alexander Robertson from Hibernian, three days later United signed an Alexander Robertson from Middlesbrough. To avoid confusion, the former was known as Alex Robertson, the latter as Sandy Robertson. In the close season, United then signed Thomas Robertson from Dundee and a Thomas Robertson from Darwen, the former was referred to as Tommy, the latter as Tom.

Greenwell did well. In September 1912, Northern League club, Crook Town, informed wing-half, Jack Greenwell, they had received an offer for his services from another club - Barcelona. Crook Town accepted the offer, Greenwell left his job as a miner in a local colliery, moved to Spain and made his Barcelona debut on 29 September 1912 in a 4-2 win over FC Espanya. Greenwell played 88 games for Barcelona and on his retirement as a player in July 1917, was appointed manager. Greenwell oversaw 492 games as Barcelona manager, leaving the club in 1923 to manage local rivals RCD Espanol. In 1931, Greenwell was manager of RCD Mallorca when the Mallorca club president informed him they had received an offer for his services - from Barcelona. As a consequence, Greenwell returned for a second spell as Barcelona manager (1931-33).

The oldest player to command a transfer fee is Billy Meredith who was days short of his 47th birthday when he joined Manchester City from Manchester United at the end of 1920-21. Stan Matthews was 46 years and eight months old when he rejoined Stoke City from Blackpool for a fee of £3,000 in October 1961.

A similar 'Patton'. When Tom Parker was transferred to Arsenal from Southampton in 1926, he left with a message for Saints fans, 'I'll be back'. Parker did return to Southampton, eleven years later when he was appointed as the manager in 1937. Parker ended his stint as manager in 1943, informing Saints fans, 'I'll be back'. In August 1963, Parker returned to Southampton as Chief Scout, thirty seven years after originally being quoted as saying 'I'll be back'. Parker remained Southampton's Chief Scout until 1975.

No Papist conspiracy. In February 1925, Albert Pape was part of the Clapton Orient team that travelled to play Manchester United. At 1pm, United manager, John Chapman, informed Orient manager, Peter Proudfoot, that Manchester United wanted to buy Pape. A fee of £1,070 was agreed and the details wired to the Football Association and Football League at 1.30pm. Although Pape had been named in the Orient line-up, he was confirmed as a Manchester United player at 2.30pm and took to the field as a United player. Pape scored on his debut for United against his old club in a 4-2 win.

Following Stoke City's 3-1 home victory over Bristol City in Division Two on 11 April 1931, the directors of cash-strapped Bristol City invited Stoke City to have any Bristol player of their choosing for a fee of £250. Stoke manager Tom Mather took up on Bristol's offer and chose Joe Johnson, who went on to play 184 league matches for Stoke City (54 goals) and win five caps for England.

During the period 1933 to 1938, Bournemouth signed 25 players all of whom, at one time, had played for Wolves.

In September 1939, Sunderland sold goalkeeper, Matt Middleton to Plymouth Argyle. Before Middleton could move south to Plymouth, however, World War Two was declared and the Football League programme suspended. Following war service, Middleton signed for Bradford City in 1946, having never played a game for Plymouth Argyle despite having been registered as a player with the club for seven years.

The first player to be transferred from a British club to a foreign club for a fee was Paddy Sloan who, in the close season of 1948, was transferred from Sheffield United to AC Milan for £10,000.

Bored of pies? In the 1947 close-season, goalkeeper Norman Malan was transferred from Middlesbrough to Darlington for a year's supply of pies for the Middlesbrough boardroom.

Dundee once held the world record for a transfer fee paid. In 1950, Dundee paid Derby County £23,500 for Scottish International Billy Steel.

Albert Nightingale played against the same opposition on the same ground for two different teams in the same week. On 4 October 1952, Nightingale was in the Blackburn Rovers team that played his former club Sheffield United at Bramall Lane. Two days later, Nightingale was transferred to Leeds United and he made his Leeds debut later that week, away to Sheffield United.

Alan Fox was included in the Hartlepools United team to play at Bradford City on 30 October 1965. Bradford City were keen to sign Fox and a deal was completed on the Friday night. Fox travelled to Bradford on the Hartlepools United team coach, but, played for Bradford City. Hartlepools won 3-1.

Dave Hickson signed for Ellesmere Port in 1945. Following a successful league career with Everton, Aston Villa, Liverpool, Huddersfield Town and Tranmere Rovers, Hickson re-signed for Ellesmere Port in January 1965, 20 years after originally signing for the club. The signing was conducted by the same club secretary who had signed Hickson in the first instance, Stan Jenkins.

In loo of a transfer fee. In June 1975, Mick Cullerton was transferred from Stafford Rangers for what was to be a second spell at Port Vale. The fee was £5,000, which Stafford Rangers used to build new toilet blocks at their Marston Road ground. On his 'second' debut for Vale, Cullerton scored a hat-trick in a League Cup tie against Hereford United.

John Barnes signed for Watford on 14 July 1981 from Middlesex League club Sudbury Court; the fee was a set of strips.

In August 1994, Paul Peschisolido was transferred from Birmingham City to Stoke City by his fiancee and soon to be wife. Karen Brady was Birmingham City's managing director. It was she who negotiated and oversaw Peschisolido's transfer to Stoke City for £400,000 plus the player exchange of Dave Regis.

In August 1995, Coventry City sold Paul Williams to Plymouth Argyle and replaced him with Paul Williams signed from Derby County. In the same month Coventry also sold John Williams to Wycombe Wanderers.

Following his move to Wycombe Wanderers in 1995, John Williams went on to have at least one new club every season until his retirement as a player in 2008. In total Williams played for 16 clubs in the remaining eleven years of his career, including Swansea City, Cardiff City, Exeter City and Walsall, none of which were on loan.

Jamie Stevenson had played only two games for Alloa Athletic when, in the summer of 2003, he was transferred to Real Mallorca, signing a three-year contract. A year later, Stevenson returned to Alloa.

Manchester United paid Real Madrid £59.7million for Angel Di Maria in 2014. The Argentine's first transfer occurred when he joined Rosario Central from Torito FC for 35 footballs.

In 2016-17, Scottish junior club Kilwinning Rangers demanded a fee of £1,500 from Alloa Athletic for striker Ross Stewart. Bereft of funds, Alloa were unable to pay the fee. So keen was Ross Stewart's father for his son to play Scottish League football, Mr Stewart, along with some members of Alloa Athletic Supporters Club, paid the transfer fee.

On 29th June 2018, Wigan Athletic signed full-back, Reece James, on loan from Chelsea and released full-back, Reece James, who subsequently joined Sunderland.

On 1 July 2019, Queens Park Rangers sold striker, Matt Smith, to Millwall and signed midfielder, Matt Smith, on a season-long loan from Manchester City.

In the summer of 2021, Pierce Sweeney was transferred from Exeter City to Swindon Town. Four weeks later, still in the close season and not having played a game for Swindon, Sweeney was transferred back to Exeter City. At the end of July 2021, Swindon enquired about taking Sweeney back to the County Ground, only to be informed the defender was not available for transfer.

Perhaps you'd forgotten he also played for...
Ossie Ardiles for Blackburn Rovers; Alan Ball for Bristol Rovers; John Barnes for Charlton Athletic; Peter Bonetti for Dundee United; David Beckham for Preston North End; Steve Bould for Sunderland and Torquay United; Nicky Butt for Birmingham City; Mick Channon for Newcastle United; Ashley Cole for Crystal Palace; Johan Cruyff for Feyenoord; Rio

Ferdinand for Bournemouth; Gerry Francis for Cardiff City and Swansea; Trevor Francis for Manchester City; Charlie George for Bournemouth; Mark Hateley for Ross County; Geoff Hurst for West Bromwich Albion; Jermaine Jenas for Aston Villa; Harry Kane for Norwich City; Frank Lampard for Swansea City; Ally McCoist for Sunderland; Malcolm McDonald for Djurgardens; James Milner for Swindon Town; Paul McGrath for Sheffield United; Bobby Moore for FC Midtjylland; Danny Murphy for Crewe Alexandra and Spurs; Charlie Nicholas for Clyde; Martin Peters for Sheffield United; Jordan Pickford for Carlisle United; Peter Reid for Queens Park Rangers and Notts County; Kasper Schmeichel for Darlington; David Seaman for Peterborough United; Paul Scholes for Swindon Town; Peter Shilton for Bolton Wanderers; Frank Stapleton for Aldershot and Huddersfield Town; Mike Summerbee for Blackpool; John Terry for Nottingham Forest; Denis Tueart for Stoke City; Chris Waddle for Sunderland; Ray Wilkins for Millwall and Leyton Orient; Ray Wilson for Bradford City; Ian Wright for Nottingham Forest; Wilfred Zaha for Cardiff City.

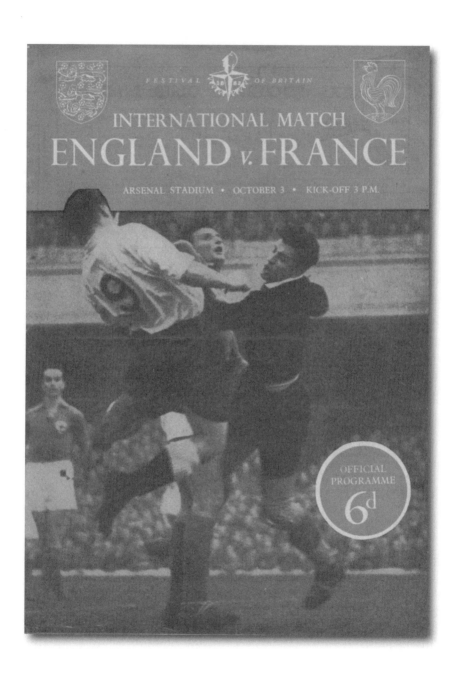

INTERNATIONAL MATCH
ENGLAND v. FRANCE

ARSENAL STADIUM · OCTOBER 3 · KICK-OFF 3 P.M.

OFFICIAL PROGRAMME 6d